Beyond Separateness

BEYOND SEPARATENESS

The Social Nature of Human Beings— Their Autonomy, Knowledge, and Power

RICHARD SCHMITT

WESTVIEW PRESS

Boulder • San Francisco • Oxford

Excerpts from *To the Lighthouse* by Virginia Woolf, copyright 1927 by Harcourt Brace & Company and renewed 1954 by Leonard Woolf, reprinted by permission of Harcourt Brace & Company. Acknowledgment is also gratefully made to the estate of Virginia Woolf and The Hogarth Press, publisher of *To the Lighthouse* in the United Kingdom.

Published in 1995 in the United States of America by Westview Press, Inc., 5500 Central Avenue, Boulder, Colorado 80301-2877, and in the United Kingdom by Westview Press, 12 Hid's Copse Road, Cumnor Hill, Oxford OX2 9JJ

Library of Congress Cataloging-in-Publication Data
Schmitt, Richard, 1927–
     Beyond separateness : the social nature of human beings—their autonomy, knowledge, and power / Richard Schmitt.
        p.   cm.
     Includes bibliographical references and index.
     ISBN 0-8133-1224-8.—ISBN 0-8133-1250-7 (pbk.)
     1. Individualism.   2. Autonomy.   3. Social choice.   4. Power (Social sciences)   I. Title.
HM136.S393   1995
302.5'4—dc20   95-8126
                                                                                      CIP

Printed and bound in the United States of America

 The paper used in this publication meets the requirements of the American National Standard for Permanence of Paper for Printed Library Materials Z39.48-1984.

10   9   8   7   6   5   4   3   2   1

She told them that the only grace they could have is the grace they could imagine. That if they could not see it, they would not have it.

—*Toni Morrison,* **Beloved**

Contents

Preface

Looking back over the twentieth century, we see an uninterrupted string of crises: wars, mass murders, famines, systemwide collapses. That perhaps does not distinguish our era from earlier times: Throughout history human beings have suffered many calamities. But in our century the experience of these crises has become very self-conscious. Crises have become occasions for serious theoretical efforts at understanding and diagnosing our ills and prescribing remedies. These efforts have not had an overwhelming success, but neither have they been shown to be useless. This book makes a contribution to this continuing reflection about ways of improving the human lot by ameliorating our ways of living in society.

The task of social amelioration has been approached in three different ways. Most familiar are the thinkers who point with justified pride at the accomplishments of capitalism and liberal democracy and urge us to improve on the details of that economic and political system to usher in a less tortured era of human history. In economics they defend laissez-faire capitalism; in the political arena they recommend subtle improvements of the electoral system in Western democracies. Their social theories interpret a wide range of phenomena as quasi–market exchange relations.

This project comes under attack from two sides. Both sides deplore the rootlessness and fragmentation of life in modern capitalist society. Both sides echo Marx's words that capitalism, "wherever it has got the upper hand, has put an end to all feudal, patriarchal, idyllic relations. It has ... left remaining no other nexus between man and man than naked self-interest, than callous 'cash-payment'" (Marx and Engels, 1978:475). Capitalism, whatever its accomplishments, has been spectacularly destructive of the social fabric. It has depersonalized relationships and thereby allowed free rein to the worst human impulses of selfishness, cruelty, and disregard for the needs of the poor and the weak. The central principles of social organization of the capitalist democracy need to be replaced.

But these sorts of criticisms take two diametrically opposed forms. First, there are the backward-looking critics: They find models of future, more humane social institutions in past societies that capitalism and liberal democracy have destroyed. Such are "communitarian" theorists. These critics of capitalist democracy point to the ways in which capitalism has robbed the world of its magic and has replaced it with a world animated by individual interest and structured by contractual relations. They want to renew our world by re-creating some earlier social structures in which community came before individual interest and tradition was stronger than (quasi-)scientific rationality.

Attacks from the opposite direction come from thinkers who identify with Marxism or have, in one way or another, been moved by Marxism to believe that there is no reason to glorify the past. The knowledge that life in feudal society was oppressive as well as the bitter memories of large-scale communitarian experiments of the fascist and communist variety support them in that stance. Critical theorists use vocabularies that range from an orthodox Marxian one to the vocabulary of communicative ethics, or of feminism, to look into the future for some hope for amelioration and possible paths toward fulfilling those hopes. They are united by the commitment to an emancipatory project. In each case the replacement of the "idyllic" relations of an earlier era by the "cash-nexus" of capitalism is the target. But different theorists take different aspects of that transformation to be the most fundamental.

Orthodox Marxists have drawn attention to the exploitative nature of capitalism. When the cash-nexus becomes the tie between employer and worker, the worker is exploited. The system that promised to increase the well-being of all, if only each would pursue his or her self-interest rationally, instead is bringing misery to the many and excessive wealth to the few. Accordingly Marxists offer as their remedy class struggle and socialist revolution designed to end exploitation: The means to a better world is to be found in class-based political action aiming at the transformation of the political landscape and bringing economic transformation in its wake.

Habermas and the Frankfurt School turned their attention to the conception of rationality that predominates in capitalist democratic societies. Replacing the older idyllic relations with the cash-nexus of capitalist contracts has replaced a more generous form of rationality with strictly "instrumental" rationality—the exclusive use of reason for calculating appropriate means to each individual's ends. The "lifeworld" of traditional ways of understanding and tackling social problems is "colonized" by the rational practices of experts and bureaucrats. Such a diagnosis of our problems leads to proposals to reform our practices as rational (political) agents by reconsidering the nature and uses of rationality.

Another focus of attacks has been the conception of persons as separate individual actors. Marx often talked as if it were simply false that human beings are as separate from one another as, implicitly or explicitly, the defenders of capitalist democracy describe them. But elsewhere, for instance, in his discussion of alienation, he suggests a more complex and interesting view: We who live under a capitalist democracy are, indeed, separate individuals, but that is determined by social institutions, not human nature, and is therefore alterable. If we are separate individuals today, we need to not be quite as separate tomorrow. The replacement of traditional, complex relationships that were constitutive of persons by the purely external relationships measurable by their economic value came about through human choices and can be undone by making other, better choices.

This last claim has gained further interest and complexity in recent feminist theory that has pointed out that men in our society are considerably more likely to conform to the image of the separate economic or political actor whom we encounter in the theory of capitalist democracy than women. Their role has traditionally been to build bridges and to establish bonds between these separate actors. Male separateness has not been open to women because they were not supposed to be separate but to supply the social and affective connections destroyed in the public sphere by capitalist democracy. The relationships of women were not uniformly replaced by the cash-nexus of the capitalist marketplace because women did work they did not get paid for, regardless of whether they also hired themselves out for wages. Work in the home was not contracted for. The older "idyllic" relations were said to have found a refuge there, even if only in the practices of women. That suggests that separateness is not natural and inescapable but is a way of being that has been chosen, mostly by men.

This attack on separateness is new. At the same time it is continuous with prominent themes in earlier views. The attack on separateness continues a long-standing tradition of being critical of the individualism that underlies the theory and practice of liberal democracy. The Marxian complaint about the destruction of social bonds became a staple of nineteenth- and twentieth-century social thought. Sir Henry Maine argued that the history of law manifests a transition from "status" to "contract." Ferdinand Tönnies distinguished the "society" in which we live from an earlier "community," and Max Weber deplored the "disenchantment" of our world by the new capitalist rationality. Fascism in the 1920s and 1930s gave a thoroughly conservative interpretation to these complaints, as do the advocates of traditional religion and morality today. Individual license is to be restrained by giving new force to traditional communal values. Individualism is overcome by subordinating individuals to communal regimes. At the other end of the political spectrum, protests against capitalist rationality point to its oppressiveness and look toward greater equality and more genuine democracy as cures. Capitalist individualism is said to have fragmented social structures and left the weak helpless against the depredations of the powerful. Collective decisionmaking at work and elsewhere is expected to cure the destructiveness of an atomized society.

Both the backward-looking and the liberationist critics of capitalist democracy agree that individualism is seriously in error. But a good deal of the debate over individualism suffers from vagueness. The reflections that follow about separateness and being-in-relation will help to clarify some issues in the debate over individualism.

Most of this book concerns itself with the argument about separateness and its opposite, "being-in-relation." In the first two chapters, the issue of general social amelioration may seem quite far removed. These chapters provide the necessary conceptual toolkit for the argument that follows. But then we come back, in Chapter 3, to the oppressive effects of separate autonomy on women and in Chapters 7 and 8 to the destructive effects of separateness on those without officially accredited expertise. From then on, the project of social amelioration is never too far in the background. More promising relationships to others, being-in-relation, occupy Chapters 4 and 5. Chapter 6 compares the kinds of intimacy available to the separate individual with the love that being-in-relation can bring. Also in the final chapter, I will approach that central issue of social and political reform very directly by examing the concept of power. The conception of power that goes with the prevailing doctrine of human (read "male") separateness is inevitably power that dominates. If we are to envisage a society where solidarity carries more weight than domination, we need either a society where power is evenly distributed—a completely utopian conception—or one where power differentials do not inevitably end in domination. That is possible only if being-in-relation is chosen more often than we choose it today.

Much of the current discussion of separateness, and of the relations that women sometimes have to one another, is too general. I will try to examine the opposition between separateness and being-in-relation in more concrete terms, to see whether the central opposition is still discernible and reasonably clear when we look at it in some detail. Hence I begin in Chapter 1 to talk about autonomy, a concept of considerable importance in contemporary philosophy in the English-speaking world. I will raise certain difficulties about prevailing concepts of autonomy that arise because autonomy is explicated against the background of the assumption that human beings are irremediably separate from one another. In the first three chapters, I argue that that assumption is an error. It is moreover a complex error. Human beings are not as separate from one another as many mainstream philosophers assume. In addition, whether we are separate is not a question of fact but a matter of how we choose to be. (So is the precise way in which we choose to be separate.) Insofar as human beings are separate from one another they are so by choice. We could choose to be different, namely, in-relation. The two chapters that follow, Chapters 4 and 5, develop being-in-relation in some detail and begin to present some reasons for preferring being-in-relation over separateness. The final three chapters will try to strengthen those arguments against choosing separateness by discussing different forms of being-in-relation: in empathy, love, knowledge, and, finally, power.

If many of us chose to be in-relation more of the time than we do now, would emancipation be closer to our reach? Would our social life be humanized? This book lays some of the foundations to an affirmative answer to those questions.

*   *   *

Many persons have listened to me talk about these issues and have read what I have written. They have patiently waited for the issues to clarify themselves while insistently pointing to the difficulties in earlier formulations. I am very grateful to Linda Alcoff, Doug Allen and his colleagues and students at Orono, Maine, anonymous reviewers for Westview Press and *Hypatia,* Stuart Barnum, Steve Beck,

Lorraine Code, Murray Code, Steve De Witt, Lisa Feldman, Connie Mui, Kai Nielsen, Amelie Rorty, Justin Schwartz, the members of SOFPHIA who commented helpfully on the very early and the very last pieces of this book, Bob Ware, and, particularly, Tom Wartenberg for many important comments. A review of an earlier book of mine by Iris Young gave me the initial impetus to take up this entire train of thought. Spencer Carr has consistently been both sharp-eyed critic and supportive friend.

Lucy Candib has worked at her computer six feet away from mine on problems very much like these. We have talked about them over quiet lunches when our children were in school and daycare or over their noisy interruptions when they were at home. I would not have been able to write this book without the joy and turmoil of life with Lucy, Addie, and Eli. May it be of use to them.

Richard Schmitt

◀ 1 ▶

Autonomy

Marx, Maine, Tönnies, Weber, and, in our day, Habermas, each in their different vocabulary deplore the modern world in which life ruled by tradition and established human ties is replaced by planning, calculation, and rational choice. Each author draws our attention to the specific kinds of human relationships characteristic of the modern social order and contrasts those with earlier and very different ties between persons. In the modern world contracts are the dominant examples of relationships. Contracts are specific and limited. One person contracts to perform a certain service if the other provides adequate compensation, agreed on beforehand. Contractual relationships are reciprocal and they are expected to benefit each partner. They are entered as a result of calculation concerning the satisfaction of one's own preferences. The relationships that are most common in our world are motivated by self-interest. Each person's responsibilities are limited to performing the action contracted for. There is no call to worry what this contractual arrangement will mean for the other, in the long run, or whether the exchange was beneficial for the other. Each participant in this large social marketplace is expected to be self-sufficient, to take care of herself or himself. Autonomy is an important concept and ideal in this picture of human society.

Implicit in the sets of contrasts drawn by these authors is the idea that in an earlier age human relationships were less self-regarding, not as carefully circumscribed, and that one's ties and obligations to others carried more weight than calculations of one's own interest. Pointing to that contrast does not endorse feudalism as preferable to life in liberal democracies. It says, much more modestly, that some aspects of the feudal society, perhaps only as we imagine it, are preferable to our way. Specifically, these authors look for (or despair of) a future in which human beings will not be primarily calculating their own interests in their relationships with others but will openly acknowledge their dependencies on others and thereby put their ties to other humans in the center of social life, giving them more weight than rationally calculated self-interest. Such a world, one hopes, would be less callous toward the suffering of others. It would reject mass murder as an instrument of government policy and would be sensitive to the suffering of children. Today their health and well-being seems to matter less than the health of large corporations and the well-being of their owners.

The difference drawn in all these canonical texts is the difference between separateness and being-in-relation. That difference has seemed important to many people. It is acknowledged more and more frequently that many ills of our world are connected with the preponderance of separateness among persons. There is a hope that in a world that applies itself to fostering being-in-relation, human beings will be prized over encouraging economic statistics and relationships between persons will count for more than the accumulation of property. The hope is not that if only we transform relations between individual persons we will enter a more harmonious world: What relations we can and do have to one another depends in large part on the institutions that structure our lives. Replacing separateness with being-in-relation does not short-circuit the need for institutional change. It only lays down one of the requirements for such change.

But so far the contrast between separateness and being-in-relation is both ambiguous and vague. The contrast is ambiguous in two ways: Separateness is often thought to be an essential quality of human beings, but at other times we talk about someone being separate from others, more or less as a consequence of his or her choices. Sometimes separateness is an essential characteristic that we have by virtue of being human. At other times it appears as something we can choose. Connected with that ambiguity is another: Insofar as separateness is an essential quality it is simply given. We have no choice in the matter and we cannot recommend that people try to be or refrain from being separate. But if separateness is chosen, it is important to ask whether that is a good choice. In the first case discussions of separateness are mainly descriptive; in the second they are normative.

But the contrast between separateness and being-in-relation is also vague. There is a sense of separateness in which it is inescapable, namely insofar as our bodies are distinct from one another. But there are other senses of the term. Those must first be illuminated. This chapter will begin to clarify this contrast between separateness and being-in-relation.

DISTINCT BODIES AND SEPARATE PERSONS

The most important facts about ourselves are often least examined. We rarely reflect about the distinctness of our bodies and what, exactly, it means. Each one of us has a body distinct from that of all others. I feel my pains directly but not yours. My thoughts are present to me whereas yours must be transmitted through language or must be inferred. I think my thoughts but not yours. My decisions eventuate in actions, unless something comes to interrupt the easy move from decision to execution. I decide to take a walk and off I go. But should I decide that you go for a walk with me, the connection between decision and action is more complex. I must ask or order you to come for a walk. I must overcome your hesitations. I must wait for you to comply.

Thoughts and actions are mine or they are yours. The same is true of a wide range of feelings, attitudes, and conducts. I think my thoughts, and you think yours. I feel my anger and pain and you feel yours. You walk; I walk. But each of us walks his or her own walk. So far everything is clear. But many philosophers infer from that that *all* my actions and inner states—walking, thinking, fearing, and fleeing—are mine and only mine and that the same is true of yours. They infer from the fact that our bodies are distinct that we are separate as persons. They infer from the fact that each of us thinks his or her own thoughts that there are (can be) no thoughts that we think jointly. There are no thoughts, or walks, that do not belong to one person or another exclusively.

At first that seems clearly false. Surely there are actions that one cannot perform by oneself. I cannot play tennis alone or truck and barter alone. Playing tennis or exchanging goods is not something that I do by myself. It makes no sense to tell my tennis partner, "I play my game and you play yours." All we can do is play our game of tennis. Many human actions are relational: They can be done only with one or more persons. It is hard to see how one can, literally, deceive oneself, defraud oneself, or be one's own benefactor. I can learn alone, but it is not clear that I can teach myself. I can neither enslave myself to nor liberate myself from myself. But philosophers who assume that human beings are separate have no problem with those sorts of relational activities: They are simply series of separate actions that take place in a certain prescribed order. Playing tennis and buying and selling are perfect examples of that. The names of relational activities such as "exchanging" goods are simply the names of sequences of separate actions by separate persons. (That view, though widely held, is open to serious objections [Gilbert, 1992]. I will return to this entire debate in more detail in the next chapter.)

This claim to separateness does not, however, follow from the distinctness of our bodies. Having distinct bodies is quite compatible with doing actions that are neither mine nor yours but ours or with having thoughts that do not belong exclusively to me or to you but are genuinely ours. So I want to argue in this book that our bodies are distinct; many of our thoughts and acts are separate. But others are, or can be, joint actions or thoughts. They can be, as I shall say, "in-relation."

Readers who are not professional philosophers, and even those who are, may want to stop reading right here because the question raised seems excessively esoteric. Does it matter whether joint actions can always be decomposed into the several actions of separate persons or whether in some cases there are joint actions that are just that, actions that belong to more than one person at the same time? Yes, it does matter a great deal. This can be seen by considering the concept of autonomy, which plays an important role in contemporary philosophy. It is usually understood against the background assumption that human beings and their thoughts and actions are separate from one another. But if we make that assumption and define autonomy accordingly, we shall soon find that we do not know whether we ever are autonomous. Ordinary convictions that autonomy is attainable, that some people are, sometimes, autonomous, and that autonomy is very important are put in question. So are the many implications that philosophers draw from the assumption of human autonomy.[1]

THE AUTONOMY OF THE PHILOSOPHERS

The concept of autonomy plays an important role in contemporary philosophy. Philosophers have insisted steadily that human beings when they are at their best are autonomous. Over and over we read that one is autonomous when one's life is "one's own" (Gibson, 1985:144). The autonomous person is his or her "own person." What it means for one's person, or aspects of it, to be one's own is explicated in a wide range of ways as being in charge or control of one's person or one's life, as self-determination, as choosing one's own life-plan, or one's own moral principles. "Autonomy" is used "as an equivalent to liberty ... as equivalent to self-rule or sovereignty, ... as identical with freedom of the will. It is equated with dignity, integrity, individuality, independence, responsibility, and self-knowledge ... qualities of self-assertion, with critical reflection, with freedom from obligation, with absence of external causation, with knowledge of one's own interest" (Dworkin, 1988:6).

Autonomy in the political arena refers to the independence of the citizens from their government or to their ability to run their own lives without interference from other members of the society. Here autonomy is relatively limited: One is autonomous if one's legal rights are respected by the government and by fellow citizens. Often *political* autonomy involves a distinction between a public and a private sphere. Autonomous citizens have the right to run their private affairs as they please, as long as they do not violate the corresponding rights of others (Lukes, 1973). *Social* autonomy consists of being free from pressures that may not violate one's legal rights but restrict one's ability to think for oneself and make major life choices. In ethics, autonomy often includes *moral* self-legislating (Benn, 1975–1976; Kuflik, 1984). *Personal* autonomy consists of having a will of one's own or choosing one's own personality.

Political and social autonomy are more limited than ethical or personal autonomy. One may well be politically autonomous in a society where one's rights are scrupulously respected but not be personally autonomous. For personal autonomy requires one to have legal integrity as well as be one's own person—one's thinking and acting are not shaped by external pressures, or at least not shaped by them exclusively. Political and social autonomy demand external independence: that others treat one as an end, not merely as a means (Callahan, 1984). In practice this amounts to such things as absence of undue political, economic, or social coercion and freedom from exploitation and oppression (Frye, 1983). Often certain minimal levels of economic well-being are included in external independence (Dworkin, 1984). If one has political and social independence one is "one's own person" insofar as no other person or institution interferes with one's external independence. One may be said to be autonomous but only partially or externally.

Full autonomy requires, in addition, personal and moral autonomy—that one not be conformist, manipulated, brainwashed, neurotic, self-indulgent. "Everyone equally has a life to live. ... Living a life does not necessarily mean that one will say or do great things, but rather that one will say or do one's own things, or be like the rest only after one has taken some thought" (Kateb, 1989:188). Here internal conditions must be met in addition to the external conditions of political autonomy. There is a long list of requirements that different authors insist on: One must have all the relevant facts for decisionmaking. People who are constantly being lied to cannot be considered autonomous; neither can people whose desires are manipulated and distorted (Friedman, 1986; Grimshaw, 1988). One must also have accurate information about one's own desires (Agich, 1990). But that is not sufficient for personal or moral autonomy: A person might not be coerced, manipulated, or misled but still be thoroughly conformist, taking opinions, values, and habits slavishly from others. Such a one would not be autonomous. To be autonomous then, one must also form one's own personality (Feinberg, 1989). The process of self-creation is often described as giving the (moral) law to oneself. But some philosophers use a different metaphor and speak about identifying with a particular aspect of oneself (Bergmann, 1977; Frankfurt, 1971). Others think that competences are necessary for having a self (Haworth, 1986; Meyers, 1989) or that a life plan that one has made for oneself is necessary (Nussbaum, 1980; Kupfer, 1987). However the self is created, if one succeeds in having a firm self one needs also to take responsibility both for the rules one lays down and one's compliance with them (Dworkin, 1988). Thus one must live one's own life or live one's life "from within" (Gutman, 1989; Kymlicka, 1989). Beyond that some authors insist that one's preferences must be chosen by oneself. Preferences are autonomously formed if they are not conformist or not just a "sour grapes" reaction (Elster, 1985b:22). In addition, one must be self-reliant (Code, 1987a) and one must be principled by sticking to one's choices when they are challenged by circumstances or by one's enemies (Feinberg, 1989). Also important is self-control. The person whose emotions run riot is their victim and to that extent not autonomous (Hill, 1987; Meyers, 1989). One particular variant of that is control over one's bodily sensations. In Martha Nussbaum's description, Socrates' autonomy consists of being a "rational stone"—a man who retains his serenity in spite of severe physical deprivation and in the face of death (Nussbaum, 1986). Another aspect of autonomy is control over one's prejudices: The autonomous person is capable of making impartial judgments (Hill, 1987).

The central claim about autonomous persons is that their decisions, plans of life, and moral and other principles are exclusively their own. Autonomy is to have beliefs and values and to make decisions that are all one's own and *are by that token not anyone else's.* Thereby one comes to be one's own person.

But what if our best thinking turns out to be mistaken? The common answer is explicit: Better to be mistaken than to derive ideas from others (Hill, 1987:135). "If a person possesses any tolerable amount of common sense and experience, his own mode of laying out his existence is the best not because it is the best in itself, but because it is his own mode" (Mill, 1948:60). When liberal appeals, such as Mill's, were manifestoes for emancipation from authoritarian political or religious regimes, they were very powerful and needed no support. But today we must surely ask, Why is it so important to live by one's own life plan? Why is this more important even than having a good life plan, one that is productive for oneself, one that makes one a valuable member of a community? Why is it more important even at the risk of being in error or of having a life plan that is totally inappropriate or, in the long run, unsatisfactory? The answer given today is clear: If you do not live by your own ideas, if you depend on others for direction, you are not your own person and therefore do not deserve respect! Rawls insists that having a rational life plan, one that one has adopted autonomously, is a condition of respect. Autonomy is a necessary condition for respect (Rawls, 1971:440). It is supremely important that my ideas, values, life plans be *mine*, that they not be yours, and that no one made me adopt them.

How does one get to be one's own person? There are three different answers to that question.[2] The first claims that one is, as a matter of course, one's own person. Two reasons are given for that. One asserts that we are our own persons because we are all owners of ourselves. If one lacks autonomy that is always a result of being prevented by others from exercising the rights that we have by virtue of being self-owners. On this view we are, as it were, born as self-owners, and whether we are allowed to grow up to be adult self-owners depends on the social and political arrangements. I shall examine that claim in the next section.

A second view considers one's self—what makes one this particular person—as a collection of inborn traits. The thought is that everyone is born a certain kind of person. But the self that one is born as is merely a complex potentiality. One becomes autonomous by developing that inborn self. To become one's own person is a "coming to itself, to produce itself, to make itself (actually) what it is in itself (potentially)" (Hegel, 1953:23). External factors may prevent one from living out those native characteristics or of fully developing them. One is, in that case, not autonomous.

A third view holds that regardless of how we are born we become autonomous by making ourselves into "our own" persons. What is "mine" is what I make, what I choose, when not under anyone else's domination. To be free is to be "self-contained" and not "dependent" (Feinberg, 1989; Benn, 1982). The autonomous person is what she or he has made herself or himself be. "The autonomous person is a (part) author of his life" (Raz, 1986). Autonomy is one's competence to make oneself be who one wants to be (Dworkin, 1988:17; Haworth, 1986; Meyers, 1989).

AUTONOMY AS SELF-OWNERSHIP, SELF-REALIZATION, OR SELF-CREATION

Ever since the early seventeenth century, it has been assumed that individuals—at first that meant only white, male, property owners—are, at best, autonomous. John Locke's defense of constitutional government begins with that assumption of individual autonomy: Anyone is able to decide what would be for himself or herself the best life to lead. Those choices can be made, as Locke tells us, "without asking leave or depending on the will of another."

Locke wanted to explicate autonomy, being one's own person in property terms. Persons, he said, own themselves. That explication provides a plausible reason for why we ought to be allowed to be autonomous. Property rights are, in general, uncontroversial. No sane person would deny that each of us has the right to ordinary, everyday private property. Now, if it turns out that in being autonomous one just exercises one's ordinary, everyday property rights in one's own person, then surely demands for autonomy are also uncontroversial.

In our day that attempt at explicating autonomy has been revived by Robert Nozick (1974). Some of his readers have thought that this conception of persons as self-owners is plausible (Reiman, 1976) or even terribly important (Cohen, 1986a); others believe that it is a "red herring" (Kymlicka, 1990:125).

At first the talk about self-ownership seems very plausible. After all, I "have" abilities and all sorts of characteristics. We even talk about "being one's own person," living according to "one's own life plan" and that does sound a lot as if one's person or one's life plan were something that one owned, that was one's property. What is more, ownership involves a certain kind of exclusion. My ownership rights allow me to exclude you from using what I own. Similarly the characteristics that I have as this human being seem to many philosophers to be mine exclusively.

But having something is not the same as owning it. Having "one's own" life plan is not the same as owning that life plan. A lot more is "my own" than only my private property. The concept of self-ownership does not help to clarify our understanding of autonomy but instead confuses it because the notion of owning oneself makes no sense. Ownership of property, as we usually understand it, involves the freedom to buy and to sell, to give away, and, perhaps, bequeath one's properties to others. Property is alienable (Kernohan, 1989). But my relationship to myself, to what is "my own," is, in many cases, much more intimate than my relationship to the things over which I have property rights.

I can sell you my car or give it to you, and you may drive off to California in it, and I will never see you or my car again. But my self is, not in that way, alienable. I cannot give myself to you in the sense that you will disappear out West and I never see you and my self again. Well, you say, but I can sell you my talents by hiring myself out to you. But what I do, in that case, is not to alienate my talents to you, but to allow you to tell me how to use them. Although you can drive off in my car, you cannot go off in full possession of my talents. You cannot even rent them, because renting puts you in full control, if only for a limited period. The most you can do with my talents is to hire *me* to put them at your disposal for a time. If my talents were a car, you could only hire me to drive you around in my car. You could not rent the car to drive it yourself, nor could you buy the car and take it with you forever.[3] One can put this point very succinctly: Property is by definition alienable. My self, and its various constituents, are not alienable from me.[4]

In addition, property rights are not unitary but are an entire bundle of complex rights (Reeve, 1987):

> ... the legal right to property is not a single right; it is a bundle of rights, privileges, duties, and liabilities. What has been called the "full" or "liberal" concept of ownership entails the right to possess, or "exclusive physical control of the thing owned"; the right to use; the right to manage; the right to income from the thing owned; the right to the capital, that is, "the power to alienate the thing and to consume, waste, modify, or destroy it"; the right to security from expropriation; the power of transmissibility; ... (Dahl, 1985:76)

Accordingly, the political process involves complex negotiations about the limits to different property rights. If I buy property that includes a swamp, state regulations concerning wetlands seriously curtail my rights to use that property. So do regulations about siting of septic systems, regulations about logging to protect certain endangered species, and so on. All of these limitations on my property rights have a direct effect on my ability to buy and sell the property as well as on the uses I might be able to put it to. Once we take property rights *concretely,* the claim that we have property rights, of that kind, in our self is transparently ludicrous. If intended to suggest that our property rights, for example, in wetlands, ought to be as unqualified and unaffected by state "interference" as our relationships to our own persons, such a claim has rhetorical force. But it throws no light on our relationship to ourselves or on our autonomy.

The matter becomes clearer, even, when we remember that property relations are social and political creations. The power of the property owner to exclude others from use of her or his property does not reside in the property, or in the owner, but in the state that decrees and enforces property law (Nedelsky, 1990). There is property only where there is a state of some sort and power to enforce rules governing property. Shall we say that there is autonomy only in a state because autonomy consists of self-ownership and because ownership of self or of other presupposes a state? I think not. More generally, if persons are self-owners, we must say that prior to the establishment of a state, and of the legal machinery to enforce rules of property, there were no persons. But I do not think that we want to say that persons are the creatures of a state as is property.

Talk about self-ownership appears plausible to many people because they think that slaves are owned by others (Cohen, 1986a:109). They argue that if some people can own others, as property, then everyone ought to be able to have property rights in himself or herself. In some obvious sense it is true that plantation owners had property rights in their slaves, but only with a proviso that is usually left out in discussions of self-ownership: The slave's status was maintained only by constant supervision, threat, and coercion. The slaves did not accept being owned except under continued coercion. When I buy a car it will drive for me as it did for its previous owner. When I "buy" a person I must apply constant coercion and threats and must live in a society where everyone else will cooperate to keep my slave enslaved.

Owning a person is not like owning a thing. Instead, it involves living in a particular kind of society where the dominant class severely oppresses the subordinate class. The entire governmental and legal system that treated slaves as property was an elaborate attempt to justify the institution of slavery. Tables and chairs cannot be oppressed; only human beings can be oppressed. As long as a range of social institutions, mainly courts and police and lawyers, all pretend that slaves are items of property, the fact that white persons oppressed black persons bitterly can be concealed behind the facade of property relations.

One denies the essential personhood of slaves to the extent that one ignores that they are *coerced* into slavery and that they *resisted* regularly. Taking the claims of the slavers that they *owned* slaves at face value is to accept their denial that they are engaging in wholesale oppression of fellow human beings. When the systematic coercion involved in slavery is overlooked, the self-ownership view of persons goes a ways toward legitimating ownership of other persons. Slavery is, after all, only one example of that. Men often claim property rights over women. The attempt to justify claims to autonomy as an exercise of self-ownership not only rests on a bad metaphor but also has a grim history of justifying slavery and other forms of oppression. After all, John Locke believed that slavery could be justified in some cases.

Self-ownership, if defensible, would explain the provenance of certain rights. It would therefore support political and perhaps social autonomy. But even Nozick's self-owner might be a thorough conformist and thus not be autonomous in the stronger senses of personal or moral autonomy. But a self that is ours from birth may also be made the fundament of personal and moral autonomy if we claim that each of us is born a certain sort of person. We attain personal autonomy to the extent that we fully develop that self in the course of a lifetime. Thus philosophers have thought that one's conscience or one's free will are moral capacities that are ours from birth and that conformity to one's conscience or the exercise of the free will made one fully autonomous.

A similar view regards the self as the product of self-creation. We make ourselves be who we are, at least sometimes. We are autonomous when we choose our own ideas and values, create our own life plans, choose our own moral principles, and in all these ways create our own selves. A self is not something that comes with us at birth but is of our own making. According to the former view, all people have selves although not everyone develops them; according to the latter, only some people create firm selves for themselves. Here then are two other answers to the question of how we get to have selves of our own and thus get to be autonomous. We acquire selves either through self-realization or through self-creation.

IS AUTONOMY POSSIBLE? THE PROBLEM OF SOCIALIZATION

It seems clear that we do not acquire our selves merely by virtue of the fact that we own ourselves because we do not, in fact, own our selves. My relationship to my self is more intimate than property relationships are. The language of ownership is inappropriate in the context of having a self. The alternative views of how we acquire a self hold that we either develop an inborn self or create one for ourselves.

Both of these views of autonomy—self-realization of a set of inborn traits or the making of a self in the course of a series of careful life choices—is threatened by the fact that we are subject to socialization. We are, after all, social beings: We are raised to be particular persons as members of specific societies, classes, or other groups within specific societies, socialized into the society at large, or socialized into our particular subgroup or our family. Can we claim both to be the authors of ourselves, either by developing ourselves into who we always were from birth or by creating our selves, and to have been socialized into a particular situation and role in our society? It would appear that our apparently autonomous choices are, actually, determined by values and beliefs that we have accepted, more or less uncritically, from others (Young, 1980).

Although everyone acknowledges that problem, few philosophers are moved by it (Bernstein, 1983; Friedman, 1986; Wolf, 1989). Most philosophers believe that one can claim autonomy for oneself even if much of one's thinking is directly affected by one's social context and situation. Of course, our character and outlook are formed by the influences and the training we receive as children from parents and teachers. Of course, we do not think in isolation from others. Of course, we learn from others, consult them on difficult issues, and ask them for advice. But we are nevertheless capable of thinking and choosing for ourselves. Socialization does not prevent us from being autonomous.

Some philosophers insist that whatever the origins of an opinion, we are autonomous to the extent that we "identify" with it (Frankfurt, 1971; Bergmann, 1977; Agich, 1990) rather than passively acquiesce in it. Opinions, even if derived from others, or from the unquestioned "common sense" of the community, can become genuinely our own when we identify with them, that is, adopt them firmly and passionately. They do not become our own when we remain lukewarm or even cold in relation to them.[5]

Others stress our rational ability to examine moral and other principles and to evaluate them for their correctness and thereby make them ours (Benn, 1982). A related view leans on a very traditional distinction between reason and emotion and claims that as long as we think and act rationally, holding disturbing emotions at arm's length, we can consider ourselves to be autonomous (Benson, 1983).

A slightly different version of autonomy stresses that we fall short of being autonomous to the extent that we are manipulated by others, or lied to, or coerced into states of actions that we would not choose without coercion. Self-reflection that lays bare those forms of domination is the first step toward freeing ourselves from these extrinsic influences and thus toward autonomy. Thus autonomy is promoted by critical self-reflection, perhaps by various therapeutic techniques, and so on (Christman, 1987).

All of these philosophers lay down fairly stringent conditions for achieving autonomy in the face of the complex social influences that shape each of us. But in a variety of ways all of them echo Feinberg's verdict that "we may all be, in some respects, irrevocably the 'products of our culture' but that is no reason why the self that is such a product cannot be free to govern itself as it is" (Feinberg, 1989:22). We are shaped by childhood socialization, but while we are being so shaped we are also developing an autonomous self. Growing up is not a totally passive process and thus while we grow into adults we accept a good deal from others but we are also busy making ourselves into certain kinds of persons. Most philosophers seem confident that however powerful socialization is, it is not all-powerful.

I do not think that that confidence is justified. I do not think that one can claim with any degree of confidence that we are autonomous *in the sense in which autonomy is used in the preceding discussion*. In one way or another, each of these accounts of autonomy maintains that we make desires, values, beliefs, and principles our own by thinking about them carefully. On some views we think about them in relation to facts or values. On other accounts we think about them in relation to other beliefs and values we have or in relation to other desires, impulses, or whatever. In all these accounts it is the thinking that makes something our own.

It seems to me, though, that we are not in a position to ever assert with full confidence that we accepted some particular principles, adopted a certain outlook, made a certain choice, for reasons all our own. For, in the light of hindsight we often change our minds about that. Examples abound: In recent years it has become very clear to many thinking persons that what they had regarded as their own, autonomous opinions were infected by societywide racial prejudices, by societywide misogyny. A prime example of that are traditional philosophical discussions of political or personal autonomy. Philosophers had thought that they had developed them independently of social preconceptions. But it turns out that these traditional ideas of autonomy owe a great deal to the prevailing misogynist beliefs about the nature of men and of women (Okin, 1991; Grimshaw, 1986). Similarly our sexual desires have been shown to be influenced by social pressures to conform to socially sanctioned models of being a "man" or a "woman." It is only reasonable to be much less certain, than we once were, of what is our own in our thinking or feelings.

All philosophers acknowledge that our thinking is influenced by social pressures of many kinds. Some think that we can emancipate ourselves and push through to autonomy, and others do not. But neither side has very strong evidence. Among autonomy theorists some believe that one can be addicted to drugs and still be autonomous if one has deliberately chosen to have the desires that constitute the addiction (Dworkin, 1989:61). Others believe that a person's endorsement of his or her perverse desires does not show that they were autonomously adopted (Wolf, 1989:143). Theorists can hold either opinion because it is extremely difficult to tell in any given case whether a trait of a person is genuinely that person's own trait or is caused by external influences of some sort. Philosophers here are telling us stories about imaginary persons, and they can make up their stories to fit their philosophical positions. But those stories are extensions of their preconceived notions, not evidence for the truth of those ideas. At issue are *empirical* questions to which answers are difficult to find and always carry a certain degree of uncertainty.

Consider a man who is certain, on mature reflection, that homosexual relations are unnatural or immoral. Can he be certain that that conclusion is not affected by pervasive homophobia, by his fear of being thought unmanly by other men or women, or perhaps by his unease with what he suspects in himself are homosexual impulses? But then you say, what about men socialized in very similar ways, who nevertheless find prohibitions against homosexuality among consenting adults unobjectionable? Are these persons not clear examples of persons who have emancipated themselves from the prevailing prejudices of their society? Well, they may be, but it is not easy to be sure. One can be liberal about homosexuality in order to give oneself permission to have homosexual impulses that one grew up to regard as abhorrent. Or, one may *say* that one is neutral toward the sexual behavior of consenting adults but find in actual cases that one's protestations do not fairly represent one's sentiments. To what extent does what one says, and says with perfect sincerity, represent one's own attitudes rather than being adopted in order to fit in in a liberal social setting? Sexual feelings may not be the exclusive source of all our beliefs and attitudes, but surely Freud was right that they are very complex and affect one's beliefs, particularly about matters of sexuality itself, very powerfully. To the extent that one's sexual feelings are heavily influenced from early childhood days, it would be difficult to claim with confidence that one's beliefs and principles about sexual conduct are all one's own as the result of careful rational reflection.

Well, you say, that may be true of principles concerning sexual behavior but what about more abstract questions such as the nature of autonomy? But look at what happens: A wide range of philosophers who disagree about almost everything all agree that autonomy is attained by careful thinking about what one likes and wants, about what one does, about who one is. But thinking is always done in a context, even thinking about autonomy. Philosophers are not impartial judges when it comes to assessing the merits and efficacy of careful thinking. Can one really consider unprejudicedly whether thinking emancipates us from social pressures if one has committed oneself to a life of thought and shares that with others who have the same commitment? Now maybe we are correct in this commitment. But it does not seem clear to me that one can be certain that one's life choices, and the social world of the university in which one operates, may not have affected the high value philosophers place on autonomy as well as their rather cerebral conceptions of autonomy.

But, you say, my life choice to become a philosopher, or a professional intellectual, was a fully rational choice, one that I made my own by careful deliberation. What kind of autobiographical account of oneself would it take to support that claim? How detailed would that account have to be, and is anyone in a position to provide a sufficiently detailed account?

I do not want to argue, as some philosophers have, that the fact of socialization proves that we cannot in fact be autonomous in the sense in which philosophers currently claim that we are (Bernstein, 1983; Archard, 1992). But it seems to me that the knowledge we have of ourselves and of others is sufficiently fragmentary and shaky that we cannot claim with any confidence to be autonomous in the sense of not depending on others in the final choice of moral principles or of desires. We simply do not know enough about ourselves to assert that.

The question whether persons are socialized so completely that they cannot claim autonomy is clearly an empirical one (Christman, 1987). It must be studied in concrete, individual cases, one by one. But it is very difficult to answer because a good deal of the relevant evidence is not available. We do not, in fact, know the step-by-step process by which some external event—for instance, some parental remark about my not touching my penis—is translated into a component of my attitudes about masturbation and sexuality. We therefore also do not know directly how such parental remarks influence us. Whatever beliefs we have about that are quite circumstantial and often rest on theories that are not proven.

Whether socialization prevents us from being autonomous must be left open until we know a great deal more about the processes of forming a human person. But that is a serious problem for all those who want to say that a human being is most human when autonomous, that we need to strive, each of us, for autonomy and we need, each of us, to respect the autonomy of the other. For as long as we do not have solid grounds, as we surely do not, for claiming that we are indeed capable of autonomy in the sense defined, the recommendation that autonomy be our personal goal and be respected in others is on a par with recommendations of how to treat visiting aliens from outer space. It is not clear that either recommendation applies to beings like us.

The problem is aggravated by the fact that we are also quite certain that there are genuinely autonomous people, that there are genuinely autonomous acts, even of persons who are, taking their life as a whole, only very feebly autonomous. What is more, there are persons who are unjustly deprived of their autonomy and it is a legitimate and pressing goal to transform social arrangements in such a way that those persons also are enabled to lead autonomous lives. Now this conviction seems true to all of us. It is central to much of our best political and moral reflection.

This confronts us with a genuine dilemma. On the one hand there is our conviction that autonomy is sometimes real, that it is achievable and therefore worth striving for.[6] On the other hand we cannot be certain whether we ever are genuinely autonomous because we lack the requisite empirical information that any action or belief that appears autonomous is not actually influenced by the beliefs or actions of other persons. The claim to autonomy, to having desires, beliefs, outlooks, decisions that are exclusively one's own and do not depend on any other person, is not proven and given the current knowledge about the development of person not provable. The relevant body of empirical information is simply not available. That seems to invalidate our confidence that we are genuinely autonomous.

Many philosophers respond to that dilemma by standing pat on their belief that we are, at least sometimes, genuinely autonomous. They infer from that that socialization *cannot* be so pervasive that it impairs autonomy. Hence their confidence, noted earlier, that autonomy is genuine and that it is a realistic goal. But that is a very bad argument for this reason: It gives an abstract argument that rests on our definitions of terms to show that certain empirical claims—namely, that some of our actions and beliefs are exclusively our own—are true, even though we do not have the empirical information to verify them. That is a "philosophial" argument in a pejorative sense, that is, it predicts on purely conceptual grounds what scientific study will show. The notorious example of that is Hegel's claim to have shown by means of an abstract argument that there could not be more planets in our solar system than were known at the time. An additional planet was discovered soon afterward. This strategy for escaping from the dilemma is unacceptable.

We have several other options. We can surrender our confidence that autonomy is a real possibility. That might not be very damaging in fields like medical ethics, where demands for patient autonomy often amount to no more than the demand that patients be allowed to make important decisions for themselves rather than being coerced, bullied, or manipulated by doctors, nurses, or relatives. That demand can stand even if autonomy, in the broader sense of being one's own person, seems perhaps unattainable. (But even in medical ethics the defense of these demands would probably be more difficult if we could not appeal to the thesis that all human beings are entitled to political and/or personal autonomy in that broader sense.)

But in ethics or politics, we would have serious problems if we were to say that we do not know whether we are ever autonomous. It would be much more difficult to resist intentional manipulation of our opinions and values by a government if we suspected that our beliefs and values were shaped by unintentional manipulation by all sorts of social forces. Why should I claim exclusive control over my private sphere if it turns out that my most intimate desires and most hallowed beliefs may well not be "my own" but may simply reflect the values and opinions of those in my immediate environment? Autonomy theorists distinguish between desires and so on that I have and those that are genuinely "mine." Only the latter are constitutive of my autonomy. But if we cannot settle the worry about socialization, that distinction collapses and so does my claim to have a sphere that is exclusively mine and therefore ought to be only under my control. Corresponding problems would arise in ethics.

We can follow existing philosophical practice by making up facts to compensate us for those we do not yet possess. But that, we have already seen, would substitute abstract, conceptual argument for patient empirical investigation. That is a thoroughly irrational move and therefore unacceptable.

But just as we think that we are caught on the horns of this dilemma, we notice that the phrase "one's own" in "one's own person" or "one's own self" is being given a very specific interpretation: Having a belief, a value, a life plan, a self of one's own, is interpreted as having something that is *only* one's own. What is one's own is assumed to be exclusively one's own. Our confidence that we are autonomous, in that sense, is weakened by the fact of socialization and by the fact that we do not understand the process by which social forces shape us.

Here we encounter the notion of human separateness. Underlying the entire preceding discussion of autonomy is the idea that any personal characteristic belonging to one person can *therefore* not also belong to another. Persons are separate from one another precisely insofar as the characteristics of one are characteristics of *only* that person. There is no such thing as a characteristic that belongs to more than one person because it is jointly owned by several. Most philosophers take separateness to be self-evident. It is that assumption that generates this dilemma.

For suppose we gave up separateness and with it that very specific interpretation of what is "one's own" and said that having a belief, a value, and so on of one's own is compatible with that same value also being someone else's. In that case, our ignorance about the empirical facts about personality formation would not be so troublesome. The fact that a belief of mine was not only mine and was, moreover, adopted jointly with someone else would not longer count as proof that I lacked autonomy, for now being a person in my own right may in some situations be compatible with sharing ideas and even with adopting my ideas together with others. Of course, we would have to give an alternative account of autonomy. We could say, for instance, that most of our beliefs are shared because beliefs are, after all, social products: They emerge from elaborate discussions among sizable numbers of people. Whether I am autonomous thus is not a matter of whether some beliefs are all my own and no one else's but is a matter of what role I play in the social process in which beliefs are formed. Do I contribute actively, by engaging others in discussion, for instance, and are my contributions valued? Or do I simply accept what everyone else says? That sort of alternative understanding of autonomy needs working out. If it can be made clear, socialization ceases to be incompatible with our claims to be autonomous. I will provide such an alternative account of autonomy in Chapter 5.

For the present we need to pay more detailed attention to what is the critical assumption in the entire preceding discussion of autonomy; namely, that we are separate from one another, that each of us has his or her beliefs and desires, and that to the extent that I accept any beliefs or desires from another person, they are not mine and I fall short of autonomy. All mental states, character traits, actions, or other characteristics of persons belong to only one person. Underlying this whole discussion is the assumption that there are no values, beliefs, desires, and so on that are not just mine or yours but are genuinely ours. Were we, on the contrary, to accept that possibility of jointly owned characteristics, the fact that some belief, value, or action is not only mine would no longer necessarily infringe on my autonomy.

This notion of separateness requires clarification. It will become clearer in the next chapter, where I will argue that it is not by any means self-evident that human beings are separate from one another. In the chapters that follow I will argue, in addition, that separateness is not given but chosen and that different persons choose to be separate in rather different ways. In rare cases, one cannot help but admire that choice because it requires exceptional fortitude. But such far-going separateness is, indeed, exceptional. The separateness of the philosophers, however, tends to be faintly disingenuous. It is not a good choice.

◀ 2 ▶

Separateness

PREVAILING CONCEPTIONS of autonomy presuppose that human beings are separate from one another. In this chapter I investigate that assumption in some detail. We will see that the assumption of separateness consists of two thoughts—one clearly true, the other dubious—which are not always distinguished as clearly as they should be. We shall also see that separateness is not an ineluctable fact but is something that some persons choose. In the chapter that follows, I will provide some good reasons against making that choice.

WHAT IS SEPARATENESS?

The prevailing descriptions of autonomy reiterate over and over that persons are separate from one another. I have my ideas, life plans, and values, and you have yours. What is more, if we are autonomous, you shape your life and I shape mine. If, on the contrary, I adopt your ideas or allow you to shape my life plan or bow to your criticism of my way of life and alter it to suit you—not as a matter of rational choice but from fear of your anger or rejection—then your ideas, not mine, determine my life. Then your decisions shape my activities, not mine; your thought or your prejudice is in control of my days and my person. I am then not autonomous. Underlying the entire extended discussion of autonomy is an assumption that any of the attributes that we use to describe persons—thoughts, ideas, values, choices, decisions, actions, and so on—always belong to a distinct individual. They are either mine or yours or hers or his. But never are they, literally, ours. Human beings are separate in that sense: Whatever attributes they have[1] are always the attributes of a distinct individual. This is a very pervasive assumption in philosophy. But it is rarely stated and never fully argued. (I will examine some implicit arguments below.) It comes to the surface in various places when philosophers describe the autonomous life in more detail.

Here is an example of this unquestioning assumption of human separateness. Cohen tells us that "it is an intelligible presumption that I alone am entitled to decide about the use of this arm and to benefit from its dexterity, simply because it is my arm" (Cohen, 1986a:112).[2] The fact that my arm is under only my direct control, and that only I am directly aware of its kinaesthetic feelings of fatigue and pain and so on, does seem to argue that I should be in control of it. It is so intimately mine that it should not be under another's exclusive control. But does that, in turn, mean that I should control it all by myself—that "I alone am entitled to decide about the use of this arm"? There is surely a clear difference between my having control over my arm and my having *exclusive* control so that no one else is participating in that control. We need to consider more closely the sense in which the arm is "my" arm and not yours. This arm is my arm insofar as my body is distinct from all other human bodies.[3] Our bodies are distinct and therefore so are our nervous systems. Our nervous systems are not connected. As long as I am healthy, I feel my big toe, but I cannot know the pain in yours unless you tell me about it. I may know you well enough to make a good guess about your pain but I owe that knowledge to what you have told me in the past. Even if I know what you feel, I do not ordinarily feel it. I only feel what I feel. Similarly, my thoughts are internal to myself and are not yours, and so are, in the end, acts of will, decisions, or choices. If I want to raise my arm, I do so—as long as I am healthy. For you to get me to raise my arm is a more complex undertaking. You have to ask, entreat, cajole, threaten. You can raise my arm by grabbing hold of it, but then you raise it and not me.

Since our nervous systems are distinct, so are the physiological bases of our interpretations of experiences. We do not automatically share experiences; in addition, we put names on them by ourselves. Thus what we each think about those experiences is also distinct from what another thinks of his or hers. The feelings each of us associates with experiences are also distinct, and thus we build up distinct meanings of experiences, often different for each of us, as layers upon layers of experiences and interpretations are sedimented in memory. Since our bodies are distinct we do not move in tandem. Thus each of us tends to have different histories from every other. Not only do our distinct bodies provide slightly different points of view from which we observe the world and provide different interpretive grids to lay on that, but since those bodies describe distinct trajectories, each of us acquires a distinct history. That history in turn shapes our experiences and what we make of them. The consequences of having separate nervous systems are profound and far-reaching.

Some philosophers think that because our bodies are distinct no one can make a decision for me (Dilham, 1987:97). In one sense that is true, but it is also a pretty trivial claim. It is quite likely that what we ordinarily call "making a decision" involves some sort of mental event that we could compare to throwing a switch. Somewhere in my nervous system a switch is closed and that sets in motion a series of other changes that eventuate in my doing something. That internal event is obviously mine alone. But it is so much mine alone that no one else could claim it as hers or his because their bodies are distinct from mine. Thus it is not a very interesting assertion that decisions, in that sense of a change taking place in my nervous system, *must* be made by me alone. That is perfectly evident as long as our nervous systems remain distinct.

But Cohen is not claiming that my decisions about the use of my arm are mine in that trivial sense. The question is not whether anyone else can make my decisions in the sense of flipping that switch for me. Instead the question is whether another can make decisions for me by supplying me with the reasons that will move me to decide. Decisions are not momentary events but processes. I weigh different alternatives and consider reasons for each. Which reason is more persuasive? And why is it more persuasive? To what extent do I incline to decide in one way because that would please another, remove a threat of harm from them, protect against certain punishment that would follow if I decided differently? Decisions made under threat or coercion are not mine. Here the reasons I adopt are not my reasons but are imposed on me. Now when Cohen claims that he is entitled to make decisions over his arm alone, he claims that the reasons that move him to decide must be *his* reasons—the reasons that appear to be most cogent in the light of his own needs, interests, and moral conceptions. They must not be reasons imposed by others' entreaties, by guilt feelings they arouse in me, by their threats or outright coercion. At first that seems perfectly plausible. The distinctness of our bodies makes my arm closer to me than to you. Its connection to me is so intimate that it is a part of who I am. That is precisely why it makes no sense to say that I have property in myself.

But that does not imply that it therefore should belong *exclusively* to me, unless we make another assumption, namely, that any decision is made either by me or by another person—decisions are never made jointly. Could it not be that some decisions regarding me are made only by me and that many are made by the two of us together in such a way that they are not yours or mine alone but are ours? It is clear from the passage in Cohen that he believes that *there are no genuinely joint decisions.* By that I mean a decision with respect to which whatever I do alone does not suffice to complete the decision. The decision is made jointly; that is, it is made only by virtue of a number of more minute actions that you and I make together and/or separately. Neither of us does enough of those to have made the joint decision.

But Cohen, and most other philosophers, believe that decisions are either this person's or that person's own decision. If one shares that assumption, then indeed my right to decide over my arm means that I may decide over my arm alone because all decisions are, after all, the exclusive decision of some one person. If a decision is not exclusively mine then it is exclusively another's, and my intimate relation to my body does seem to entitle me not to be subject to another's exclusive control.

That suggests that the conception of separateness implicit in the description of autonomy has two parts: I am separate insofar as (1) I am distinct from you—we have separate nervous systems—and (2) any decision of mine (and presumably any other suitable attribute of mine) is either mine or someone else's. My decisions are not just mine; they are *only* mine. There are no genuinely joint decisions. Talk about joint decisions either is a way of misleading someone about the fact that another has decided for her or him, or is a way of trying to escape re-sponsibility for one's decisions, or is perhaps just a way of being muddle-headed, of not seeing that, in the end, when you and I make the same decision we still make two decisions—you make yours and I make mine.[4]

Philosophers move insensibly from the distinctness of our bodies to the sepa-rateness of our lives in the complex debate over ethics and political theory. They argue that "different people live different lives. Each life consists of experiences that are not shared with other lives. These facts are sometimes referred to as the 'separateness of persons'" (McKerlie, 1988:205). Here the movement from bodily distinctness to the separateness of actions and persons is made as if it were utterly unproblematic. The next step is then to use the separateness of person to argue against utilitarianism (Rawls, 1971:27) or for utilitarianism (Parfit, 1986:321ff.) or for libertarianism (Nozick, 1974:32). In each case the distinctness of bodies is used as reason for saying that goods are goods of each person separately and so are harms.[5] Now it is, of course true, that physical pains are directly felt only in the body of the creature in pain. But goods and evils are not the same as physical pains and pleasures. Once moral or political philosophers come or talk about "pleasure" and "pain" or "happiness" and "unhappiness" or about "human flourishing" and its opposite, they are not self-evidently talking about attributes owned exclusively by separate persons. A person may be flourishing as far as his or her life is concerned, but flourishing in a social world that is not functioning well is considerably more restricted than personal flourishing in a world where most others are also doing well, where existing institutions are working and sup-porting the well-being of individuals. Participating in successful projects with others is a significant part of flourishing or of happiness. That such happiness is nevertheless exclusively owned requires extended argument. It cannot be taken as self-evident.

GROUPS AND THE DEBATE OVER INDIVIDUALISM

A frequent objection to the separateness of persons is that there are other ways of thinking about the actions of groups. One need not assume that each member of a group is a separate agent. Sometimes group members act separately; sometimes the members act jointly.

> There is a distinction largely ignored, or mischaracterized ... between matters which are for me and for you, on one hand, and those which are for us, on the other. ... A conversation is not the coordination of actions of different individuals, but a com-mon action in this strong irreducible sense; it is *our* action. It is of a kind with ... the dance of a group or a couple, or the action of two men sawing a log. Opening a con-versation is inaugurating a common action. (Taylor, 1989:167)

I believe that that is absolutely right, but we need to say much more. We need to try and make clear in what way the actions of groups are different from the ac-

tions of separate individuals. In some ways it is perfectly obvious that not all actions are actions of individuals. After all, there are not only individuals but also
groups in the social world and groups act; groups have characteristics all their
own. Soccer teams win or lose. It is neither the forward, the defense, nor the
goalie who wins, but only the whole team. Conversely, the whole team does not
catch the ball before it hits the net but only the goalie. But how are we to understand sorts of expressions like "the team won"?

There has been a great deal of debate about that, and two sorts of answers are
popular. On one side are the people who say: If teams win, then teams are distinct
entities from their members. It is not individual members of the team who win
the game but the whole team. Thus groups should be regarded as individuals distinct from the members that constitute them. There are not only facts about individuals but also facts about social entities such as teams, banks, associations. In
some situations that is clearly plausible: Banks are rich even if, and often because,
their employees are not rich. But there is nothing mysterious about that since
banks are persons before the law. Because of a legal fiction, banks can count as individuals. But in other cases that answer seems less plausible. Sports teams are not
in the same sense legal fictions, even if their owner is. But sports teams also have
attributes that are not attributes of the team members separately. A team may play
like a well-oiled machine, but that is not because each of its members plays like a
well-oiled machine. A team may be outstanding even if not all of its players are,
but in that team even ordinary players turn in extraordinary performances. That,
theorists believe, shows that teams are individuals in their own right, distinct
from the individual persons that are their members.

But the opposing theorists reply that teams, banks, or associations are very odd
sorts of individuals since they do not exist separately from their members (except
as legal fictions). The president of the bank cannot introduce you to the bank—
only to the other executives and board members. Fans cannot honor the members
of the team and then honor the team separately, because there is no team apart
from the members. Hence, to say that the team wins must be taken as an elliptical
way of saying that the members win. Teams, and groups in general, are referred to
as a sort of shorthand for its members and their actions.

That debate has been carried on for some time and has become quite complex.
What we need to notice though is that both sides to the controversy assume that
all individuals are separate. The action of each person is that person's action
alone. That assumption leads one to the conclusion that if one can say that "the
team won" then there must be some individual that is the team, which is not identical with all the team's members. The opponents of this view, being leary of such
collective individuals, instead claim that what we call the actions of the team are
instead the actions of separate individuals. Both views maintain the prevailing assumption of separateness.[6]

In recent years, another view has been widely discussed: methodological individualism. It makes a contribution to that debate by moving out of the arena of

ontology—What sorts of things are there in the world?—into the arena of explanation—What sorts of things do we need to talk about when explaining the world to ourselves? The methodological individualist has no problem with facts about groups. Some banks are strong; others teeter on the brink of bankruptcy. The methodological individualist accepts that such claims may be literally true or false. But when we come to explaining facts about groups, methodological individualism insists that groups do not figure in rock-bottom explanations. A bank failure may be explained, to begin with, by reference to facts about the bank; for example, that it made a lot of speculative loans and investments. But sooner or later we need to explain those facts, in turn, by statements about particular persons who acted in certain ways that produced the present unfortunate results.

The debate over individualism, methodological or ontological, shows that the thesis that persons are separate—in the sense defined at the end of the preceding section—is not as easily refuted as Charles Taylor, for instance, thinks. Just gesturing at the activities of groups proves nothing. It only raises new questions; namely, how we are to understand and explain the actions of groups, whether as linguistic fictions for more cumbersome expressions listing the actions of individual persons or as the actions of separate super-individuals such as teams, banks, or philosophy departments.

All three views—methodological individualism, ontological individualism, and their opponents (who are often called ontological wholists)—presuppose that human beings are separate. To show that these different forms of individualism are mistaken we need to show that persons are not separate and that there may well be genuinely joint actions. This demonstration will have two steps. I will first show that the sorts of more or less implicit arguments philosophers offer for separateness are unimpressive. Next I will show that we can choose to be in-relation. Joint actions are possible.

So far the discussion is cast in terms of whether people are separate. The question appears to be whether persons *are* always separate or whether they sometimes belong to social wholes, which are not merely aggregates of individuals and their actions. The question seems to be—to put this in slightly different terms— whether the events in the social world are always explicable by reference to the states and actions of individuals alone or whether there are causes that are not individuals. But as we examine the individualist stance in detail, we begin to see that the issue is not purely about what is or is not. Whether we are separate or not depends on whether we *choose* to be separate. At issue are not facts alone but possibilities that are actualized because of human choices and actions.

Separateness is not a given, a fact about the universe, but is a complex set of conducts that some people choose to engage in and many others, as we shall see in the next chapter, pretend to engage in where such a pretense is convenient. We can act, and we do act, in such a way that what we do is done by the group of us, not by the separate members—it is done by us jointly. That does not commit us to reifying groups and ascribing thoughts, beliefs, and actions to groups or claiming that groups have minds besides the minds of each of the group's members. But it is saying that decisions can be made jointly by groups if the members of the group, and the group as a whole, choose to conduct affairs in this way.

THE DEFENSE OF SEPARATENESS

The thesis that human beings are separate is taken so much for granted that it is never challenged explicitly. There are therefore also no elaborate controversies about that claim and no detailed defenses of it. What defenses there are must be inferred from the asides of philosophers, from remarks incidental to other claims. On that somewhat speculative basis, we can unearth several defenses of separateness: Separateness is a quasi-logical given or separateness is rooted in quasi-natural facts about human beings.

Separateness as a Quasi-Logical Given

Feinberg claims that a "powerful case" can be made to show that autonomy is a precondition for "dignity, self-esteem and responsibility" (Feinberg, 1980:20). Autonomy amounts to being in control of oneself, all by oneself. Autonomy is here defined as self-rule and thus the absence of rule by another. If I am to be autonomous, I must meet two conditions: I must be internally in control of myself and not be controlled externally, that is, by anyone else. There must be internal rule without external domination.

The autonomous person needs internal constraint. It is difficult to regard a person as autonomous who is at the mercy of his or her desires, whose life has no shape or order, and who lacks all sense of direction. But why must I be free from external rule to be autonomous? Because external rule is always rule by another. The possibility that external rule may *also* be internal rule because it is *joint* rule is not envisaged. Clearly Feinberg believes, along with many other philosophers, that there is no such thing as joint rule because we are separate from one another. Ruling oneself is something we do all by ourselves. If someone else is involved in ruling me I am under external constraint and therefore not self-governing or autonomous.

To the extent that we can find any argument for this position at all here, we can discern an implicit argument that seems to be quasi-logical: Control must be either internal or external, and these two possibilities are mutually exclusive. Self-control is internal control. Any control that is not internal control is external control. Therefore self-control, autonomy, is not external control, QED.

Separateness as a Quasi-Natural Given

Mill argues that we are entitled to self-determination within the private sphere because "with respect to his own feelings and circumstances, the most ordinary man or woman has means of knowledge immeasurably surpassing those that can be possessed by any one else" (Mill, 1946:68). We have direct knowledge about ourselves that no one else has and are intimately connected to our bodies in ways in which no one else is. We are, in short, distinct from one another in our bodies. That fact, Mill claims, gives us a right to self-determination in the sphere in which we are more intimately connected to ourselves than anyone else. Cohen, as we saw in the preceding chapter, presents a very similar argument. He infers from our bodily distinctness that we each have the right to exclusive decisionmaking with respect, for instance, to the use we make of our bodies and our abilities. Cohen, like Mill, moves from a fact about our nervous systems, namely, that they are not interconnected, to a very different matter, namely, who is to make decisions that affect me in a serious way (Cohen, 1986a).

That transition is eased, as I pointed out earlier, by the assumption of separateness, which likens all our acts and characteristics to states of our nervous systems: Neither can be shared in a full-blooded sense. Just as your proprioception is not shared by me, so your decisions, beliefs, values, actions are said to be all yours. What is more, separateness is so closely assimilated to distinctness that it too appears to be just a given. Only here it is not so much a logical given, but rather a natural one. Separateness—that no acts or conditions of persons can be joint acts or conditions—is so much like distinctness—that bodily states belong either to your body or to mine—that both have the force of natural conditions known to all.

Separateness as a Biological Fact

Kant claimed that women were less able to reach maturity, to become autonomous rational thinkers, because they were more prone to conformism, more emotional, more easily swayed by the opinions of others. Kant seems to have attributed this failure of women to achieve autonomy, and thus separateness, to female character, to laziness and lack of courage. Freud echoed Kant in proclaiming that women were less principled and more ready to respond to emotion than men but then provided a psychological explanation for that difference: Men's ability to draw clear lines between universal principles and private inclination is learned very painfully when fear of castration by the father deters them from trying to sleep with their mothers. Female children, not having a penis, experience the Oedipal traumas differently and resolve them more gradually. They are thus never shocked into becoming principled, rational, autonomous human beings. They never achieve the separateness that the oedipal drama forces on men. They remain more closely attached to the mother, try to substitute a baby for the penis they lack, and are, therefore, always ready to nurture children and the fathers of those children. Separateness or the lack of it derives from biological facts (Lloyd, 1984:68ff.; Gilligan, 1982:7). Here separateness is treated as a given because it is the effect of a biological difference between the sexes. Having female reproductive organs brings with it a specific set of character traits or a specific psychological history. Women's character or their psychological history makes them incapable of men's separateness.

In all of these cases separateness is a given; that is, it is not something we can choose to adopt or reject, it is not a posture whose value we can question. We have no choice with respect to being separate because it rests on the logical structure of the universe, or because it depends directly on the inescapable distinctness of our bodies, or because it is the effect of central biological facts about men and women. Whatever support is given in these fledgling arguments to the claim that we are separate, the outcome is always this: We can no more choose not to be separate than we could choose a different logic, or choose to link our nervous system with that of others, or choose that the human species not be divided into biological males or females. Separateness is inescapable.

These three arguments are less than impressive. It is hardly self-evident that all constraints are either external or internal. In fact, whether those alternatives are exclusive, or whether there are constraints that are both external and internal because they are constraints jointly imposed by myself and others, is precisely what is at issue. The quasi-logical argument begs the question. So does the attempt to argue for separateness on the grounds that our bodies are distinct because what is at issue is just this: There are no joint pains or joint secret thoughts. Are there, in the same way, no joint decisions? The Mill-Cohen argument does not argue for separateness but takes it for granted.

The Freudian claim that men are separate because they have penises is logically more respectable, but there is overwhelming evidence that it is not good biology or psychology (Stiver, 1991). The oedipal drama, we are told, plays itself out very differently for boys and for girls because the boys have penises and girls do not. Thus male separateness is interpreted as the direct effect of being a biological male. But feminists observe that female roles, as well as male roles, have been imposed and maintained by force and often by means of violence. There is still a controversy whether "biology is destiny," but we would not argue about that if biology really *were* destiny. Truly biological traits, such as male and female roles in biological reproduction, are not imposed forcibly. We do not prevent men from getting pregnant by beating them up or ostracizing them; neither does social disapproval and condemnation from the pulpit dissuade women from impregnating men. Biological differences are given. No one needs to be coerced into having the appropriate biology. It is not a matter of choice and therefore not a matter of controversy. But women's and men's roles in having and raising children are imposed by complex and oppressive regimes of childhood socialization and policing of adult behavior. The different behaviors of stereotypical men and women are learned under pain of violence and ostracism. Men are not separate because they live through that great crisis, but are made to live through that crisis so that they may grow up to believe that real human beings are separate. If separateness were not a matter of choice, none of this effort at disciplining people into the "right" behaviors would be necessary.

Separateness has long been taken for granted. We can now see that there is no pressing *intellectual* reason for doing so. What there is by way of argument for separateness does not overpower us. Separateness is not a given. On the contrary, it is often something we choose. At other times we choose to be in-relation.

JOINT ACTIONS

Methodological individualism asserts that events in the social domain are explicable by reference to the acts and states of individual persons. This means that what appear to be the acts or states of collectives such as banks or teams are properly explained as the aggregates of acts and states of individual persons. But how shall we explain the acts of individual persons? Presumably, states and acts internal to each individual person will explain those.[7]

But it is easy to see that that is not correct. Suppose we have a group of people sitting in a room. Most of the people face in one direction. But at one end of the room is a long table and people sitting behind that table face in the opposite direction. People speak. Now this one, then another. Then one of the persons at the table says something and some people raise their hands. Then one of the persons at the table seems to count the raised hands. The person who spoke before speaks again and others raise their hands, which are then counted. What goes on? A meeting taking a vote? A public criticism–self-criticism session in which persons publicly confess to their errors? A planning meeting where people volunteer for different jobs? Are these commodity traders, offering to buy or sell? Or is it some ritual whose rules we do not understand?

Suppose it is a town meeting where a vote is being taken. Each person raising a hand, or keeping it down, does so in view of certain conventions, understood and shared by the members of the group, about taking votes in meetings. The significance of what each does is explicable by reference to those conventions and by those conventions being shared by all or most persons in the room (Taylor, 1985). The people in that room (or most of them) must have some sort of shared understanding with each other of what they are doing. The action of each person is an act of voting because the act refers to the acts of others and to the shared understanding of what they are doing in this room.

Here the explanation of individual acts does not consist merely of statements about events internal to the person. What the persons voting are doing is determined by the shared understanding of what they are doing. Voting is a joint action in certain respects and is not a joint action in certain other respects, which we will see below. Joint actions are performed when the actors conform to certain conventions and understand those conventions. Everyone knows what is being done; for example, "we are taking a vote" or "some people are volunteering to cook for the next town picnic."

This shared understanding differentiates two people doing the same thing at the same time in proximate places from two people doing something jointly. If I sit on the subway behind a man reading the newspaper, I may read the page he is reading over his shoulder. It does not matter whether he is aware of it. We are reading the paper together, but his acts and mine are perfectly separate. I can stop; he can go on. I can read while he, in fact, has closed his eyes and fallen asleep, which I notice when the paper disappears from my view and falls to the floor. That is very different from you and me reading a particular piece together, commenting to each other, looking for a particularly outrageous passage someone told us about. Here there is a common project. I read. You read. But that is not all there is to it. What makes it our effort is the understanding that we are doing this together. If you start reading something else, or your conversation drifts off toward a different topic, it is clear that we are no longer reading the paper together.

Now this common understanding is not just the aggregate of our separate decisions. I decide to read the paper, and second, I decide to read the paper with you. You make the corresponding decisions. But that still does not make us read the paper together, because we have not told each other what we decided. So then we tell each other. Whether we now have a joint decision or a joint project remains to be seen. When your attention drifts, I complain, saying, "I thought we were reading the paper together." And you reply that that does not mean that we read the same story. We are just looking at the same newspaper together. Well, now there are two different understandings of what we are doing. So it may turn out that we are not doing anything together, except in a separate sense, or it may turn out that we decide what kind of reading the paper this is going to be. If we do that, then the actions of each of us are going to be shaped by the ideas and desires of the other. From now on the decisions each of us makes are determined not only by our own separate reasons but are shaped by what we jointly agreed that we would be doing. You come back to reading the same piece as I and the conversation about it continues. You think that that is going to be fun, after all. The project is jointly defined.

We remain distinct. Insofar as decisions, thoughts, and desires are internal to our bodies, the decision of each of us is different from that of the other. But in making a joint decision these internal events are, by our own choice, brought under the control of the other's desires and thoughts. You begin to read the article I was reading to please me or because you stop being distracted and my reminder brought you back to your previous state of mind, in which you wanted to be reading with me. In a joint decision, the persons remain distinct but the decision is no longer under the control of each person separately: it is now controlled by the decisions of various persons together. Persons making such a joint decision form a "we," according to Margaret Gilbert. They form a "plural subject" (Gilbert, 1992). As we come back to reading the paper together in the sense in which we had originally intended, before your mind wandered and I complained about that, what we say and do (pointing to a sentence, joking about a turn of phrase, clowning around) "refers" to the other. What you and I say and do we would not do were we not reading this newspaper article together with the other. Were we separate agents, we would act very differently (Waldron, 1993:354).

I want to develop these ideas by talking more about conversations. Many conversations are conversations between persons who are perfectly separate. These are, for instance, conversations in which each free-associates on something the other has said. One person talks. The other barely listens and then responds with some remarks only remotely related to what the first person said. Neither person responds to the other except in the most minimal way that some remarks made by one were prompted by some word or phrase used by the other. Extreme examples are conversations in which the partners talk at the same time so neither can pay any attention to what the other is saying.

Equally separate are the parties in a legal or philosophical discussion in which each member offers a view and defends it unto death. Many sentences begin with "My view is …," and it is accepted by all parties that the purpose of the conversation is well served by everyone defending his or her views.

Conversations in groups that have to make a decision frequently follow that model. For instance, in a college faculty group trying to reach a practical decision, different proposals are made. They are argued for or against, amendments are offered and accepted or rejected, and then a vote is taken. All of this is interspersed with professorial jocularity and appeals to Robert's Rules of Order. But the final outcome is determined by counting the separate expressions of equally separate opinions.

Here we have a "common" action in two different senses:

1. The conversation among the faculty is a conversation they have with each other and is therefore, in a purely formal sense, a "common" conversation. But these are joint conversations only in a quite trivial sense: A conversation is, by definition, something you have with someone else. If I talk to myself in the course of a complex philosophical argument with myself, I pretend to be another person who is being critical of my views. There are still two of us, but one of them is being impersonated by me. Thus the faculty vote comes after a conversation that is (possibly) common only because more than one person was talking and listening.

2. The purpose of this conversation is not to be witty and entertaining but to come to a decision. Many persons make one decision and so there is a "common" product. What that, formally common, conversation brings forth is a common decision, and so we have a second reason for talking about this conversation as common to the participants. That decision is made by means of a vote, which aggregates the decisions of individuals. Professor Lardbottom's motion as amended by Professor Coldfeet carries.

Here making a decision means that you make your decision and I make mine and that we then count up the different decisions to generate a common decision by rules accepted beforehand. That is one way of talking about "deciding together" that would not invalidate the basic conception of separateness, that everyone decides for himself or herself—or their decisions are made for them by someone else. As noted earlier, there is a shared understanding of the process of voting presupposed, but the vote itself is making a decision in a perfectly separate sense. There are many activities done in groups in which each of us is a separate agent. Participating in groups and being separate are perfectly compatible. Being-in-relation is not coextensive with being in a group; in addition, many group activities are not done in-relation. There are very different ways of "doing something together" and only some of those are examples of being-in-relation.

Benn talks in that way about a cooperative editing project among a group of philosophers: Each persons writes and edits his or her piece of the whole book. Each chapter in the book has a discrete and readily identifiable author (Benn, 1982). Then the papers are put together by the publishing house, printed, bound, and sold. If that effort merits the name of a "cooperative" project one can well cooperate and remain perfectly separate.

But what if we acknowledge that we have learned from each other? Criticisms you raised induced me to reconsider my views; suggestions you made were new to me but on reflection seemed worth accepting. What I write owes a lot to you, but the decision to accept certain ideas and to reject others is clearly always made by me, albeit only after you talked to me. Here consultation is necessary for my developing my views, but they are still exclusively mine in the sense that I decided, by myself, what to accept from you and what to ignore or reject. Your actions are causally necessary for mine, and our editing project is a collective one in the causal sense noted above. We could even say that there is a stronger sense of "deciding together" in which each makes his or her contribution to the final outcome, but the process has been so extended and complex that we can no longer identify who said what when and how what each said or did affected the other's thinking and decisionmaking.

Some philosophers want to argue that the principle that each person makes his or her decision separately is maintained here even though the contributions of each person to the actual decision can no longer be disentangled (Nozick, 1974: 187). But it is not obvious that that is true any more. For such an interpretation overlooks that the conversations about the different contributions to a common book always presuppose some shared understandings about the goals and content of this book. Now it may be that different contributors have very different ideas about the book and no shared understandings, but the comments of one may prove helpful to another contributor, more or less by accident. But it may also be that there is a shared understanding of the book that motivates all, that they all have worked toward this goal as a precondition for putting the book together. These conventions, as I said earlier, are shared in a sense that is not compatible with separateness. Certain conversations or shared projects cannot be explained except by reference to such conventions.

It is not the common product that makes this conversation different. Many different kinds of conversations have that depending on what the goal of the conversation is. As noted earlier, conversations that aim at making a decision produce a common product if successful. What is important in this type of conversation is not that decisions are thought of as one person's or a number of persons' ideas prevailing over the ideas of others but that decisions are thought to arise out of the conversation. Here there are, of course, separate persons contributing, and participants are well aware of who contributed what. But these contributions are not added or subtracted from one another; they form a whole through the effort of the group, and the original contributions often are transformed in the process so as to make them more or less new. Here one does not defend the integrity of one's original suggestion but happily sees it transformed into a richer, more complex suggestion or one that is more consonant with the entire course of the group's reflection. Hence, although we can identify the authors of some of the building blocks of the final consensus, what finally emerges does not belong to any individual but is the accomplishment of the group as a whole. It is a genuinely joint action.

Margaret Gilbert points out that in these sorts of conversations the final outcome is different from an aggregation of the beliefs of the individual members of the group. The group may adopt a certain policy, and I may support that decision since it seems to correspond most closely to a consensus under which the group could function and even thrive. Thus I identify with the consensus finally arrived at. But for myself, I may have some reservations about the policy adopted (Gilbert, 1992:289). I may not be totally happy with it and have doubts about its effectiveness. This does not put me in the position of a person who lost in a vote because I do support the joint decision made. If it came to a vote, I might vote against it. But we are not aggregating individual beliefs, or voting, but reaching a joint decision, and that is a totally different project.[8] Nor is it what the skillful politician does; namely to compromise on the best resolution that she or he believes can be obtained from this particular group at the moment. If the votes are not there for the resolution the politician would ideally hope for, then she or he will compromise and accept the best it is possible to get. But what we have then is one more vote. Suppose the group is trying to decide how to conduct its meetings. If we vote, I vote for the best resolution I can get, but I have not committed myself to following the policy adopted. If I join a consensus in which the group decides that it will henceforth, say, begin meetings on time, even if some members are absent, I commit myself to act in appropriate ways in the future, even if privately I may have doubts that the consensus will last, that others are fully committed to it, that it is a good idea. Here the joint commitment is clearly distinct from the individual beliefs I have. The former is not an aggregation of the latter.

This points to another aspect of joint decisions: Underlying certain collective actions is a shared understanding that the members of a group have a goal in common, in this case to resolve the problem of meetings starting late and the more fundamental goal to resolve difficulties consensually. Everyone knows that this is one of the group's goals, and everyone knows that everyone else knows that. Everyone has given the others to understand in more or less explicit ways that they share that goal (Gilbert, 1992:163). (Voting may have such a common goal behind it but need not do so. There are elections held even by governments that do not believe in elections but must pretend to do so.)

A different aspect of joint actions is illustrated by Jeremy Waldron's analogies between individual acts and the parts of an opera. As the curtain rises on the opera, the opening aria is infused with meaning by being the opening aria. It foreshadows events to come, the intrigue, the drama of the plot, the music one anticipates. Each portion of the opera gains its significance, in part, from being a portion of a whole. Similarly, events in a person's life gain significance from being events in this person's life (Waldron, 1993:356). In similar ways, in the process of a joint conversation each contribution to the conversation acquires particular meaning as a step in the collective process of resolving a certain matter and arriving at a policy that all will accept as the policy of the group.

Groups reach joint decisions by what is commonly called "consensus" decisionmaking. Here different persons make suggestions, and one builds on the other. Some contributions to the conversation are off the train of thought and thus are ignored. The persons who offer those do not continue to defend them but instead join in the shared train of thought. (One may insist that a point one makes be heard when at first it is not. This is not because it is *my* point that is not being heard but because it belongs at this particular stage of the process—one defends not one's point but insists that the common suggestion that is being developed would profit from this particular addition, emendation, or transformation.) Other suggestions strike a chord with several participants and are eagerly embraced, developed, repeated. At a certain point a decision is made. Often this is felt not so much as *making* a decision but that the decision emerges: It is more or less suddenly there. After that there may well be more conversation offering clarifications and offering specifications in which the decision is worked out in greater detail.

Such conversations have a different ethos from a conversation that is collective free association or from the decision made among separate persons: One does not defend one's ideas against all rivals, because there is a common project that is on a certain track. One does not attack the view of the other, although one does of course offer conflicting ideas and views. One's responses to the other are not to suggest that the other is mistaken but to offer different views of what the other has said, to transform the other's ideas to fit them into the decision that is emerging. Early in the conversation there may be alternative suggestions of the direction in which the decisionmaking process should go. But here too the alternatives are not offered as conflicting alternatives as much as beginnings of what may become a common decision. The effort will then be to find a common direction that does justice to the different initial proposals.

It seems clear that the process requires a certain homogeneity of the group. I don't have to like everyone, but I have to trust them not to be exclusively on their own parade—otherwise I will find myself used by them. Thus not all conversations are of this sort; nor can they be. But that is not important at this point.

What matters is that there are genuinely consensual decisions that are not in whole or in part some particular person's ideas but are the joint product of a number of people who have worked them out together. That suggests strongly that separateness, in decisionmaking at least, is not self-evident and is not pervasive. Instead there are decisions made by groups in which everyone remains a separate decisionmaker and there are decisions made jointly by groups.

The crucial difference between separate and consensual decisions is that each is chosen. If we take a vote we choose to count separate opinions. If we strive for consensus we try to adopt a very different process of decisionmaking in which we talk until it is clear to everyone what has been decided, at least in general. The vote insists on the separateness of persons. Consensus stresses being-in-relation. Whether the decision is separate or in-relation is, therefore, a matter of choice. It is not an individual choice, one that each member of the group makes separately, but one that is constitutive of the group. Only among persons who are willing and eager to make joint decisions can decisions be made jointly.

Here we get a first glimpse of being-in-relation. From this very beginning it is clear that separateness and being-in-relation are chosen. Separateness is not given; it is not a fact. Neither is being-in-relation. The assumption of separateness is not best countered by asserting that we are "really" in-relation. Instead we need to unmask the frequently disingenuous choices of separateness that underlie a great deal of mainstream philosophy.

It will take a good deal of effort to link this description of making a decision in-relation to the more familiar descriptions of being-in-relation: affiliation (Miller), caring (Gilligan, Noddings), empathy (Jordan), permeable ego boundaries (Freud), and so on. I will undertake that task in the fourth chapter. But the following passage from an article by Jean Baker Miller will serve as a preliminary characterization of being-in-relation:

> It is the interplay between people that is important. They have both created the interplay. ... Each contributes to it. It is something more than what is done by each individual or what goes on in each individual. ... Both created something new together. Both are enlarged by this creation. Something new now exists, built by both of them. This is the "connection between," the relationship. It does not belong to one or the other. It belongs to both. (Miller, 1986:7, 15)

Autonomy as usually understood in philosophy presupposes separateness. Separateness has two parts: that our bodies are distinct and that we make our decisions alone and, more generally, that we have a wide range of capacities and conditions that belong to each of us exclusively. The first of these is an empirical truth. Our nervous systems are distinct. We can indulge in a science fiction fantasy of a world where there is only one nervous system because we are each only a node in a universal neural network. If that came to pass, human life would be quite different from what it is now. But the second part, that we have our attributes exclusively, is not a simple truth. It may seem, and does seem, very plausible to many because it does describe their actual practices and the way in which they think about and enact their relationships. Others find separateness foreign and implausible, because they conduct their relationships in very different ways.

I have so far merely shown that in the case of decisionmaking, joint decisions are possible. It is not inevitable that all decisions be made separately. Some are, in fact, made jointly. But that is only one case. What about separateness in all the other areas of our lives? In the chapters that follow, I will show that there are separate and in-relation ways of doing many other things we do. I will contrast separate and in-relation versions of empathy, emotions, knowing, and power.

◄ 3 ►

The Critique of Separateness

I WANT TO SHOW THAT the prevailing assumption that human beings are separate is not defensible on either descriptive or normative grounds. Human separateness is not a simple given, of some sort, but is chosen. It is chosen in different forms, and the most common forms of separateness are not to be recommended.

But no one chooses to be separate without also choosing to be autonomous in a specific way, or to have empathy in a particular way, or to love, or to know, or to hold power in a separate manner. Hence the critique of separateness is best undertaken by examining separate forms of more concrete human attitudes. In this chapter I will look at autonomy as it is understood and practiced by those who have chosen separateness. The critique of separateness will focus on a particular embodiment of separateness, namely, in autonomy. Other forms of separateness will be examined in later chapters. Later we will also see that there are forms of autonomy that do not presuppose separateness, and the same is true of empathy, love, knowledge, and power. But in this chapter, the word "autonomy" refers to separate autonomy.

Autonomy is thought to consist of being the "author" of one's life, as living according to a "life plan" that one has chosen for oneself and is now executing. Careful choices and rational weighing of alternative courses of action figure prominently in many descriptions of autonomy, as do freedom from coercion, manipulation, and constant material distress. Not too long ago autonomy was explicitly considered a male attribute. Philosophers wrote books and papers about "the autonomous man." In recent years, that sort of language has come to be considered improper and writers about autonomy now dutifully vary the gender of the personal pronouns in their writings, referring in some examples to "him" and in others to "her." This is a welcome acknowledgment of the feminist movement and its revisions of mainstream philosophy. But other than that, feminist criticisms of prevailing conceptions of autonomy have been pretty much ignored.

These criticisms are, however, extremely powerful. I will begin to examine them in this chapter and continue to develop them in detail in the chapters that follow. I will begin this extended discussion with a case history, Virginia Woolf's portrait of an autonomous philosopher.

A CASE HISTORY

Virginia Woolf's *To the Lighthouse* (1927) is a sustained critique of the prevailing ideal of autonomy and the separateness it presupposes. Although Woolf has long been celebrated as a great writer, her critique of the ideal of autonomy has been ignored by philosophers. They have taken little notice of Woolf's impressive demonstration that separate autonomy, so far from being an ideal for all human beings, is an ideal only for some men. They have continued to insist that separate autonomy is morally admirable and is the foundation for liberal political institutions.

But *To the Lighthouse* tells a very different story: Men pretend to be autonomous but are actually intensely dependent on women not only for the care of their physical well-being but to replenish their spiritual resources. They live off women; their pretended autonomy is a form of parasitism. They are incapable of genuine intimacy with either women or men. Men mistake their distance from other humans for autonomy, and their addiction to abstract thought for rationality. Their constant preoccupation with abstract issues and competition unfits them for maintaining any sort of human environment for themselves, let alone for children and for women. Women, by contrast, are forced into the role of caretakers, of providing what men need but are unwilling to provide for each other or for children. As thanks they receive sneers for being different from men, for not sharing in the abstractions of men. Deprived, by men, of the chance for autonomy, women are then devalued for lacking autonomy. The autonomy of men is oppressive to women.

To the Lighthouse opens with Mrs. Ramsay answering James's question whether they would go to the lighthouse tomorrow.

> "Yes, of course, if it's fine tomorrow," said Mrs. Ramsay.
> "But you'll have to be up with the lark," she added. ...
> "But," said his father, stopping in front of his drawing room window, "it won't be fine." (9)

The little boy is crushed, and his mother tries to reassure him by saying that the weather might still change. That enrages Mr. Ramsay:

> The extraordinary irrationality of her remark, the folly of women's minds enraged him ... she flew in the face of facts, made his children hope what was utterly out of the question, in effect, told lies. He stamped his foot on the stone step. "Damn you," he said. But what had she said? Simply that it might be fine tomorrow. So it might. (50)

Mrs. Ramsay, from her perspective, is appalled:

> To pursue truth with such astonishing lack of consideration for other people's feelings, to rend the thin veils of civilisation so wantonly, so brutally, was to her so horri-

ble an outrage of human decency that, without replying, dazed and blinded, she bent her head. (51)

Mr. Ramsay pursues truth.

He was incapable of untruth; never tampered with a fact; never altered a disagreeable word to suit the pleasure or convenience of any mortal being, least of all his own children, who, sprung from his own loins, should be aware from childhood that life is difficult; facts uncompromising. (11)

The Ramsays disagree not merely about the importance of truth as weighed in the balance of human pain that truth causes: They also differ about what truth is. Mr. Ramsay is a philosopher. He writes about "subject and object and the nature of reality ... a kitchen table when you are not there" (38). The world not seen by human beings—that is Mr. Ramsay's but not Mrs. Ramsay's reality. That reality is very abstract, and Mr. Ramsay is very abstracted. Mrs. Ramsay is neither:

His understanding often astonished her. But did he notice the flowers? No. Did he notice the view? No. Did he even notice his daughter's beauty, or whether there was pudding on his plate or roast beef? He would sit at table with them like a person in a dream. (107)

Mr. Ramsay's truth does not have to do with the everyday world that he inhabits *with* other human beings. Hers does. In her world the disappointments of children matter, as do their budding beauty and intelligence. The connections and currents between persons matter. But none of that is truth for Mr. Ramsay. His truth is impersonal and quite abstract. Hers is enmeshed in the constantly changing interplay between all the persons around her. His truth is eternal; hers evanescent and ephemeral.

Seeking this impersonal truth, trying to know the kitchen table when no one sees it, is inevitably a very solitary pursuit. To catch a glimpse of the world that is unobserved, one needs to distance oneself from oneself at one's most human, from one's emotions, from one's blind prejudices, from one's likes and dislikes. One shares that work with others who have similarly distanced themselves. Thus one moves in a world where all disregard the personal and hide behind the mask of objectivity.[1] Mr. Ramsay is not only abstracted: He is also distant from those he loves best. He does not notice his daughter's beauty. Truth, as he understands it, is more important than the desolation of his little boy, who has his heart set on going to the lighthouse tomorrow.

Abstract truth comes before human bonds. In fact, human bonds tend to interfere with its pursuit. One of the guests at the Ramsays' summer house in the Hebrides is Augustus Carmichael, who "should have been a great philosopher but he had made an unfortunate marriage." (19) Never mind that the marriage had been a good one. It interrupted a promising career in the pursuit of abstract, objective truth.

Relations to other men are impersonal; they revolve around their work. Between Mr. Ramsay and other philosophers, relations are always competitive because the issue of how good his work is preoccupies him continually. Men in other fields are friends because one has known them for a long time, even if they stopped being intimates many years ago. Friendships become habits. They involve no feelings. Men's conversations, therefore, are either about ideas or academic gossip, about

> who had won this, who had won that, who was a "first rate man" at Latin verses, who was "brilliant but I think fundamentally unsound," who was undoubtedly the "ablest fellow at Balliol" ... (15)

Men believe women to be irrational because they do not participate in this world of work. Not being dedicated to the pursuit of men's "truth," women are considered unable to achieve greatness in any of the cultural pursuits. Mr. Ramsay keeps telling Lily Briscoe, another guest and a painter, that women can't paint, can't write. A woman is meant to be married and to "manage ... her husband, money, his books" (14). Men negotiate treaties, rule India, control finance. Women are excluded from all of that. Women guard and support. It is for them to make "the whole effort of merging and flowing and creating" (126) because when it comes to establishing and maintaining connections between persons, men are, as Mrs. Ramsay says to herself, "sterile." Of course, men love women, but even in loving they are distant.

Men's relations to women are those of domination: contempt mixed with insistent demands for affection, support, and so on. Women are at best adored, at worst used to perform a wide range of services. Watching Mr. Banks looking adoringly at Mrs. Ramsay, Lily Briscoe thinks that "no woman could worship another woman in the way he worshipped" (75). Women are not as distant from other women and thus see them more clearly. Men's love for women is the love of the dominant male who never takes the trouble to seek to know the object of his affection seriously; for men to maintain domination, women must be kept at an emotional distance. They are kept out of the male world and that makes them utterly different. They, therefore, remain incomprehensible to men. Women, by contrast, have much more complex understandings of others; they see the faults as well as the virtues of other people.

Here are two very different ways of being a person. Mr. Ramsay values his work above all. What makes his work so valuable is that it is what counts in the world of men. There, a man is respected for what he does, whether he writes books, is a steady worker, or is a good athlete. Marriage, children, ties to family are outside that men's world and always represent a slight threat to the man's freedom to strive and succeed in the male world. Augustus Carmichael is an example of that. In the world of men, a person is what he is by himself. Mr. Ramsay's books, his lectures, his relations to students and colleagues are his, chosen by him, and are what he alone has made. What is his alone, Mr. Ramsay believes, constitutes his person. The same applies to things: Their reality consists of what they are "in themselves." Hence he is working on "reality"—what the kitchen table is when no one sees it; that is, what the kitchen table is all by itself, independently of any relations. In Mr. Ramsay's world, relations are extraneous to the essence of a thing or person. Only what is all one's own makes one oneself.[2]

THE TROUBLES WITH SEPARATE AUTONOMY

Virginia Woolf's portrait of Mr. Ramsay levels a number of distinct charges:

1. Separate autonomy is self-centered.
2. Separate autonomy unfits one for genuine intimacy.
3. Separate autonomy therefore either demands that one live one's entire life very separately or—which is much more common—demands that one pretend to be autonomous while actually being dependent on others.
4. Dependence is exploitative of those others on whom the separate person depends for many services.
5. Such separateness is not a morally admirable quality.
6. Separateness distorts the search for knowledge.
7. Separateness falsely devalues all but the knowledge of persons with professional credentials.[3]

Separate Autonomy Is Self-Centered

This is true in two respects. The autonomous person is self-centered insofar as her or his decisions are always the most decisive sources of choice and action. Nothing else—moral obligations, prior promises, love, or desire—can overrule the careful, deliberate, and rational choices of the autonomous person. But the autonomous person is also self-centered in a second way: The decisions that shape his or her life are never joint decisions made with another. They are always made by this particular autonomous person alone. This brings with it that the choices of the autonomous person are overwhelmingly self-regarding. His or her own good is the primary guide. The first of these senses of self-centeredness is explicitly acknowledged by some philosophers (Dworkin, 1988:23) whereas others deny it. The second is less frequently attended to.

Mr. Ramsay was not a very considerate man. Neither are many other persons. But that, one may say, is not to be blamed on their autonomy. Autonomous persons only strive to avoid conformism or to protect themselves against domination by others. They want to make their own choices by themselves. But that does not commit them to being self-centered. They might well choose to be altruists; they might choose to be saints, to be utterly self-sacrificing. There is, philosophers often object, no necessary connection between autonomy and the sort of exploitative self-centeredness that Virginia Woolf describes.

If we define autonomy on the assumption of separateness, the choices an autonomous person makes must always be what that person chooses alone. No one else has a deciding voice in the decisions of the autonomous person. Such a person can decide to be altruistic but that choice is always conditional. The moment I change my mind, my altruism comes to an abrupt end. But what sort of altruism is that? Autonomy cannot mean what it means now and, at the same time, allow us to subordinate our own desires and choices permanently to the desires and choices of others.

Many philosophers deny that. Autonomy, they say, does not consist of doing *whatever* one does in view of one's separate decisions and values. An autonomous person may well choose to follow a guru (Mason, 1992). Autonomy requires only that the original choice be made autonomously and that, in addition, one open one's major choices to occasional open and rational reevaluation. I am not sure that such a description of autonomy is defensible (I will return to this later in this chapter). But even if we adopt this restricted concept, it yields a very peculiar kind of altruism. The altruist cares for others. Should such an altruist also be an autonomous person, then that caring for others is always conditional. It is never a reliable commitment. The autonomous person, whether altruist or not, cannot promise anything without qualification. Promises hold only until the next period of reconsideration of one's life goals. The autonomous person still comes first. All ties and commitments to others are always open to reconsideration and suspension because the autonomous choices of the separate person take precedence over all prior obligations and commitments. One's own autonomy remains the supreme value. One's own condition of independence always comes first.

But the obstacles to genuine altruism are even more serious for the person who seeks autonomy. For the autonomous person, his or her decisions are not only the ultimate source of authority but are also decisions made by this or that person alone. But that has interesting implications for one's understanding of altruism. Is altruism best thought of as doing what the other wants one to do, as giving the other's needs and desires precedence over one's own? The autonomous altruist decides all by himself or herself to place the needs of others higher than his or her own. What if the other does not want that? Suppose what the other wants is that decisions about his or her life be made jointly. The autonomous person cannot accede to that without giving up autonomy as defined with the assumption of separateness in the background.

This sort of difficulty comes up most naturally in the relations between parents and children. Parents, by and large, do love their children. Much of the time they genuinely decide what is best for their sons and daughters. But who decides what is best? For the autonomous person the answer is clear. She or he must decide alone how to be devoted to their children's well-being. But surely a good case can be made for saying that what is the best for children is to be active participants— in ways appropriate to age and inclination—in deciding what is best for them. That is very different from saying that parent and child discuss a question and then the parent decides alone and so does the child. If their separate decisions co-incide, there is a "joint" decision. But what if they do not agree? Will the parent have the stronger voice? That is the best the separately autonomous person has to offer. But it hardly counts as wanting to do for children what is best for them.

It seems that altruism requires a lot more than just valuing another's needs or desires higher than one's own. It requires that one be genuinely open to the other's needs and desires, even if they are not stated clearly in so many words (as they rarely are). It involves not only the value one places on the needs or desires of others, as compared to one's own, but also one's attitudes toward the other. To what extent is one attuned to the other, open to hearing what the other does not say clearly or even appears to be denying? To what extent is one willing to make genuinely joint decisions with the other—decisions that are neither one's own nor the child's exclusive decisions? That sort of openness requires that one have a very specific kind of relationship to the other, that one give some thought and atten-tion to that relationship and cultivate it. What one needs here is what Sheila Mullett, following Iris Murdoch (Murdoch, 1970), calls "unselfing." This moves us away from "our feelings of anxiety, hatred, jealousy, envy and vanity and takes us out of the confinement of our needs and desires. ... [The result is that] ... we are able to care to the extent that we can be pried away from self-obsession" (Mullett, 1987:318). It moves one away from the separate self, whose concerns are for her or his needs, desires, wishes, and decisions into looking at the world through the eyes of a "we."

But that is not possible for the autonomous person who understands auton-omy as requiring that she or he decide and act by herself or himself alone. For such "unselfing" requires minimally that one create a "plural subject" with the other, that one enter a joint project with the other where decisions are no longer mine or yours but are ours. Caring for the other person, and for the other person to allow himself or herself to be cared for, is a form of being-in-relation. But the autonomous person's commitment to separateness does not allow such a rela-tionship. Separate autonomy is in those respects irremediably self-centered.

I will discuss the next criticism, that separate autonomy unfits one for genuine intimacy, in Chapter 6.

Separate Autonomy Usually Conceals Dependencies

While Mrs. Ramsay is comforting James and reading to him about the fisherman and his wife, Mr. Ramsay walks back and forth in front of the house reciting snatches from "The Charge of the Light Brigade." Brooding about his accom-plishments as a philosopher, which have fallen short of what he had expected to achieve when he was young, he drifts into a fantasy of being the brave captain of a ship going down in a storm or the leader of a doomed expedition in arctic wastes—courageous, proud, solitary, living up to his own standards to the end, facing the worst with equanimity—and never denying for a moment that his own choices put him in this dire straight but reaffirming those choices as death closes in. In his fantasy, he is "his own man": His decisions are his own, and he is "the captain of his soul." He is an autonomous man.

Woolf's criticisms of autonomy, and separateness, begin with the observation that men are not always as autonomous as they believe themselves to be. Rather, their much-vaunted autonomy rests on support by women. Mr. Ramsay was very much his own man in the sense that his work was of paramount importance to him and his relations to others weak and impersonal. But Mr. Ramsay was also dependent on Mrs. Ramsay, or on the support of other women if his wife was not available at the moment.

That dependence was, moreover, of a peculiar sort because it had to remain hidden. Mr. Ramsay was "afraid to own his own feelings, ... [he] could not say, This is what I like—this is what I am" (Woolf, 1927:70). Thus he could not go to his wife and tell her that he was feeling low because his last book was not as good as earlier ones and have her talk to him about his problems about self-esteem. As a philosopher he could, no doubt, discourse eloquently about the Self, but his own self was not a topic for discussion or thought. Instead he would come around and mutely wait for her to guess what was on his mind and what he needed.

> Mrs. Ramsay, who had been sitting loosely, folding her son in her arm, braced herself ... to pour erect into the air a rain of energy ... and into this ... fountain and spray of life, the fatal sterility of the male plunged itself, like a beak of brass, barren and bare. He wanted sympathy. He was a failure, he said. ... Mr. Ramsay repeated, never taking his eyes from her face, that he was a failure. She blew the words back at him. "Charles Tansley... ," she said. But he must have more than that. ... But he must have more than that. ... (Woolf, 1927:58)

For two painful pages, Woolf describes Mr. Ramsay demanding more and more extravagant encouragement in his misery without ever using his vaunted rationality to articulate, let alone to think about, his feelings and possible remedies. When he leaves, finally pacified, "Mrs. Ramsay seemed to fold herself together ... and the whole fabric fell in exhaustion upon itself. ..."

Male autonomy is, at its very center, emotional dependence on a woman's support, flattery, or admiration. Conceived against the background of separateness, male autonomy is adamant that one's projects need to be chosen and begun by oneself. But completing the project and bearing the burdens it imposes can be shared or even given over to others. Autonomy does not include self-sufficiency in the pain of self-doubt. Philosophers repeat again and again that the autonomous make their own decisions, but healing their own wounds is never mentioned as part of the autonomous person's repertory. My decisions are to be all my own, but not my pains. Decisions are all that autonomy requires.

Nor are men only emotionally dependent on women. Many of their other projects may have been chosen autonomously, that is, all alone. But once the choice has been made someone else needs to do a substantial amount of the work to bring the project to fruition. The choice of a project, or of a life plan, may be autonomous. But the execution of the project—actually living according to the life plan chosen autonomously—depends heavily on the work and thought of others. What is more, that project is not regarded as a joint project. Autonomy of the single chooser is preserved even though he does not do a lot to execute the project to which he has committed himself.

In the eyes of philosophers, Mr. Ramsay is autonomous. He is "is obedient to the law that he prescribes to himself ... these [beliefs, values, and principles] are his, because [they are] the outcome of a still continuing process of criticism and re-evaluation ..."(Benn, 1975). One would expect him to have chosen carefully when he decided to marry and to father eight children. But that is all he needs to do. The autonomous father need not change diapers. Mr. Ramsay's autonomy does not require that he learn to be more than a nominal father to his children. Being unable to take care of the infants one begets is nowhere cited as a failure of being autonomous. It does not show that the project of fathering is not "all one's own." Nor does this autonomous man leave only the drudgery to Mrs. Ramsay. The creative and demanding work of rearing children that makes great demands on both intelligence and imagination is also left to her. Being unable to make things "merge and flow," Mr. Ramsay is unaware of his children's feelings. Mr. Ramsay is not attuned to the needs and sentiments of his children. He is not only unwilling and unable to see to their bodily needs but he is also quite incapable of seeing to it that they grow up sane and happy human beings. The autonomous man need not be an *effective* father and husband. He can leave that to others and still be autonomous.

According to this conception of autonomy, autonomous men live according to their own life plans (Dworkin, 1988:31; Nozick, 1974:49). And in the formulation of these life plans, the opinions of others are "counted merely as advisory" (Rawls, 1971:448). Others can help, "but their help is, by and large, confined to securing background conditions" for autonomous choices (Raz, 1986:407). The autonomous man determines his own life plans. He may extensively consult with others, but in the end the decision is all his own.

How does that work out when someone chooses a project that essentially involves other persons? Rawls understands that life plans do not chart out one's future life in complete detail, once and for all. On the contrary, one lays down the general outline and "the details are filled in gradually" (Rawls, 1971:410; see also Raz, 1986:374n) Life plans are developed and perfected as they are being followed. As the plan is executed it also gets filled in: Every day there are more choices to be made. Many of them are not made over and over ad hoc, but one of the available alternatives is adopted for a period of time: Will the baby be fed on a rigid schedule or on demand? If it cries in the night, will they let it cry or will someone go down to sing or walk it back to sleep? Who will do that? The details of the life plan are filled in as we begin to execute the plan and then confront a host of new decisions that need to be made and that, once made, make the plan much more concrete. But that means that to form a life plan, one needs to act on it. There are not two distinct projects, one to adopt a life plan and the other to put it into practice. One has adopted a life plan only if one is actually trying to realize it, if it is constantly being worked out and rendered more specific.

Life plans that involve more than one person are acted on by more than one person. The other affects my life plan, not only in an advisory position but in the concrete working out of the plan. A life plan may start out as mine, but once I take on projects in accord with that life plan that essentially involve other persons, the development and realization of the life plan is no longer all mine. There is a genuine incompatibility between the traditional philosophical claims about autonomy and any reasonable understanding or practice of friendship, love, marriage, parenting. Choosing to be friends or lovers with another is to make a life plan that one cannot execute by oneself. Insofar as life plans consist not of the initial resolution or choice, but of the life as it is lived deliberately, the plan is no longer the plan of a separate individual. It is a joint project. (I will return to that point in Chapter 6).

There are a number of ways of trying to escape that difficulty but none of them are satisfactory. For instance, the joint decisions required of marriage partners about the conduct of family affairs and the rearing of children can, of course, be made in different ways. One can insist that all decisions are separate. Father decides, mother decides. If their separate decisions coincide, there is what they call a "joint" decision. If there is disagreement, father has the last word. Or they can adopt a strict division of labor in which different persons have the final say in different areas of the family's life. Mother takes care of house and children and must make the relevant decisions. Father decides about money matters. But is that division of labor itself decided jointly? As we shall see below in the discussion of Mrs. Ramsay's autonomy, it is usually imposed by means more or less overtly coercive. But at some point there must be a genuinely joint decision or the entire arrangement rests on the superior power of one family member, usually the father. The entire arrangement of separate spheres must rest on a shared understanding that these persons will conduct their affairs in this way. A joint decision always underlies projects shared by several persons, even if the execution of the project is very separate.

One could try to avoid these difficulties by saying that Mr. Ramsay chooses to be a distant father. After all, he reasons, he has rare abilities and training that might enable him to make an important contribution to our understanding of reality. He must not waste his energies on child care. But the matter is not quite so simple. Suppose Mr. Ramsay does consider himself a father. He is, in his own way, devoted to his children. But is he autonomous? Does he father in his own way, does he think about being a father and act on that thinking in ways that are not conformist? There is little evidence that the absent fathers in this world have chosen their form of fathering after careful consideration of other ways of fathering and rejecting them in favor of being distant. In the same way, Mr. Ramsay has not chosen the specific aspects of his role as a father at all. His abstract choice of becoming a father has remained abstract. But he cannot *be* a father in the abstract, and thus the father he really is is not his autonomous choice but the result of what everyone else in the family chooses for him.

Add to that that he has whatever autonomy he does have only because his wife and his children let him be the distant father he is. His autonomy is at the mercy of the others. If his wife and his children refused to put up with his distant fathering any more he would have to change or leave. Either choice would change his father role, and the choice would be constrained, not autonomous. In the end, Mr. Ramsay can be married *and* autonomous in his very separate sense of autonomy because Mrs. Ramsay lets him have his autonomy. Separate autonomy, if it is combined with love, friendship, and other human ties, is incoherent autonomy because it is dependent on the toleration of others, on their willingness to do the work, on their willingness to allow the autonomous person his or her separate decisionmaking.

But incoherent autonomy is a poor autonomy: We expect autonomous persons to be more or less "all of one piece." We expect them to be aware of their inner conflicts and to be striving to settle them, not by compartmentalizing their persons but by making a clear choice of what really matters to them and what they are willing to give up. That requires serious attention to the internal signs of conflict: depression, anxiety, anger, frustration. Mr. Ramsay's autonomy and that described by some philosophers pays too little attention to the importance of emotional self-awareness in striving for autonomy. Mr. Ramsay can be childishly dependent on his wife while basking in the illusion of being an autonomous man. However, insofar as the autonomous person strives for unification of the person, his autonomy cannot rest on massive and persistent self-deception (Meyers, 1989). But being autonomous (in the separate sense) and being married and a father are not compatible. Married autonomous men must deceive themselves about some aspect of their projects.

This does not mean that separate autonomy is inherently unattainable. There may well be persons who have chosen to be completely separate. They have chosen to think of themselves as separate; that is, to identify their selves with what is theirs alone. They have also chosen to act consistently with that view of themselves. They work alone, and they have no serious relationships to other persons. Their life plans can be truly said to be theirs alone because no one participates in their lives in significant ways. There are few if any encounters with other persons in their lives that affect the course of their lives. Such persons have chosen to be *openly* separate.

Nor is this only a conceptual possibility. Alice Koller's account of her life comes close to describing such a genuinely separate life (Koller, 1990). Barbara McClintock not only never married but also, by her own account, never thought that that was something she wanted to do. Lovers or children never figured in her life plan. Much of the work in biology to which she devoted her life was done alone. When she collaborated with others, it was usually with a much younger and less experienced person who took the methods and ideas from her. She was in a position to claim that her life was hers alone (Keller, 1983). At the same time, these are rare persons. One has to look hard for instances of lives that are, perhaps, more separate than in-relation. But most of those who claim separateness for themselves are, in fact, covertly in-relation.

The implications are clear: Except for those who are willing to choose to be separate in all respects of their lives, separate autonomy is not a good choice. Defining autonomy against the background assumption of separateness makes it difficult to engage autonomously in projects that one does not take up all alone, for which the choices and decisions made cannot be "all one's own." The ordinary separately autonomous male is deceptive and self-deceived: His autonomy conceals many forms of dependence on others for emotional support, for executing the autonomous man's decisions, and for allowing him to pretend to be autonomous.[4]

This is a difficulty for many current philosophical accounts of autonomy. Philosophers speak of autonomy in terms of living according to one's own life plan (Rawls, 1971) or living by one's own moral rules (Benn, 1975). They speak of self-determination (Mason, 1992) and self-creation (Raz, 1986:369), of shaping one's own life (Waldron, 1993:155) or of being independent (O'Neill, 1992). Young defines autonomy as the ability to "direct one's life" together with determining oneself what one's preferences are: "The autonomous person in popular parlance is his own man or her own woman" (Young, 1980:566). Here autonomy includes, at least, acting in the world and acting in relation to or in concert with other persons. Autonomy involves, as one element, careful consideration and reconsideration of values, life plans, actions, moral codes. But it also involves acting on them.

But that conception of autonomy is in trouble.

> To be committed to a friend or a cause is to accept the fact that one's actions, and even desires, are to some extent determined by the desires and needs of others. Even one's beliefs may be to some extent affected as in the case of a wife who refuses to believe that her husband has done something evil. ... To be devoted to a cause is to be governed by what needs to be done, or by what the group decides. It is no longer to be self-sufficient. (Dworkin, 1988:23)[5]

Philosophers have thought to resolve this difficulty of being both autonomous and engaging in projects that one cannot execute by oneself—such as marriage and parenting—by redefining the concept of autonomy. They have proposed to substitute a "procedural" conception of autonomy. Since one cannot engage in projects that are all one's own and still be husband or father, or belong to a political party, religious community, and so on, they have proposed that we limit autonomy to those areas of one's life where one can, indeed, choose and decide all on one's own. Now the only realm where one is thus alone is the internal one, the realm of thinking about one's choices. Autonomy then becomes, as Dworkin says, "procedural." It concerns only the internal processes in my mind that preceded coming to a choice, perhaps to adopt certain opinions or to engage in certain projects (Dworkin, 1988:18; Haworth, 1986). Action, the execution of decisions, is no longer something that can be said to be autonomous or not autonomous. The concept of autonomy refers exclusively to the ways in which one has adopted one's desires, values, and projects. To the extent that one has thought about them, considered them in relation to one's other projects and choices, to one's history, and to values one has chosen earlier, those values and projects make one into an autonomous person. Autonomy lodges exclusively in the privacy of one's mind.[6]

Such an explication of autonomy seems acceptable as long as one talks about autonomous decisions or choices, because those terms are conveniently ambiguous. On the one hand they refer to something that goes on in my mind: I notice my options, I reflect on them, I decide. If I follow the correct procedures, then I can be said to have decided autonomously and to that extent can be said to *be* autonomous. But on the other hand, suppose I announce my decision, say, to write another book. My friends are pleased and excited. But then I do not begin to write, I do not read any relevant works, and I do not take notes. Instead I am building a miniature pagoda in my backyard. My friend says: I thought you had decided to write another book. I reply: I did. My friend may well be puzzled because deciding to do something involves doing it—not perhaps immediately but at some time, at whatever time is the appropriate time (and what is the appropriate time is often part of what I decide). There is something decidedly odd about my announcing the decision to write another book and then taking up a totally different project. That requires an explanation. Thus procedurally autonomous persons commit themselves to actions. If they do not act, we conclude that they changed their mind or that they had "not really" decided. The proof of the decision is the action. Autonomous decisions must lead to autonomous action. If they do not, then no decision was made, or it was reversed.

But these actions are not just the consequences, or effects, of the act of decision. As we saw earlier, that decision is elaborated, filled out, developed in one direction rather than another by the way we put that decision into practice. As the example of Mr. Ramsay shows, moreover, many decisions are not elaborated by oneself but are elaborated by joint actions, actions together with others, and so on. According to the procedural conception of autonomy, though, all of that is not relevant to the question whether the decision is autonomous or not. The only fact that is relevant is that I reflected, carefully, we hope, on my original decision. It does not matter whether I do the work or let someone else do all the work. Whether I am helpless and dependent in the execution of the project or take a leading and original role is not important. I am autonomous because I reflected some time in the past.

But the clash between being separately autonomous and being a husband and father cannot be done away with by redefining "autonomy." We are not free to explicate the concept of autonomy in any way that squares with the underlying assumption of separateness unless we are willing to admit that autonomy is not nearly as important a concept as philosophers believe it to be. Philosophers widely regard autonomy as morally admirable. They widely argue that some form of liberalism is defensible because human beings are or ought to be (able to) be autonomous.

But the "procedural" autonomy just described is not particularly admirable, morally or otherwise. The procedurally autonomous person who weighs choices very carefully and makes his or her decisions rationally—and then does not act on them—is ridiculous, not admirable. Kant is said to have considered marriage twice and in each case weighed the pros and cons so long that the woman whom he was courting married someone else. Rational? Perhaps. Morally admirable? Hardly. Autonomy that is restricted to "reflecting on one's motivational structures" does not have a serious claim on our moral admiration. Thinking, however rational, that does not eventuate in action—that does not take the risk of action, either to avoid being challenged by others or be shown to be in error—is not an example of fine moral character. It is perverse. You may call "autonomous" the person whose thinking is careful and independent. But if that thinking leads to being slavish, or dependent, or completely conformist in one's conduct, it is going to be difficult to persuade us to admire one who is autonomous in that very restricted sense. (I will return in Chapter 5 to the normative inadequacy of redefining autonomy as purely procedural.)

Liberalism—a political view that demands far-ranging freedoms for each of us—is not defensible on the grounds that human beings are *procedurally* autonomous. The liberal creed is often put as the requirement that government policies not favor one way of life over another or that alternative and incompatible life plans be allowed to coexist in a society—subject to elementary and comparable protections for adherents to each way of life. Such a demand is often justified on the grounds that human beings are autonomous. Sometimes that means that autonomy is simply a fact; at other times it means that it is a moral value. Human beings ought to be autonomous or human beings are autonomous, and that is good. Hence they require a social and political order in which they will be able to be autonomous, that is, live their lives according to principles of their own choice (Raz, 1986:373).

That argument will not succeed if all we mean by autonomy is that people think carefully about their desires and values. For one can do that sort of thinking even in solitary confinement. Autonomy justifies a liberal polity if autonomy involves actions with others, commitments to common goals, and setting examples of the good life. Liberalism is intended to leave room for different religious practices, for different ways of organizing one's family, for different ways of making a living, and for building communities. But if these are what is meant by autonomy, then autonomy can no longer be understood as purely procedural autonomy. If autonomy is purely procedural, however, then we can live in ways that do not require liberal protections of rights and still be autonomous. Formal autonomy is too weak to serve as the argument in favor of liberal rights.

Male Autonomy Is Oppressive to Women

When this separate autonomy is male autonomy, it is oppressive to women. For to the extent that Mr. Ramsay makes his own autonomous choices, Mrs Ramsay's life is circumscribed by his choices. He decides to have children. She has them and rears them. He decides that he needs support. She must be ready to provide it.

It is difficult to imagine anyone more different from Mr. Ramsay than his wife. From the beginning of the story she is always in relation to someone, taking care of that other person, sensing the needs of others and trying to meet them. She is who she is insofar as she is supporting and caring for. It is essential in her view that persons be in relations: Women must be married, and children and men need watching over and nurturing. No one should be alone. To be a person is to be with and for other persons.

But is Mrs. Ramsay autonomous? We can assume that she chose Mr. Ramsay. She is in charge of house and children and runs those without interference from anyone. She does sally forth to the village to take care of various people whose problems she has chosen to make her own. Those efforts at philanthropy are all her own and under her control. What is more, she does not want to be like all the men. They are incompetent in important respects insofar as they are unable to make things "merge and flow."

Nevertheless, Mrs. Ramsay lacks crucial elements of autonomy. Her social role of nurturer to any male who needs it was not chosen by her. Philosophers have described autonomy as choosing one's way of life or choosing one's moral principles. But Mrs. Ramsay did not choose to be a full-time nurturer to all and sundry. *Not* being a nurturer simply was not an option for her. Moreover, she was not free to choose to whom she would commit herself or whose interests she would allow to take precedence over her own. Perhaps she chose to nurture Mr. Ramsay, but other men also come around and want nurturing and *take it for granted* that she and other women will be ready to attend to them when asked to do so. Many portions of her life are under her control. But she does not control what sort of life it is—a life of caring for others, of caretaking, and of putting the needs of others ahead of her own. She cannot choose her moral principles. It is not for her to decide what her obligations are, for instance, whether the time has come for her to replenish her own resources and it is therefore all right to tell Mr. Ramsay that he needs to take care of himself for a while. Nor is she free to choose to whom obligations are owed. (Must every adoring graduate student of Mr. Ramsay's become her charge?) She is not autonomous in the sense that philosophers have given to that term. (I will qualify that view in Chapter 5.)

But, some might insist, Mrs. Ramsay likes her life, likes what she is doing, and prefers her life to that of men. But liking what one is doing is not evidence of having chosen that activity or way of life. Some people like the conditions they find themselves in without having chosen them. Many persons do not. Neither like nor dislike has a bearing on autonomy.

Mr. Ramsay's autonomy is oppressive to Mrs. Ramsay in many ways. On the one hand, men regard women with an "arrogant eye," in Marilyn Frye's phrase (Frye, 1983:66). Men define the context in which women live and work by determining values—what is good and what is bad, what is healthy and what is sick—and determining all those in the light of male interests. Victorian women could be married and lead a life like Mrs. Ramsay or they could be "spinsters" and be the object of pity and ridicule. What women did was judged by the extent to which it served male ends. If she were to complain or refuse, she would be judged abnormal or sick. Thus the choices that Mrs. Ramsay has are prescribed for her by others and are dictated by the needs and interests of those others.

On the other hand, stereotypical men see women as different. Women are not like us, men insist. (And secretly they fear that they may not be as different from women as the male ethos demands.) Now one can react to difference in more than one way. One can try to understand the other across the difference; one can enrich one's understanding of oneself by trying to see oneself as others see one. Men can try to see what they look like through the eyes of women and learn a very useful lesson. They can see what they look like with their male privileges and their ill-concealed neediness, thinly disguised by flamboyant rhetoric about autonomy (Lugones, 1991:43). But those lessons are not welcome to most men and so they choose the other road: They allow difference to be a wall that conceals the other. The other is not recognized but instead remains unknown. In the world of men, women are therefore indistinct and incomplete. In similar ways, in the world of white men and women, persons of color lack full reality because they are perceived as different, but few make the effort to bridge that difference (Lugones, 1987).[7]

But none of that must ever be said openly. For to admit that women are oppressed by male dependencies would be to admit that men are not autonomous either. A woman must not only be available when needed, but she must also act as if the man did not need her or ask for anything. The dependence on women's love and homage is not to be stated openly. The demand is made silently. The woman has to guess what is wanted. The reason for this shamefacedness is obvious: If autonomy is the ideal, and autonomy means that one be "one's own man," one cannot very well come around and admit needs and weaknesses and ask for help. Jean Baker Miller has stated that very clearly:

> A man wants ... first of all, to sail through every situation "feeling like a man"—that is, strong, self-sufficient and fully competent. He required of himself that he always feel that way ... at the same time ... he harbored the seemingly contradictory wish

that his wife would, somehow, solve everything for him with such magic and dispatch that he never would be aware of his weakness at all. She should do this without being asked. ... (Miller, 1976:32–33)

Separateness Is Rarely a Morally Admirable Quality

In the remainder of this book I will argue this in a variety of different ways by showing that separateness is exploitative, oppressive, and usually self-deceived. The striving for that kind of separate autonomy tends to make persons self-centered. Autonomy, as actually practiced, is not a very desirable trait. The word "autonomy," being "one's own man," suggests independence, running one's own life, being able to take care of oneself, not being beholden to anyone, not being either lender or borrower. Very few, if any, men, however, are autonomous in that sense. The autonomy they lay claim to is most often rather different: It involves being unaware of the feelings and needs of others as well as one's own. It involves living in a rather impersonal world, where the daily details of food and clothing are left to women to take care of and where women also remember birthdays and anniversaries, arrange for celebrations and gifts, and, generally, maintain relationships. Male autonomy does not mean genuine independence but means getting what one needs without contributing fully to the maintenance of all the relationships that one depends on. It is self-absorbed and does not carry its weight in the work of caring for those who need care, maintaining relationships, or, generally, humanizing the world. The autonomous man tends to be a "narcissist who sees the world in his own image" (Benhabib, 1987:84).

Autonomous man, being a narcissist, can function only because women are not autonomous. Were the pursuit of such autonomy genuinely to become a universal human trait, instead of being the province of some men, its effect on our social world would be devastating:

> There is every reason to react with alarm to the prospect of a world filled with self-actualizing persons pulling their own strings, capable of guiltlessly saying "no" to anyone about anything, and freely choosing when to begin and when to end all their relationships. It is hard to see how, in such a world, children could be raised, the sick or disturbed could be cared for, or people could know each other through their lives and grow old together. (Scheman, 1983:240)

In a world populated exclusively by Mr. Ramsays, no one would make things "merge and flow"; all would be too preoccupied with their own concerns and their own intellectual pursuits to heed their sons' feelings or notice their daughters' beauty. There would be lots of good, abstract conversation, but who would comfort the little boys who wanted to go to the lighthouse? It would, to be sure, be a world that one could not but view with alarm.

Separate autonomy is usually not admirable. But there are exceptions. I noted earlier that a few persons are really serious about separateness and they draw the proper conclusions from that. Their lives are pretty solitary. Their projects, except for quite trivial ones, are not shared with others. They make deliberate efforts to avoid situations where one's activities require joint decisions or the sorts of understandings that make joint projects possible. A person who seeks that sort of autonomy will make sure that most of her or his life is lived alone. The work that is most important in such a life, the occasions that bring greatest joy and deepest satisfaction, are solitary ones. In this life there is no family, no daily life shared with others, no work that depends in significant ways on the help and support of others. Such persons may well have friends and may be on cordial terms with neighbors, but these relationships are peripheral to what counts in their lives. Such a very solitary life is hard to lead and clearly requires persons of exceptional fortitude. Choosing to be genuinely separate is a rare accomplishment. Most of the advocates of separateness have in fact wisely not chosen to be so rigorously separate. Their separateness is much more qualified. It is incoherent, self-deceived, and exploitative. It is not morally admirable.

IS SEPARATENESS CHOSEN?

Separateness is clearly chosen. But what sort of choice is that? There are different sorts of choices, notably direct and indirect ones. In making an indirect choice I choose something by choosing something else, either because the thing I choose is the consequence of what I choose directly or because it is a whole of which the action chosen directly is a part. Neither separateness nor autonomy is chosen directly. I choose separateness in choosing to be autonomous in a particular way or by being empathic, or a lover, in a particular way. But being autonomous consists of a whole sequence of actions: One well-considered choice does not make one autonomous. So I choose autonomy only by virtue of a whole series of other actions.

That explains, in part, why talk about choosing separateness or autonomy seems slightly odd. Separateness is not the sort of thing one chooses directly, and hence talking about choosing separateness surprises. But there are other reasons for being wary of the claim that we choose to be separate, among them the fact that we use "choice" in different senses. In a very generous sense, whatever we are not forced into, in whatever way, is said to be a matter of choice. But not everything that is a matter of choice is actually chosen, in a more restricted sense of the term. In that sense choice requires awareness that there are several options and some decisions to go with one of those options rather than another. We choose, in that sense, only if we are aware of choosing.

Human separateness is not the incontrovertible fact about human life that many philosophers take it to be. We are not constrained to be separate by any physiological or psychological facts about human beings. If we nevertheless are separate it must be something that we have chosen, in the first very generous sense of the word. But we may not have chosen to be separate in that second more restricted sense, for separateness may be something that we just happened to fall into but that we could choose to change. Most readers, unlike Alice Koller or Barbara McClintock, probably have never given the choice between separateness and being-in-relation a great deal of thought, so it is most apt to say that people just fall into separateness. Separateness is an available option and since everyone around you chooses it, if you are a man, you choose it without even being aware of making a choice. Even readers who have thought about this a good deal probably found themselves being separate in some ways and in-relation in others, and they had not chosen those ways.

But there are other senses of "choice" that further complicate the question whether separateness can be said to be chosen. There are unconscious choices and those are of different kinds. Some people make the same sort of choice over and over but are not aware of that pattern in their lives until someone points it out to them. There are choices of some sort being made, and being made again and again, but not consciously.

Separateness is a matter of choice in the sense that one could choose to be a different sort of person. But it is not as frequently chosen consciously and deliberately as the protestations of philosophers about autonomously choosing life plans and so on would make one expect.

The range of available choices is limited in a variety of ways. Telepathy is not an option because we cannot choose to feel directly the pains and pleasures of other persons. Nature sees to that by virtue of the distinctness of our nervous systems. But our range of choices is not only limited by natural fact. We are also hedged about by social conditions, and what there is for us to choose is largely determined by social and cultural facts.

Accordingly, Joseph Raz argues that we value autonomy because our culture offers us the choice to be autonomous. But choosing to be autonomous is not a direct choice. Our culture offers us the possibility of being autonomous because it allows us, for instance, to determine by oneself whom to marry; it allows us to choose whether to marry or to cohabit; and it allows us, much more grudgingly, the choice between same-sex or different-sex partners in cohabitation. Autonomy is valued where a culture allows persons a wide range of choices that they can make by themselves (Raz, 1986:392). Raz does not point out, though, that the options for autonomy are not distributed evenly in the society. There are even in our society few options that are open to everyone—and many of those are disagreeable. Certainly autonomy has traditionally not been open to women and to a much more limited degree to men and women of color. Autonomous choices are not simply permitted (or not) in a given society. They are permitted in very complex patterns for some persons, in some situations, and not for others.

Similarly, separateness is valued where choices, such as the choice for autonomy, are allowed in a separate way. Not only are we allowed to choose our own marriage partners, but we men are also allowed to marry, father children, and leave all the work to women, reserving for ourselves only the power to make important decisions. Not all couples choose that, but it is a real option in our society. Comparable ways of being friends, being empathic, and so on are also genuine options. Separateness is a choice, moreover, because alternative ways of being with others, being-in-relation, are also options. Women in their relationships with one another are much more likely to be in-relation than men are, and that is regarded as legitimate. Women are supposed to be in-relation to their children and in oddly deformed ways to their husbands.

Society lays out a series of options for us in different ways of being persons and in different kinds of relationships we can have with our fellow humans. The selection of one option over another surely is a kind of choice, even if the selection is not done quite consciously or is not preceded by anxious deliberation.

Separateness results from one's choices. Our society offers many of us more options for autonomous decisionmaking than were available to the generation of my grandparents. There is much more room for individual choice in decisionmaking, for instance, in matters of marriage, sexual life, and family life than there was formerly. Those changes, however, are themselves the results of choices others made. We live in a fairly tolerant world, as far as these matters are concerned, because others living in a much more restrictive environment chose deliberately to violate the rules and thus to begin to weaken them. In the same way, separateness was chosen deliberately by those who wanted to break out of the stifling embrace of traditional small towns, religious communities, or large families in cramped quarters. They chose deliberately to separate themselves. It is easier to be separate today. The choice may not be as explicit but it is equally a choice.

At the same time, these choices are never made in a social vacuum. Emma Goldman and Alexander Berkman were lovers without benefit of rabbinical blessing or permission from city hall, but presumably they found support for that choice among their friends. Choice and innovation do not occur in a social vacuum.[8]

Separateness is chosen, indirectly, not only because it is usually not a conscious choice but also because the very possibility of separateness is offered to us as a consequence of the explicit choices of many people, both those who chose to lead separate lives and those who were in support of that. The same applies to being-in-relation: One can choose it explicitly or one can choose it not knowing. But in either case the possibility of the choice depends on choices other people made so as to establish this as a legitimate option. Those previous choices, in turn, depended in various complex ways on the social setting in which they were made and on others who inspired, helped, encouraged, or looked the other way.

BEING-IN-RELATION: MINIMAL, COVERT, OR OPEN

One may choose different ways of being separate. There are also different ways to be in-relation. One can be autonomous, in the sense of being separate, to a very considerable extent. That choice involves careful attention to avoiding joint projects in most of one's life. There are also less draconian and more ordinary ways of aiming in the same direction. There are, after all, ways of doing something with another yet preserving almost complete separateness. A number of autonomous authors may choose to write a book together. Each writes his or her piece. Then all those pieces are printed in the same volume. Only a minimal agreement is needed to get that project started and to bring it to completion.

To be sure, participating in such work is not preserving one's separate autonomy completely, because the beginning of a joint project requires that one create a "plural subject"—that one enter an agreement to do certain things with others, that one have one's paper written at a certain time, that it be of such and such a length, that it be subject to certain outside evaluation, that royalties be divided in this way rather than that. There emerges, in Gilbert's terminology, a "we," a plural subject that makes and sticks to and executes certain joint decisions that give the group some claims against each separate individual. To the extent that each participates in the founding agreement, they cede some self-determination to the group. For participation in the group gives some determining power to the group decision over the decisions of each separate individual member of the group.

The original decision of the group members to write a book together is for each of them to enter into a relationship with the others. To the extent that they are a "plural subject," a "we," they are in-relation. But that bit of being-in-relation may well be the foundation of each going in his or her separate way to write a separate contribution to the collective volume. The relations between the members of the group may, once the original joint decision is made, revert to being as separate as they please.

Hence it is possible for two persons to be in-relation in a very minimal sense. They can, for example, decide to get married but be from then on, perhaps even by mutual consent, very separate. These separate relations take a wide range of forms. Persons are separate who have nothing to do with one another. Suppose a U.S. citizen marries a foreigner to make it possible for the other to get citizenship quickly but as soon as legally possible after the ceremony the two separate. Persons are also separate if the will of one determines that of the other. Separate relations can be coercive or manipulative. They can be relations of a complex division of labor in which some work is done by and run by one persons while the other has different responsibilities, or it may be that one does all the work and the other makes all the decisions. All of these are forms of separateness. Hence a joint decision may well be the beginning of a very unequal and uneven relationship (Gilbert, 1992:411).

Separateness, even in the context of autonomy, thus takes very different forms. When I speak of "choosing" separateness, that is a convenient shorthand for saying that separateness takes all these different forms and that that is not an accident but depends on choices one makes. It is a matter of choice, in many cases, to what extent one's projects are going to be solitary ones or to what extent they will be projects undertaken with others. If we undertake projects with others, then choices are made about the extent to which joint decisions are merely the founding moments of such projects or to what extent the entire project is formed and executed by a continuing series of joint decisions.

In corresponding ways, being-in-relation takes many different forms. Minimally, a project begins with a joint decision but then continues with each partner having a proper sphere where each is supreme. Sometimes that leaves the partners separate but equal. More commonly, one partner, the man, has potential decisionmaking power in all spheres whereas the woman's decisionmaking competence is restricted to her proper domain.

I will refer to all these sorts of arrangements as "minimal being-in-relation." Here essentially separate arrangements only presuppose an initial joint decision. Such minimal being-in-relation may be openly admitted by all. But the sort of arrangement we have been examining in this chapter is different. Here one partner pretends noisily to be separate, and the underlying joint decisions and the dependencies, needs, and weaknesses must all be denied and hidden away. This is being-in-relation, to be sure. Often it is not particularly minimal, but it is concealed. I will call that "covert being-in-relation." Covert being-in-relation is common, but it is a complex relationship. Often it begins with some genuinely shared understandings. But then the man reasserts his independence while demanding care and nurturing. Both the assertion of independence and the demand for nurturing may be accompanied by threats—economical, emotional, or physical—that may well weaken the original joint decision. But now a relationship is established, although much of it has to do with concealing that it involves genuine elements of being-in-relation.

There is also overt being-in-relation that is chosen wholeheartedly and is elaborated in further joint decisions with every new day. I will try to elaborate that sort of relationship in the next two chapters.

IS THIS ONE MORE ATTACK ON INDIVIDUALISM?

The doctrine that society is made up of separate, autonomous, and self-regarding individuals dates back, in our tradition, at least to the eighteenth century. But as soon as this individualism became widespread and enshrined in the early liberal political theories, it also became the target of philosophical attacks. Thus Hegel points out against the individualists that one comes to be aware of oneself as a separate individual only in opposition to another person. In his analysis of the relation between master and slave, Hegel puts this dramatically by asserting that only in the struggle unto death between master and slave is each aware of his distinct individuality (Hegel, 1931). Marx points out that the concept of the separate individual is itself a historical phenomenon. It was not known to the Greeks or the medievals but arose with the ascent of the new capitalist class in England in the eighteenth century. Thus the identification of oneself as an individual presupposes a social stock of ideas and thus a functioning society and culture (Marx and Engels, 1978:222). Both the arguments of Hegel and of Marx have recently been used by Charles Taylor (1992). Taylor also points out, as do many feminists, that the claims of separate individuality completely ignore our early histories as very dependent beings who need care and nurturance from caregivers and who, throughout their lives, are enriched and shaped by their intimate relations (Midgley, 1988:32).

There are two difficulties in this debate for or against individualism. It is not clear what the individualist asserts, and hence it is not always clear that the arguments offered in refutation are as devastating as their authors consider them to be. Critics of individualism describe the position as follows: "Abstract individualism considers individual human beings as social atoms, abstracted from their social contexts, and disregards the role of social relationships and human community in constituting the very nature of individual human beings" (Friedman, 1990: 143).

If that is an accurate depiction of individualism, then certainly Marx's argument is powerful: Human beings are not abstract individuals whom one can consider (and who can consider themselves) in abstraction from their social context, for in so abstracting one draws on the conceptual schemes of very specific societies. But the problem with Marx's argument is that this characterization of individualism is widely held by its critics but is rejected by its defenders. "Implicitly, all liberal writers [namely, all defenders of individualism] acknowledged the social constitution of the individual" (Holmes, 1989:238). The major disagreement between critics and defenders of individualism concerns not the truth of individualism but what it asserts.

It is therefore also not at all clear how conclusive the arguments of individualism's critics are because it is not easy to get agreement on what position is being criticized. But even if we set this difficulty aside for the moment, individualists need not be distressed by any of these critiques. To Hegel they reply that the way in which we come to know our identity has blessedly little to do with the nature of that identity. It may be true, as a matter of empirical fact (although Hegel has not given us such facts), that we come to know ourselves only in opposition to other persons. But that does not show that we are, as individuals, intrinsically dependent on other persons. Our separate individuality is not rendered questionable by the ways in which we come to discover it. Similarly, Marx's argument falls short of refuting individualism. That we have shared ideas, concepts, and values does not deny that we do not think for ourselves. Individualists do not need to deny that we learn from one another. They are interested only in insisting that we are able to decide all by ourselves whether to adopt certain ideas. The arguments offered by Hegel, Marx, or Taylor do not weaken that claim. The observation, finally, that we are all born helpless and grow up dependent does not show that we are not, as adults, capable of growing into separate individuals. The separate autonomy that individualism claims for us is a victory over the dependency that characterizes our early years. It is not refuted by it.

Individualism makes claims about human nature: Human beings are separate, they are capable of autonomy, their own interests are usually stronger motives for them than the interests of others. The arguments routinely given against that do not weaken those claims about human nature. However, I argued earlier in this chapter that the arguments for claims about human separateness are also quite weak. The familiar debate for and against individualism is unfocused because it is not clear what is at issue between defenders and critics. The debate has, in addition, weak arguments on both sides.

We have already seen the reasons for that. The argument over individualism is an argument about the essence of human beings, over what human beings *are*. There is some factual support for either side. Individualism is supported, to a point, by the fact of our bodily distinctness. But that distinctness does not entail that we are separate. There is only partial factual support for separateness. It is precisely because individualists do not see the difference between distinctness and separateness that the case for individualism remains weak. But the opponents, also, have less factual support than they are aware of. Yes, it is true that there are activities of all kinds that one cannot engage in all by oneself. Playing tennis is a trivial example; writing books together and speaking a language are important ones. But the existence of cooperative or collective efforts does not refute individualism since one can take these projects on as separate persons or as minimally in-relation. One can also, as we shall see in more detail below, choose to be fully in-relation. But our social nature is not a bare fact, a given, but is possibly chosen in a social setting that allows such choices.

As long as the argument over individualism is conducted as an argument over facts it will remain inconclusive, since matters of fact are only weak support for either position. We need to understand that being-in-relation is to be chosen before we can get out of the repetitive circle of argumentations that philosophers have been caught up in. But the whole matter of *choosing* to be in-relation or to be separate, or to pretend to be separate if one is covertly in-relation, is completely absent from the traditional debate over individualism. Both sides to the debate agree implicitly that what is at issue is an essential fact about human beings, a fact about who and what we are. But with that the central issue in the controversy between separateness and being-in-relation is overlooked.[9]

Hence the argument for choosing to be openly in-relation, which I am developing in this book, is not another skirmish in the extended war over individualism. That war arises, like most wars, from a terrible misunderstanding of the issues. Human beings are distinct but not separate. Much of what they do is done with other persons, and we have a wide range of latitude—some of us to be sure have a lot more latitude than others—to choose in what way we shall do what we do with others: Shall we be separate as far as possible, shall we pretend to be separate, or shall we work toward being openly in-relation and for building a society where that is a real possibility? These are questions that differ from the debate about individualism.

◄ 4 ►

Being-in-Relation

IN THE FIRST CHAPTER we saw that separateness denies the possibility of joint projects, decisions, thoughts, and so on. In the second chapter we discovered that separateness is not given but is chosen. The third chapter showed that separateness is, in most cases, chosen disingenuously because the door is always left open for secret dependencies. Much of the talk about autonomy conceals being covertly in-relation. One is autonomous only in one's mind but not when there is work to be done. We have seen that that kind of separateness and separate autonomy are not to be recommended. Instead, it seems clear, we ought to choose and strive to be overtly in-relation.

Considered abstractly, the difference between separateness and being-in-relation has to do with the actions of two or more persons. Separateness claims that all actions are actions of single persons. Since our bodies are distinct, so are all actions. Being-in-relation, by contrast, points to the fact that some acts, such as decisions, are *joint* acts, which are not "yours and mine" but ours because there is only one act, which you and I perform together when we decide on some course of action, on a common project. Projects that are genuinely ours are neither yours alone nor mine alone. They begin and rest in a shared understanding that this is what we will do together. Such shared understanding is quite different from you agreeing and I agreeing that you and I will do something alongside each other or in each other's company. Insofar as actions have agents, such joint actions constitute you and me as a plural subject. For shorter or longer periods, two or more persons constitute an agent insofar as they have a shared understanding with respect to some more or less specific matter.[1] Each, of course, remains a distinct person. Each is different and has his or her separate identity. They come together as a plural subject with respect to very specific acts, agreements, projects.

But this is only the structure of being-in-relation. That structure is exhibited by minimal being-in-relation as well as by being-in-relation overtly chosen. But there is a world of difference between minimal being-in-relation, where two persons agree on a joint project but also agree to conduct that joint project as separate persons, and openly chosen being-in-relation, where not only the initial understanding is a joint project but also the hope and effort go toward conducting the entire enterprise jointly. Minimal being-in-relation is everywhere. Even the ordinary autonomous, separate married man and father is often minimally in-re-lation. But openly chosen being-in-relation is an altogether different matter. It has to do with how we choose to conduct our projects undertaken together with other people when we are striving for being-in-relation throughout the common undertaking. But it also has to do with a shared understanding of how we will ar-range together the details of the project and who will do or get what. In most cases those shared understandings presuppose that the partners pay careful attention to one another. Shared understandings require that each listen carefully to the other. They cannot emerge between persons who are distracted or oblivious to the other.

Such overt being-in-relation is open for us to choose. What such a choice might look like is the subject of this chapter and the chapter that follows. First, though, I need to be more specific about the ways in which overt being-in-rela-tion may be chosen. We saw toward the end of the preceding chapter that auton-omy is accessible for choosing insofar as particular persons in particular situa-tions are faced with a range of options, some of which might be chosen autonomously whereas others, if chosen, would constitute a rejection of auton-omy. The example cited was the range of options we have for choosing partners for marriage, cohabitation, and family. It is inaccurate to say, simply, that auton-omy is an option for us in this society. It is much more accurate to say that certain persons of particular origins, gender, and class have specific choices with respect to specific life events in which autonomy may come into play or, alternatively, is barred. Choices of professional careers are open, by and large, only to members of the white middle class. Others have no opportunity of manifesting autonomy or of turning their back on autonomy in this area.

The same is true of separateness and being-in-relation. Striving for being-in-relation in a military organization, or a bureaucratic one such as a university, is liable to cause a great deal of trouble. Running a small business cooperatively, in contrast, is possible but not easy. But some cooperative women's bookstores, for instance, have flourished for some time. A small business does not have to be hi-erarchical, exploitative, and oppressive (Ferguson, 1984). But there are not very many areas of our lives where being-in-relation is a ready alternative. The reason for advocating that we choose being overtly in-relation is precisely to urge us to make more places where being-in-relation is a genuine option. As is suggested by the example of the transformation of rules concerning marriage and sexual rela-tions among those not married, such changes are slow and require the daring in-novation of small groups of active or supportive pioneers. What is needed in our world are persons who are willing to agitate for being-in-relation in their actions by trying to conduct their affairs in ways that beat back separateness and all its oppressive consequences.

The difference between being separate and being-in-relation has been much discussed in feminist writings, not all of which are the work of philosophers. Cen-tral are the work of Jean Baker Miller (1976) and her colleagues at the Stone Cen-ter in Wellesley (Jordan et al., 1991). Their approach is primarily psychological, from the perspective of practicing therapists. They start out from object relations theory, as does Nancy Chodorow (1978), but then they go beyond that to develop a clear distinction between separateness and being-in-relation. Important also is feminist work in theology (Keller, 1986), in legal theory (Nedelsky, 1990), and in sociology (Oakley, 1981). And of course the writings of Carol Gilligan and Nel Noddings are important. I will throughout cite the writings of many other feminists, who work in a variety of different fields.

Much of the discussion of being-in-relation, and the closely related discussions of the ethic of care, of women's empathy, and of the central role that relationships play in the lives of women—and should play in the lives of all of us—takes love and friendship as key examples of being-in-relation. The reasons for that are obvious: Being-in-relation has the widest scope in the area of personal and family relations. Here being-in-relation exists and is widely experienced. Prevailing ideologies, moreover, are most permissive of being-in-relation in the so-called private sphere. There it is easiest to acknowledge that one is indeed in-relation. In the public realm, separateness is the dominant mode of transactions between persons. But we shall see that the relationships between teacher and student, for instance, can be either separate or in-relation. Teachers and students can talk to each other as separate persons or can, in some instances, be in-relation, albeit in appropriately restricted ways. In the chapters that follow, I will argue that the distinction between separateness and being-in-relation applies to many more situations than merely love and friendship. It applies, for instance, to knowing and to power.

CARING

Carol Gilligan's discussion of two alternative ethics—an ethics of justice and an ethics of care—is familiar. It brings to light many of the differences in thinking, acting, and talking that are, in this book, described as differences between separateness and being-in-relation. Gilligan's ethics of care has given rise to an extensive discussion among philosophers.

The term "caring" has a number of different meanings. "I care for you" sometimes is another way of saying that I love you. But it might also mean that I "take care" of you, as one cares for children or animals. "Do you care for more Nudelkugel?" offers you another helping. In addition, one cares *about* things, which, according to some philosophers, is a bit more impersonal than caring for persons (Tronto, 1989). But in the eyes of other philosophers, caring about may be very important and consist of being deeply invested in projects and persons (Frankfurt, 1982). An older meaning of "care" comes out in such expressions as "careworn": Here "care" comes close in meaning to "sorrow" or at least to "worry." Hence "caring for" also means feeling "concern" for or "taking trouble on behalf of."

In their discussions of the ethics of care, philosophers have used "caring" in very different senses without paying much attention to these different meanings of "caring." (For some exceptions, see Fry, 1992). Some use "caring" to refer to someone's being aware of and taking account of someone else's desires and needs (Rigterink, 1992), whereas others use it in the sense of actively responding to meet another's needs and desires (Manning, 1992). But those two are very different stances. Others identify "caring" primarily with paying close and concentrated attention to a person (Dillon, 1992). That is a different sense again.

Not only is "caring" taken to be a perfectly familiar concept, but the politics of caring is also ignored. A good deal of the discussion of caring accepts prevailing differences between men and women as given and pays no attention to the disparities in power that affect the forms caring takes in different relationships. But as is well known, a good deal of women's caring is compromised by being compelled, if not coerced outright. Much of the caring women have done was caring on demand, in ways specified by those demanding care. Remember Mr. Ramsay, mute and miserable, asking for more and more extravagant affirmation! If such caring is at all "intrinsic" to women's lives, it is only of the essence of women as they are constructed in a misogynist world. Insofar as women define themselves and their worlds privately in very different terms, caring is not in their "nature" and the caring they do is different from the male-defined caring they are often compelled to do (Collins, 1991). Thus we should not be surprised that women do not always care for others. Women have cared, when they did, only for some others while being cruel and hostile to members of different religions, ethnic groups, races, and classes (Spelman, 1991:108). We should, more importantly, be alert to the possibility that there is caring that is oppressed and quite different from caring that is freely chosen. The outlines of the former are defined by a culture hostile to women. The latter is women's own creation. If we are to learn lessons about how to live well from these discussions of caring, we need to be sure that it is this second kind of caring we model our ideas on.

Because of this prevailing insouciance about the word "caring," the differences in lives and in behaviors that Gilligan points to have often been misunderstood and trivialized. Philosophers have not been very careful with the ordinary meanings of "care" but have assumed that we all know what that word means in any particular context. Hence they have also not paid sufficient attention to the fact that "caring" in Gilligan comes close to being a technical term. The shift from the justice to the care perspective reorganizes

> thoughts, feelings, and language so that words connoting relationships like "dependence" or "responsibility" or even moral terms such as "fairness" and "care" *take on different meanings*. To organize relationships in terms of attachment rather than in terms of equality changes the way human connection is imagined, so that the images or metaphors of relationship shift from hierarchy or balance to network or web. In addition, each organizing framework leads to a different way of imagining the self as moral agent. (Gilligan, 1987:22–23; my italics)

The difference between lives organized around justice and lives organized around care is much more complex than is often understood. One main difference is in the meanings of central terms. Not only do relationships play a different role, but they are also very different *kinds* of relationships—a difference reflected in the fact that "relationship" has a very different meaning for those following an ethic of justice or of care.[2]

Gilligan characterizes the ways of stereotypical women with a variety of terms: "embeddedness in social interaction and personal relationships"(8–9) versus being separate and individual; dependence versus independence; being empathic versus being less so; defining oneself by reference to relations versus by reference to work and so on; being interested in maintaining relations versus resolving conflicts according to rules(9–10); "sensitivity to the needs of others and the assumption of responsibility for taking care"(16) versus the lack of both of those; "a world comprised of relationships rather than of people standing alone, a world that coheres through human connection rather than through systems of rules" (Gilligan, 1982:29).

These characterizations are not as emphatic as they should be about the difference between male and female relationships and about male and female caring. One could read some of the passages cited as saying that men have hardly any relationships at all or that although they do have relationships, they do not value them. And whereas connections to other persons are at the center of women's lives, men work all the time and are uncommunicative, uncaring, consumed by the drive to get ahead, and pay little or no attention to family and friends. This characterization of the difference between typical men's and women's lives is often summarized in the slogan that "men are separate, women in-relation." But men reply to that, not unreasonably, that they are, after all, also sons, fathers, lovers, friends, and colleagues and thus do have many relationships of their own. What is more, they too care for parents, lovers, children, and friends.

In other passages, Gilligan is much more explicit that the differences between men's and women's lives lie somewhere else: Men's relationships are very different from those of women. Both men and women have relationships and often value them. But what each has and values is rather different from what the other has and values. Between the ethics of justice and the ethics of care, the general word "relationship" changes meaning, along with specific terms like "caring." Women's relationships tend to be of different sorts from those that men have to other men as well as to women. Correspondingly, caring by men, and among men, is of a very different character from caring by and among women.

Gilligan's use of the word "care" to characterize the women's perspective invites misunderstandings. The difference between the perspectives of stereotypical men and stereotypical women is not clarified by talking about caring in the ordinary sense of that term, as if caring were done only by women. Instead we must be clear that Gilligan's "caring" is caring in a special sense. We need to look at that second kind of caring to see what makes it different from separate caring.

RECIPROCITY

In her account of caring, Nel Noddings contributes a great deal to the clarification of the difference between stereotypical men's and stereotypical women's relationships. The latter, she tells us, are reciprocal. The woman's ethic rests in caring in which reciprocity is of the essence, and that means "my caring must somehow be completed in the other" (Noddings, 1984:4). We should not think, therefore, that persons who choose separateness are not capable of caring for others and do not, in fact, care for others. Instead we need to recognize that there is the caring of the traditional father for his children, which may well involve his not being home much and thus not being very close to his children but centers in his providing for their material needs. And then there is the caring of the stereotypical mother, in which reciprocity is a requirement of her relationship to her children. The father may well care deeply for his children. His caring consists of his emotions and his actions. He translates his feelings for his children into hard work on their behalf. That sort of separate caring, however, does not involve a reciprocal relationship to the children. His children may well, although they usually do not, grow up as perfect strangers to him. That would not in any way weaken his caring for them.

There are a variety of forms of separate caring. The person who loves Elvis cares for someone who does not respond. That caring belongs all to the one caring. His or her feelings, fantasies, and dreams are all that that caring consists of. But separate caring may well be mutual: Two persons who are very separate may care for one another mutually. The one cares for the other, the other cares for the one, and they do that at about the same time in close spatial propinquity. If one of them stopped caring, the other might well be very unhappy but could very well continue caring all alone. That is separate caring and it may be mutual. I will discuss that sort of caring in more detail in the chapter on love.

This mutuality is different from the reciprocity Noddings points out to us. The other sort of caring, exemplified more often by women and examined by Gilligan and Noddings, has very specific relationships at its center; namely, relationships that are reciprocal in the sense that what one person does in caring is not complete until the other brings it to completion. But here men will protest once more: Their relationships are also reciprocal through and through. After all, the contractual relationships that are so central to male theorizing in ethics and political theory are nothing if not reciprocal. A contract is not fulfilled until each person has done what he or she has promised to do. That is an important reminder. It turns out that not only "relationship" but also the term "reciprocity" has significantly different meanings in the perspectives of separateness and of being-in-relation. We need to clarify the ways in which male relationships are reciprocal and distinguish them from women's forms of reciprocity.

Noddings is aware of this difficulty. She insists that the reciprocity of caring is different from an ethic of contract or promises (Noddings, 1984:4). Contracts are concluded between persons who are, in the respects relevant to the contract, equal. Reciprocity between equals consists of X providing roughly for Y what Y provides for X. Equality of contribution is the central principle, although the participants to a contract or an exchange have some leeway in deciding what goods will count as equal. Some typical male relationships are reciprocal in this other sense, namely, all those that the fit the contractual model more or less closely. These are

> cool, distanced relations between more or less free and equal adult strangers, say, the members of an all male club with membership rules and rules for dealing with rule breakers and where the form of cooperation was restricted to ensuring that each member could read his *Times* in peace and have no one step on his gouty toes. (Baier, 1986:248)

Here the persons in reciprocal relationships may well be strangers to one another. When they react to one another, they react not to a particular person known to them but to some other whose presence in the confines of the club attests to his being an equal—but about whom they neither know nor desire to know anything else. The other in these reciprocal exchanges is easily replaceable by men who have the same social standing, credentials, or privileges. By contrast, the sort of caring Noddings and Gilligan talk about is a relationship between two specific people. Neither partner is replaceable by another abstract individual. As Rita Manning points out, "If my child needs my attention, I cannot meet this need by sending her to a therapist" (Manning, 1992:46).

Thus there are two very different senses of reciprocity: reciprocity-in-exchange[3] and what I shall call "reciprocity-in-completion." The former requires an exchange of roughly equal goods between persons who are, with respect to the exchange, roughly equal. (I can trade candy with a child, but the trade is not reciprocal if I get more simply on the grounds that I am bigger). Here the unit of discourse is the individual trade; it is a particular exchange that is (or is not) reciprocal. Reciprocity-in-completion prevails where an act is not complete until acknowledged and completed by a recipient. Acts are not acts of separate individuals but require, if begun by one person, that they be completed by the other. I will not discuss reciprocity-in-exchange any further but concentrate instead on the very different kind of reciprocity, namely, reciprocity-in-completion.

What matters here is that one respond to caring, that one acknowledge it, perhaps only by "glowing and growing stronger": "When the attitude of the one-caring bespeaks caring, the cared-for glows, grows stronger ... " (Noddings, 1984: 20). The one cared for accepts being cared for:

> I have claimed that the perception by the cared for of an attitude of caring on the part of the one caring is partially constitutive of caring. It and its successful impact on the cared-for are necessary to caring. Does this mean that I cannot be said to care for X if X does not recognize my caring? In the fullest sense, I think, we have to accept this result. ... It is complete when it is fulfilled in both ... [if] X does not feel that I care ...

> I must admit that, while I feel that I care, X does not perceive that care, and hence the relationship cannot be characterized as one of caring. (Noddings, 1984:68)

The sorts of relationships that, according to Noddings and also to Gilligan, involve caring are reciprocal insofar as the person who refuses to be cared for, who rejects your caring, or, worse, perhaps does not even notice your caring is not in a caring relationship with you in the sense of "caring" that is important here. If you care for someone who does not want to be cared for (by you) or does not want to be cared for (by you) in the way you care, then there is no reciprocal caring. You are not in a caring relationship with that other, regardless of your feelings for the other person or your efforts on his or her behalf. Hence selflessly caring for persons who are barely aware of your existence or caring for those who have nothing but contempt for you are not caring in the sense intended here.[4] Such selfless caring is often oppressed caring—the sort of one-sided responsiveness that women learn, as girls, and is enforced on them by a range of mechanisms from politicians holding forth about "family values" to men murdering their wives or girlfriends when they refuse to be as pliable as the men demand.

This reciprocity is not so easily understood. Some careful and sympathetic readers of Noddings have pointed to the striking similarity between her description of caring and the traditional nurturing role of women who take care of everyone except themselves. Such readers have expressed concern that Noddings's and Gilligan's ethics of care come perilously close to describing and validating the traditional exploitation of women by dressing it up in feminist language. For if the reciprocity required is so minimal, such as an occasional smile or even less than that for the one caring, the fact that the person cared for is thriving will suffice to make a reciprocal relationship. But the one caring looks, for all the world, like an oppressed, exploited woman who provides for everyone what they need and gets next to nothing for herself (Houston, 1989).

Whether this is a justified worry about this account of caring as reciprocal depends very much on how we develop this requirement of reciprocity. Granted that caring is a relationship in which what one does is not complete until the other does something, what is needed to complete the act? Is glowing and getting stronger sufficient? Will an occasional smile, some flowers, or an effusive acknowledgment in the preface of one's latest book suffice ("And to my wife without whom …")? Alternatively, must I respond to every smile, to every expression of affection? Must every kindness be acknowledged or repaid? We see here two versions of reciprocity-in-completion that would clearly not be adequate: If the requirements for what one must do to complete an act of caring are set too low, almost anything will count as caring and thus even one-sided, coerced, separate caring would count as reciprocal. Yet caring that requires an immediate response, an immediate return in a similar act of caring, strikes one as too unsure of itself and too demanding for return or affirmation to count as caring at its best. Caring does not call for the anxious bookkeeping and keeping accounts of everyone's contributions to make sure that they all balance out. We need to try to clarify this concept of reciprocity in more detail.

In exchanges, there are impersonal rules that set the measures of what goods and services are equal to others. But the reciprocity that is essential to relations of what Gilligan and Noddings call "caring" is not definable as an exchange of equals. The conventions of comparability that govern contracts do not apply here. How then can we discern the difference between reciprocal relationships and those that are not? When a member of a caring relationship wants to complain that the relationship is not reciprocal, how will she or he frame the grievance? Questions of ordinary equality may well come up: I wash all the dishes, and I don't like it. But if partners do different work because they like different work, that may nevertheless be acceptable to both unless such a division of labor is objectionable on political grounds that both share. What will complaints about lack of reciprocity look like if equal exchange is not the definition of reciprocity?

Questions about the distribution of burdens and rewards are not central to this reciprocity (Young, 1990:18ff.). All-important, instead, are the ways in which distributions are negotiated. The reciprocity involved in caring does not presuppose conventional standards of what is equivalent to what. Instead the participants must agree what a just distribution is. What makes the relation reciprocal, moreover, is not that they agree that it is a just distribution but what that agreement consists of and how it was reached.

If one party acquiesces in order to be "nice" or to avoid the other's anger, there is no reciprocity. Nor is there reciprocity if one party acquiesces because it is more convenient and more comfortable to be in the role of the underdog. If each decides by himself or herself and it happens that they come to an agreement, reciprocity may well be minimal or nonexistent. Instead, reciprocity in the relationship consists of the fact that the rules of reciprocity are a joint product of the partners in the relationship. The problem Dinah has with Hank is not that Hank never washes the dishes but that he does not listen to her complaints, that his agreement to change is always short-lived, that he is not interested in talking to her or in making changes to their relationship. His disinterest denotes his absence; the relationship is not a shared one. Hank jealously guards his separateness. He is unwilling to make the definition of reciprocity a joint project.

Reciprocity-in-completion is not primarily reciprocity of particular acts. It is not of central importance whether you and I take turns washing the dishes or whether one of us always washes and the other dries. What matters is how our arrangements come to be. Different persons expect different completions of their acts. Some expect effusive gratitude for small acts of kindness; others are embarrassed by expressions of gratitude. Some need their feelings to be carefully monitored by the other; another person avoids all references to emotions. Reciprocity here has to do with the ways in which those sorts of differences are worked out. Do the two come to a style of responding to one another, or of acknowledging what each does or feels, that is worked out jointly? Or are the desires of one decisive and then imposed on the other? Reciprocity-in-completion is not compatible with a coercive relationship but on the contrary requires that projects be shared, that they rest on a shared understanding, and that, as they proceed, decisions continue to be made jointly.[5]

When there is a joint project, the participants are likely to change. Willingness to enter into joint projects is willingness to be changed. For in developing ways of going about a particular undertaking, one learns to go about them in ways one would not always have chosen had one been all alone—or very separate. I adopt your ways to some extent when I work with you in a joint project. What is more, I adopt them not because I have been forced to do so, and now work unwillingly in a way that is alien and uncomfortable to me, but because I have learned to see things from your point of view. I have adopted some of your ways of thinking. I ask your questions, which before I did not ask; I provide kinds of explanations that before would not have occurred to me. I emerge from our joint project a somewhat different person and so, of course, will you. (I will return to that point repeatedly in later chapters).

We have come back here to the terminology developed in the preceding two chapters: Reciprocity, of the noncontractual kind, turns out to be the same as being-in-relation. A relationship is reciprocal to the extent that it is a joint project of two or more persons. The assignments of tasks and the distribution of goods must be worked out together. Reciprocity here has to do with the ways in which members of a group assign work and leisure, set goals and strategies, and assess their situation and frame their projects. Who does what and who takes care of whom in what way and on what occasion? Who decides what individually, and what decisions must be made jointly? To the extent that these and myriad other assignments are chosen jointly, the relationship is reciprocal in the being-in-relation sense. To the extent that each makes decisions by himself or herself, reciprocity is purely contractual. There is separate reciprocity and a being-in-relation reciprocity. It is the latter that is characteristic of caring relationships (as discussed by Gilligan and Noddings).

There is, then, not only separate decisionmaking and decisionmaking in-relation, as we saw in an earlier chapter, but there is also caring in-relation and separate caring. Persons care for each other in very different ways. Some of this caring is very separate; some involves reciprocity. Reciprocity, in its turn, may involve more or less equal exchange of acts, gestures, favors, and so on. Reciprocity that is not equal may rest on coercion, where one person imposes on the other his or her favorite ways of responding and being responded to. Or it may be genuinely in-relation because the ways in which each completes the acts of the other are arrived at jointly. The style of a relationship—the habitual acts and responses—are slowly articulated in a continuing conversation. It is therefore not useful to explain being-in-relation by reference to "caring" because, on the contrary, what we want to understand is one kind of caring, namely, caring that is in-relation. (Hence Gilligan treats "caring" as a technical term.) We cannot understand the different kinds of caring unless we already understand being-in-relation.

But does reciprocity in the being-in-relation sense then require that everything be talked about and explicitly negotiated? Two questions are being asked here: The first wants to know whether being-in-relation can allow for mutual accommodations that are made by the partners without their being fully aware of it. There surely are many of such adjustments. The characteristic of being-in-relation is that such adjustments tend to be made by both partners at different times and in different contexts. In separate or in covert forms of being-in-relation, often one partner makes most of the adjustments; the other is the model. But in a life that is genuinely shared, or in work that is done by a group, or in a game that is developed by a number of people, everyone models and everyone adjusts, at different times. But there are also, as we saw in the preceding chapter, adjustments that are understood by one partner while the other pretends that they are not there. Mr. Ramsay's autonomy was made possible by the support of his wife and children and their acceptance that that was the way he was. They knew they were making allowances for him. Only Mr. Ramsay did not know that. That sort of adjustment also is marginal to or even inimical to being-in-relation.

The second question is this: Must all the aspects of a shared project be discussed explicitly? To that we need to say the following: In some way reciprocity needs to emerge from the joint life of two distinct persons. Where the initial expectations of each person are different from those of the other about how they want the other to respond to him or her, a new form of responsiveness needs to emerge that belongs to both. How two (or more) persons create their forms of being attuned to each other differs enormously from case to case, of course. Conversations about common matters go on intermittently for years and differ with the style of talking of the participants. What emerges in a reciprocal relationship may well be a peculiar kind of conversational style that suits both of these particular people. Thus being-in-relation does not require an endless turning over of how each person feels about this or that or about the feelings of the other. One does not need to talk forever about one's childhood, about archetype and symbol—but one may if that is central to the life one shares with another.

Many changes in each partner take place without elaborate conversation. One insensibly takes over the other's ways because one likes them, or one yields on something one cares little about because it matters to the other. Whether that is a freely adopted change or just being submissive or conformist depends on the relationship as a whole. Are power differences out in the open? Are they sometimes contested? Is there agreement that each should strive to avoid using coercion or intimidation or should strive not to yield to them? Is each really trying to do that? There is much here that does need explicit discussion. To the extent that these discussions have done their work, less and less talk may well be needed.

There is a second reason why being-in-relation is not well explained in terms of caring. "Being-in-relation" is a much broader term than "caring." Unlike caring, being-in-relation is not always peaceful. Conflict is an inevitable ingredient in this project. What is more, conflict—open, unabashed conflict—is important. Women have not been allowed to be angry and/or have found it difficult. That has made it harder for them to resist coercion and refuse to be submissive. On the road toward being-in-relation one must at times stand up for oneself, outline one's differences as clearly as possible, or articulate one's difficulties. It is not always possible to do that without anger and animosity. Being-in-relation is not all love and quiet exchange of civilized opinion. The joint project is in part constituted by serious disagreements and differences. Our relationship turns out as it does because we share these views and habits and because we differ in those other ways. Some of those differences are complementary. Others strike sparks.

In some relationships, shared projects, beliefs, and habits outweigh differences. In others, animosities and aspects about each other that one cannot stand are more powerful than common stances. Both kinds of relationships may be in-relation. I can be in-relation with friends or lovers. But I can also be in-relation with someone I am very ambivalent about. Nietzsche understood this: "You should have eyes that always seek an enemy—your enemy ... you may have only enemies whom you hate, not enemies you despise. You must be proud of your enemy ... (Nietzsche, 1976:160).

To be sure, Nietzsche confuses hate with ambivalence. Hate depersonalizes. The hated enemies are not quite human; they are indistinguishable from all the others. They are all the same. The only thing known about them is what makes them into enemies. Hence the surprise at finding a Jew, a Puerto Rican, or a black one likes. But they are only exceptions to the rule. In the end, enemies must be kept in subjection or eradicated. It makes no sense to say that one should be proud of them.

But ambivalence about one's opponents is different. There are opponents who are "one's own," persons one knows well, persons one even respects—ones "you hate but do not despise"—who stand for the opposite of what one oneself takes to be valuable. One's ambivalence toward them may take very different forms. Here is a person I like, and admire in some ways, but in other respects he is incomprehensible to me. I do not understand the ways he goes about his work; I cannot imagine what he is thinking about. All I know is that in some ways his outlook or his values are very different from mine—so different, in fact, that I am not sure we will ever be able to talk about our differences.

I may have quite pleasant relationships with such a person. We may be friendly but distant with one another. But in other relations, the differences between us stir up my emotion. I admire this woman's intelligence and originality, but her consuming ambition and what seems to me shameless self-promotion stir up my anger. In other cases, again, the emotion may be fear, contempt, or envy. Thus ambivalence may be primarily cognitive in that I just do not understand the other in some respects or it may be primarily emotional or a combination of both. In all of these cases I have a good relation to the other in some situations but do not understand or am repelled by the other at different times.

Such ambivalence may be covertly or openly in-relation. Often the separate male has ambivalent and covertly in-relation ties to women. Mr. Ramsay goes around saying, "Women can't write; can't paint." Like many men he forever displays his misogyny but at the same time he needs Mrs. Ramsay. The open display of hostility helps him pretend that he is "his own man" and conceal that he is not. But the expressions of hostility and the forms taken by his pretenses of separateness are to some extent a function of the relationship. His need of her limits how he can be negative. Mrs. Ramsay does not mind too much, one suspects, if he denigrates the intellectual power of women. But if Mr. Ramsay took to drink and embarrassed her with drunken displays in front of the children or guests, she might very well withdraw some of her support. That expression of his hostility and disrespect for her would not be acceptable. Thus Mr. Ramsay must watch the forms of his ambivalence. (To be sure, in oppressive relations, the limits to that ambivalence are very narrow, but they are there nevertheless).

But ambivalence may also be openly in-relation. Over many years, I have had philosophical opponents whose attitudes and views are offensive to me. We have struggled to good effect. My opponents and I have learned from each other. We have been aware that this struggle, however difficult at times, has been good for us. In struggling with such an opponent one becomes a better defender of one's own causes and becomes clearer about what makes one be who one is. The relationship to him or her is clearly ambivalent: It involves love and hate, respect and total rejection. But the relationship is nonetheless a joint project. We both execrate the relation and nevertheless hold on to it and work at it because we both know—and sometimes even acknowledge openly—that the loss of that relationship would be painful. Ambivalence is a perfectly acceptable example of being-in-relation.

Noddings's account of what she calls caring has invited criticism because what she requires of the other who completes an action seems very minimal. That is a real difficulty. But the critics have not taken account of the fact that Noddings takes on a particularly difficult case of being-in-relation, the relations between adults and children. Among adults, contested practices or assignments of tasks and rewards and costs can all be talked about, and more acceptable agreements can be reached in the course of conversation. But such techniques for working out relationships are, by and large, not available when dealing with small children. They are also not always appropriate in more restricted forms of relationships such as relations between teachers and students. Hence in those situations it is not as easy to say what is meant by saying that two or more persons have a joint project, that they form a plural subject. After all, small children are just learning what it means to have joint projects.

CARING FOR CHILDREN

Being-in-relation takes many different forms. Caring in-relation between adults emerges, in part, from joint conversations that themselves have a style all their own created by the participants. Being-in-relation with small children is very different. Here the available means for establishing joint projects and for achieving reciprocity are very limited. Even small children who are quite articulate don't do well in discussing their relationships to their parents. They are just beginning to learn the language of motives and of interests. Their perceptions of who their parents are is very different from, say, the parents' perception of one another. What could reciprocity mean in that context?

The scope of these relationships is limited by difficulties in mutual understanding. I do not completely understand Eli's world, which is populated by monsters and other creatures of his fears and desires. I don't need to sleep with a night-light on; he does. My older brother troubles me in very different ways from those in which Eli's older sister troubles him—to Eli she seems to be so much more powerful than he. I cannot remember what it felt like to be just two and a half feet tall, to have a very vague sense of time and of what is in the past and the future, and to have next to no control over the ways in which the day unfolds. In corresponding ways, Eli does not understand me.

But we do have a language that I do not share with other adults in quite the same way—the language of bodily contact. We rarely go anywhere without holding hands or my carrying him for stretches. Embraces, at that age, speak louder than words. Then there are games. They solidify a reciprocal relationship because they are something we do together, as are reading books, singing songs, making up stories, and playing in the bathtub. Bringing up little children is contentious business and it needs a firm foundation of shared projects. These projects are fun. Because they are genuinely shared projects they support a relationship that the vast discrepancy of power makes inherently difficult. There is no other person in the whole world to whom I tell just those stories, sing those songs, or with whom I play just these games. These stories and songs are not mine; they are ours.

More needs to be said about this, however. There are different kinds of shared projects and not all of them are instances of being-in-relation. Mr. and Mrs. Ramsay's life together is, in spite of his fantasies about his lonely and autonomous victories over adversity, a joint project. But it is only covertly in-relation. So are the many relationships in which each partner makes certain adjustments just to be "nice" or to avoid conflict or because of a genuine desire to "make the relationship work." Here there is mutual adjustment, there is a certain kind of reciprocity perhaps, but it is the reciprocity of exchange, of giving up something at one point to get a concession at some other. Often relations between adults and children are of the same sort. Children adjust to the demands of parents in order to get love and escape punishment. Parents give in to children in order to get love and keep the peace.

Here it is very important to be clear that "caring" can be used in very different senses. Mothers and fathers have, in different ways, cared for their children from time immemorial. That means both that they have loved their children and that they have taken care of them. In many cases it even meant that they liked them. They have fed and nurtured and been alternately stern, playful, patient, and self-sacrificing. But all of that is well compatible with being quite separate. The obvious example is the distant father. But mothers too can care without being-in-relation. There are mothers who keep their houses immaculate, are good cooks, and keep track carefully of everyone's schedule but who, often from suppressed anger at inept or absent husbands or abusive parents, are not available affectively. Their caring for children is their separate project. They are not engaged in-relation with their children.

What matters is not the love, the patience, the self-denying sacrifices for the child but the effort to teach the child how to engage in joint projects. From very early in their lives children are capable of responding to others and engaging in some sort of reciprocal activities (Candib, 1995). What differentiates different kinds of maternal (and paternal) caring is the extent to which parents encourage those abilities and try to foster in the child the ability, willingess, and even eagerness to engage in joint projects rather than in remaining largely separate. One does that by engaging the child in games in which each contributes to the course of the game or to the rules and where thus a joint project is coming into existence. One does it by consulting children about matters that concern them. But this consultation, too, can take different forms. Some parents replace the old parental authoritarianism, under which they suffered, by letting the children decide many things that they are not old enough to decide. Domination by children replaces domination by parents. But a useful kind of consultation encourages conversation. Useful kinds of conversations encourage the child (and the parent) to consider the matter under discussion from the other's point of view and encourages each to give due weight to that other point of view. One continuing task is to encourage children to participate in thinking up compromises to settle disagreements: You want to wear shorts to school? But it is really cold this morning. Can you wear long pants now and take the shorts in your bag to change into them later? After a while the child will offer those compromises and the matter is resolved in a manner more in the spirit of being-in-relation.

Teaching children to be in-relation is inherently difficult. It is made more difficult by the fact that in society at large—in daycare, nursery school, and school proper as well as on TV—images and practices are those of separate persons. Little boys in ancient Sparta cannot have been more bloodthirsty or preoccupied with murder and mayhem than little boys in the United States today. It is difficult to teach in the midst of that that one should do things jointly, with consultation, even with fierce struggle but always for the sake of developing shared projects. There is so little support for this lesson and so much that pushes children in the other way. Adults suffer from the same handicaps. Were being-in-relation uniformly practiced everywhere, we would be much more skillful in encouraging cooperative projects with and between our children. As it is, we must make it up more or less by ourselves and often prove ourselves insufficiently inventive to meet the daily crises and struggles in ways that teach our children to be in-relation.

BEING-IN-RELATION AND TEACHING

Reciprocity is a form of being-in-relation, but there are, as we have seen many times, very different kinds of being-in-relation. The tendency in prevailing discussions of being-in-relation is to put almost exclusive attention on loving relationships. But that restricts the distinction between separateness and being-in-relation unduly. More important, if being-in-relation is limited to love and friendship, it remains as exceptional as love and friendship are. Then decisions are separate, unless shared by lovers, and being-in-relation has no place in the discussion of teaching, knowing, or the uses of power. The conception of persons as separate remains fundamental.

But we have already seen that the difference between separateness and being-in-relation has a much wider scope than love and friendship: It applies, for instance, to ambivalent relations and to relations to certain adversaries. But it also applies to relations between teachers and students or between doctor and patient (Candib, 1995). There is, as we saw earlier, decisionmaking that is separate and decisionmaking that is in-relation. But we could draw the same distinction in talking about a work team, about the board of a social service agency, a political group, or a neighborhood association. In later chapters I will talk about other forms of being-in-relation that are not love relationships.

For the moment I want to look at the differences between separateness and being-in-relation in the case of teaching. There is separate teaching, the "sowing the seed" method. To the extent that I choose separateness, I think of my teaching role as presenting material as interestingly and seductively and as responsibly as I can. This teaching is best done in lectures—putting forward ideas, facts, interpretations, or even exhortations to people whom one may not know at all, who respond minimally, and about whom one does not know anything except their performance on an examination at the end of the course. Here there is no reciprocity, no being-in-relation. The alternative is teaching that tries to establish a very restricted and fairly clearly focused relation to a particular other person so that that student may learn a specific skill, solve a particular problem, or master a particular body of information by virtue of having this relationship to a teacher and/or to other students.

It is not immediately obvious what reciprocity would mean in the relation between teacher and student and how it is to be accomplished. How can there be
joint projects, joint decisions about what are fair distributions of pleasures and
pains? In the negotiations about work assignments between adults, the important
consideration is that everyone listen very carefully to everyone else, that everyone's needs and goals be as transparent to everyone as possible. Hank reasserts his
separateness by refusing to see Dinah's needs and complaints for what they are.
Keeping the power unequal is clearly on Hank's agenda. Should he change, however, and make an effort to attend carefully to what Dinah is telling him, he would
signify that he is trying to be in-relation, that he is trying to undertake a joint
project with her.

But teachers and students are not equals. They do not negotiate a joint project
as equals. Instead the point of the project is that the student learn, and the project
is determined by the basic fact that the teacher is older, knows more, and is more
powerful. One great value of Noddings's discussion is precisely that she thinks
about reciprocity in raising children or in teaching, where there are serious dis-
crepancies in capacities and in power that call for different ways of achieving reciprocity. She asks how we can talk about "reciprocity"—she sometimes also talks
about "mutuality"—in this situation. Does reciprocity, of any sort, not presuppose that each partner in the relation pay attention to the other and to the other's
needs? But both the teacher's and the student's attention are focused on the student's learning. If students start paying attention to the teacher's educational
strategies, for instance, they get distracted from the task at hand, which is learning
(Noddings, 1984:180).

Noddings answers that if the teacher is genuinely caring and the student
thrives, there is reciprocity. But sometimes I assign a piece of reading that a student reads just when that text has enormous significance for him. He feels genuinely enlightened. The text opens a new world to him. Is that a reciprocal relationship? Hardly. It is, on my part, sheer luck. The student may be in a large class. I
barely know him and will, perhaps, never know that he profited from reading that
text. Noddings is explicit that that is not what she means. What she does mean is
that the teacher receives "and accepts the student's feeling towards the subject
matter; she looks at it and listens to it through his eyes and ears" (Noddings, 1984:
177). The teacher tries to see the student as clearly as possible, to understand what
she or he is trying to say and to be helpful to that person. But what is the student's
part in this reciprocal relationship?

The effort must be to develop a joint project in which what is said and done is
jointly developed by teacher and student. The relationship has a clear purpose:
for the student to learn. Nor is the purpose for the student to learn anything
whatsoever, because a particular teacher teaches very specific subjects, skills, attitudes—whether one teaches in kindergarten or at the postdoctoral level. The
teacher-student relationship is therefore very restricted, and the teacher cares for

the student within the limits of that project. Hence it is possible to care for and do well with a student whom one does not even like especially.

But the caring is effective—that is, the student learns from the teacher—only if the relationship is reciprocal. One does not learn much unwillingly. One can amass facts against one's will and memorize irregular verbs, multiplication tables, or the catechism unwillingly but not learn what they mean. One can be fortunate and begin to learn a subject against one's will and then come to love it. But there is little to recommend taking that chance. Most people who learn unwillingly only come to dislike learning. The best learning is done where each is eager to participate: Students are eager because they will receive what they are looking for, teachers because they see the students learn. For the student to receive what is needed requires a teacher who listens carefully and a student who is encouraged to be reflective and articulate about her or his learning. Those skills develop only where learning is done in-relation.

The development of a joint project need not always be explicit. It does not require that teacher and student sit down to plan a particular course of studies. Often such joint projects develop incrementally to the extent that teacher and student(s) respond to one another. In our world where separateness is widely assumed to be a natural condition, the relation between teacher and student begins as one between two separate persons. To what extent they can transform that into a very different relationship where each pays careful attention to the other depends on many things, in part on how long they have to develop that relationship. Thus in these relations, two or more persons may be more or less in-relation. There is a wide range of relationships that fall somewhere between the extremes in a spectrum that runs from complete and consistent separateness to being totally engaged and in-relation with the other. Teacher-student relations will never be at the latter extreme and should not be at the former.

Most relationships are somewhere in between. I have spent extended periods, over several semesters, arguing conservative political philosophy with particular students. I had no other expectation than to make that person a more sophisticated and articulate conservative. I succeeded to the extent that there was some reciprocity, that the student saw both that I did not share his political stance, that I respected his intellectual gifts, and also that he responded to my demands for clear statements, valid arguments, and respect for facts. The project was to some extent a joint project: I had little interest in his particular political stance, so he set the agenda of our conversations. But I set the standards, and he was willing to follow on that. The resulting talks were something we did together, and in that particular instance, both of us learned something. For I too did not know before we started how one would give a strong defense of views that are very different from mine.

At other times, the task was to improve someone's writing skills. That too can be done only if the student is willing to accept direction. That in turn will happen only if corrections are offered in a way the student can accept. That is sometimes very difficult to do, and I have not always succeeded when I tried. Failure to offer corrections in a form acceptable to this student destroys the chance of reciprocity and one's chance to teach that person this particular skill. Here too teaching gives rise to a joint project, albeit a narrowly focused one. Central are the teacher's attempt to prove his or her accepting goodwill toward the student and the student's effort to show that she or he is responding. Once some mutual trust is established in this way, skills and information are imparted readily.

I stressed before that the choice to be in-relation is easier or much more difficult, or even impossible, in different social environments. For us whose teaching is, like most other relationships, assumed to be separate, it is difficult to establish the sorts of relationships that make in-relation learning and teaching possible. Hence it does not happen very often and requires a good deal of time. In a world more accustomed and dedicated to being-in-relation, teaching in-relation would also be easier. But even in our world it can be and is being done, as the following example shows.

In this world dominated by separateness, there are teachers who are trying remarkably hard and are successful in establishing being-in-relation as the norm in their classrooms. Here is a description of one such classroom. The teacher's name is Ms. Smith.

> The classroom was located in an urban school district near Buffalo, NY. According to data supplied by the principal, approximately 65%–70% of the children in the school qualified for free or reduced lunches. The school had a black population of approximately 20%. ... [Ms. Smith describes how her teaching style changed:] The hardest part was training myself to give up control and to learn to trust the kids. ... Sharing control with the children does not come easily and Ms Smith comments on it frequently ... [she] constantly moved about the class room, assessing and facilitating in order to establish an open, yet productive atmosphere ... [she] actively established ... guidelines: therefore student choices, negotiations, and ultimate empowerment developed within those parameters. ... (Garan, 1994:192–197)

In this first-grade classroom, the teacher makes it possible that, at the end of the year, groups of children take on some work without being prompted by the teacher and, in a situation where the teacher was supposed to participate in their group, do the work alone when she is unable to be there. The study cited shows example after example of situations in which children, if given concrete examples of how they could solve their problems together without calling on the teacher's authority, readily take in those suggestions and follow the examples at the next opportunity.

The result is a classroom where learning is a joint effort. Children who get distracted are called back to the work at hand by their classmates, and what is really impressive, they respond and get back to work. Children who need help get assistance from other children; the teacher does not need to be always the helper. Resources are readily available so that children know where to look when they are unsure about spelling a word. They can help themselves and one another. Most of that would be impossible if learning in this room had not become everyone's project. Children can be active in finding what they need or helping others, and those others can accept help because the project is a joint one. Children are no longer "being taught" by a separate teacher. No longer does each child separately have its own relationship to the teacher, because learning is a shared project of everyone in the room. The classroom ceases to the teacher's classroom and becomes the classroom of all the persons regularly in it.

Here the teacher has to distance herself from her traditional role as the one who is in control. Once again being-in-relation requires that one distance oneself from one's separate self, whose projects are one's own exclusively. Instead, one must join with others in a common effort, in this case to create a functioning classroom where children learn actively and responsibly. Teaching in-relation is not only possible. It is highly desirable.

SEPARATENESS, COVERT BEING-IN-RELATION, AND OPENLY CHOSEN BEING-IN-RELATION

It is time to take stock. I have pointed out the prevailing view that human beings are separate from one another, as a matter of logic or of natural fact. Against that I have shown that whether one is separate or in-relation is a matter of choice and that, moreover, many people who claim to be separate are, in fact, covertly in-relation. Usually that means that they require a good deal of attending from the others but retain for themselves the freedom to act separately and independently whenever that seems more convenient. People who openly choose to be in-relation, however, are attentive to the other. There are many joint projects that belong neither to one partner nor to the other but to both. Moreover, the participants choose to make them joint projects, and that means that everyone's participation is important and valued.

But now someone will say, I will grant you that talk about autonomy, and how we are all separately shaping and responsible for our lives, is truly silly. But your alternative, the critic continues, is equally silly. All this elaborate discussion of being covertly or openly in-relation amounts to no more than this: Whenever two or more people take on a common project, not everyone can have everything his or her way. Everyone has to adjust, compromise, give some and take some. Everyone wants to be loved and respected. Few people like to be in constant conflict. So children learn to say what their parents like to hear, and parents buy candy, or tolerate noise and chaos, merely to keep the peace in the house. All of this is very plain and excessively familiar, and nothing more needs to be said.

This objection misstates and trivializes the insights of the preceding three chapters. Yes, it is true: In any joint project, everyone must make some concessions, and in the vast majority of cases, everyone does. But the ordinary good advice to "give a little, take a little" ignores the fact that who gives what and who takes what is decided in rather different ways in different projects. Clearly give-and-take is very different depending on the power relationships. If one partner is more powerful than the other, that usually means that the more powerful partner takes more. But even should that not be true, the more powerful partner more often than not sets the rules and apportions gains and losses. One difference between openly and covertly in-relation projects is surely that in the former, power differences are acknowledged, thought about, and their effects either minimized or restricted to areas where they are appropriate.

Look at the relations between teachers and students once more. Teachers have more power in the world at large. They can give good or bad recommendations for other courses, other schools, jobs, grants, or other honors. But the student is not without power to wound the vanity or threaten the teacher's self-esteem by being indifferent, disrespectful, or spreading derogatory stories. Then there is power having to do more directly with their joint projects. The teacher knows more about the subject than the student, but the student may have relevant knowledge in other fields that the teacher does not have or may have intellectual or other skills that are helpful to the project and that the teacher lacks.

To talk here about give and take is not enough. In a joint project these power differences can be negotiated in very different ways. The teacher, covertly in-relation, may keep a tight rein and make sure never to relinquish control of the project. The teacher may, of course, also be very permissive if that suits him or her more and let the student run the project as that person pleases. But that too is to be, ultimately, in charge, for in either case the teacher sets the basic rules alone. The student may be allowed to make choices about the shape of the project in some respect, for example, scheduling may be both at the teacher's and the student's convenience, but be limited to accepting orders in other respects. But such a joint project can also be very different. Teacher and student can openly acknowledge the power differential but make an effort to forge a relationship in which the student can feel reasonably certain that the teacher will not use her power without consultation and, in effect, without the student's permission. But such a relationship takes time to establish. It takes work and it may always remain a bit precarious. It is, however, the basis of a very different sort of give and take. The difference between covert and openly chosen being-in-relation is manifested in very different sorts of give and take.

But the differences uncovered in the preceding three chapters are important in another respect. The image of give and take reminds us of a marketplace where exchanges are made. I give up the decision in a particular issue, and at another time you reciprocate and do things my way. In the former instance, I give; in the latter, I take. But this image represents relationships as exchanges and puts attention on who gives what to whom. From the being-in-relation perspective, however, what matter are how the givers and takers listen to one another, what sort of attention they have for each other, and the extent to which each is open to change or is, on the contrary, defending a self that does not want to change. What matters even more is how their relationship is a joint production, created and maintained by both together. Stressing what each gives to the other still stresses each as not only distinct but also separate and thus obscures the ways in which in being-in-relation each becomes, in limited ways, an extension of a joint person and personality. In being-in-relation persons make themselves permeable to the other. If the persons are thus interconnected, the give and take is quite different from the exchanges in a relationship modeled on a commercial transaction—different because of what is given and taken and different because of what giving and taking might mean. One can, to be sure, describe being-in-relation as giving and taking, but to do so only flattens out and obscures the complexities of being-in-relation.

I have made a great deal of the difference between covert and open being-in-relation. It is important to notice, in conclusion, that this distinction is in danger of oversimplifying the enormous diversity of human relationships. I have talked as if there are only two or rarely three possibilities: A person may choose to be genuinely separate, to be openly in-relation, or to be covertly so. But there surely are very many different sorts of relationships. There is a large range of different ways in which persons in face-to-face relations talk and act or just are with each other. Two or more persons may be openly in-relation in some ways and not in others. As the critic said earlier, everyone wants to be loved and often choosing to be in-relation may involve challenging the other, raising difficult or painful issues. That is scary, and it is less threatening just to "give a little." It is also easier; it takes less effort. Some people are more passive in their relations than others and thus more inclined to simply adjust or evade conflict. We need to say that any particular person may be openly in-relation in some relationships or some specific projects and not in others. In some situations we try very hard to be openly in-relation. In others we settle back to do what is most convenient or familiar at the moment. But this merely means that we do not choose to be separate or in-relation once and for all but that it is a choice that is constantly reconsidered and remade about different acts and different aspects of relationships. The complexity of the choice or the fact that it confronts us every day does not, however, detract from the fact that for most of us only being-in-relation is a defensible choice.[6]

◄ 5 ►

Examples of Being-in-Relation

BEING-IN-RELATION TAKES different forms in different contexts. It will, therefore, be helpful to discuss some other examples. I will consider empathy and autonomy in this chapter.

We have seen again and again that clarifying the difference between separateness and being-in-relation proves difficult because words as we use them ordinarily are not neutral between separateness and being-in-relation. Instead our language tends to favor separateness. The most ordinary senses of many words tend to presuppose that all human beings are separate. Language itself favors the male outlook on the world (Griffiths, 1992). I will end this chapter by reflecting about the ways in which language makes social change very difficult.

BEING-IN-RELATION AND EMPATHY

We saw in the previous chapter that being-in-relation is often identified with caring but that the ordinary everyday senses of "caring" are not helpful in explicating what we mean by being-in-relation. "Caring," as the word is commonly used, refers to the submissive caretaking that stereotypical women have been expected to do. That kind of caring occurs in relations with persons who are and mean to remain separate. It is different from being-in-relation. We must be on our guard against a similar difficulty with respect to empathy, which is often identified as a central feature of being-in-relation (Jordan, 1983, 1984). Here too we find a common sense of empathy deriving from the assumption of separateness. Before we can see the connection between empathy and being-in-relation we first need to see the failures of separate empathy and discover a very different kind of empathy that is, indeed, a form of being-in-relation.

Empathy, as ordinarily understood, presupposes the distinctness and separateness of persons. It is a response to questions like this: In empathy one enters into the life—the joy and suffering—of another. Empathy seems to imply shared feelings. But if my feelings are exclusively mine, and yours are only yours, how can there be empathy? In reply it is commonly said that empathy does not involve shared feelings at all but merely my mimicking the other's feelings in the light of my own. Psychologists tell us that in empathy one feels what the other person feels—as Chodorow wrote, "experiencing the other's needs and feelings as one's own" (Gilligan, 1982:8). Heinz Kohut understands empathy as neither compassion nor intuition. It is, instead, an attempt to understand the other by "mobilizing memories of feelings comparable to the patient's" (Gardiner, 1987:765). Roy Schafer has "spoken of generative empathy as the 'inner experience of sharing in and comprehending the momentary psychological state of the other person' ... this knowing is approximate, 'based to a great extent on remembered, corresponding, affective states of one's own'" (Jordan, 1984:3). Nor do philosophers, whether "analytic" (Ripstein, 1987) or "phenomenological" (Smith, 1989), present a different view. Empathy is always a way of "putting oneself in the other person's shoes." One feels what the other feels by virtue of having previously experienced what the other is undergoing now. In empathy one reconstructs the feelings of others in the light of one's own experiences. Separateness is bridged by guessing the other's feelings in the light of feelings one has had oneself.

There may well be some situations where empathy is only guessing at the other's feeling and having feelings that are similar. But empathy encompasses a lot more than that. Besides, separate empathy often fails and turns into some other emotion. In many situations it is liable to be not really empathy at all but, instead, a cover for very different and often less admirable feelings.

Empathy involves being in tune with other persons, but that is quite different from supposing that their feelings are like one's own. It is, for instance, not reliable to infer from another person's action that the other's motives are like one's own when doing similar actions. When I was a student I tended to attach myself to older men because I was, vaguely, looking for a father. As a teacher, I may suspect a student who shows great interest in my subject of trying to do the same. But perhaps this student is really interested in the subject rather than in me. Only if I am genuinely empathic can I accurately understand his motives. Supposing that his motives are similar to mine is not being empathic but, on the contrary, rather gets in the way of empathy. I know myself to some extent. If I assume that the other is very much like me, I also assume that I know the other as well. But then I need not make the effort, essential to empathy, of attending closely to the other because I already know him.

This kind of empathy is, besides, extremely limited. As a man I do not share the experience of women who feel unsafe in many public spaces; nor am I as guilt ridden about being an adequate father as many women are about the adequacy of their mothering. I have not had the experiences of persons in prison. Being white, I do not have the experiences of persons of color in the United States. Were empathy merely to feel what another feels by dredging up experiences out of one's own memory, the range of one's empathy would be much more limited than it, in fact, is.

At times, I feel someone's sadness because it is my friend who is sad and I want to share in his grief. But often empathy is not so much a matter of *feeling* what the other feels but knowing it. I may know, in some detail, your grief at your father's death, your worry that you should have spent more time with him during his last illness, or that you had not attended to him as well as you might have in his old age because of your long-standing anger at his failure to talk to you when you were younger and needed him. I may know that that is what you feel, but the only thing I feel is distress over your unhappiness or over my inability to help you bear your burden. I am being empathic but do not feel your feelings.

Consider also this: My knowledge of your feelings may go together with a sense that you got what you deserved and thus a certain satisfaction or schadenfreude. But that surely is not a case of empathy. That requires, on the contrary, not only knowledge of your feelings but also a keen sense that your grief is undeserved and that the universe is not dealing fairly with you. Empathy includes regret or sorrow over your suffering or happiness over your joy without necessarily feeling either of them (Scheler, 1931).

Empathy, finally, may not consist as much of knowing or feeling what you feel but of an understanding that you are in need and an alert readiness to provide for you what I can (Greenspan, 1986). An empathic person is one you can rely on to bring you a meal or flowers when tragedy strikes or who shows in other, usually imaginative and especially appropriate ways, that he or she is there to be leaned on when you need to do that. Empathic persons listen well. They hear with more precision and clarity than others what you are saying and what precise form your pain or pleasure takes. When you muddle about in a welter of feelings, unable to say what is bothering you, the empathic person—precisely because he or she does not feel the same feelings—may be able to mirror your feelings more clearly than you perceive them yourself.

However, sometimes feeling what the other feels is not empathy at all but rather suffering the effect of a pervasive atmosphere of sadness. Suppose I come to work and find everyone in a somber mood because a beloved public figure died the night before. Perhaps the news had not affected me when I first heard it, and it took the shared sadness of my co-workers to make me also feel sad. I feel what others feel through a kind of emotional contagion that is not empathy at all. Empathy is a much more complex phenomenon than the dubious "reconstructing of another's experience on analogy to one's own" that many psychologists describe.[1]

There are, of course, situations where one is guessing more or less elaborately what another person is feeling. One's own past emotions certainly provide relevant information when one makes such guesses. But such guessing is not paradigmatic of empathy. In central cases of empathy both persons are involved; there empathy is a form of being-in-relation.

Robert Bly talks to men about their grief at having had an absent father. In a videotape, he illustrates the absent father with this story: A young man, the son of a mechanic, manages to go to college and graduate school and becomes a college professor. When his father falls gravely ill, the son calls up his father to offer his support and sympathy. Here is the conversation that Bly relates in a Bill Moyers videotape, "A Gathering of Men with Robert Bly" (Public Broadcasting System, January 8, 1990):

> Son: Hi, Dad, it's John.
>
> Father: Wait, I'll call your mother.
>
> Son: No, Dad, I want to talk to you.
>
> Father: Do you want something?
>
> Son: No, but I have been thinking how hard you worked so that I could get an education, and how grateful I am to you. I wanted to say that I love you.
>
> Father: Have you been drinking?

What Bly wants us to find in this story is the stereotypical father who is emotionally absent. He leaves all communication and everything that has to do with affection and relationships to his wife because it is "women's work." He is the archetype of the separate man. There is, however, a more complex reading of that story.

It is interesting to notice, to begin with, how even if we accept the story as intended, empathy is to some extent a cooperative venture. It is very difficult for John to be empathic with his father, who rejects his approaches. Well, you may say, can't John, being a man also, feel some of his father's panic at the open display of emotion that is threatening in this conversation? But imputing one's own feelings to another is often deceptive. John may instead try to guess his father's feelings. But that would be difficult. For we know about others what they tell us or what we guess on the basis of what they have told us before. People who are generally uncommunicative are therefore hard to read. It is very difficult to empathize with someone who never allows one to see his feelings. We may know that this person is happy today and that another is angered by something that just happened, but knowing another's feelings about his son is very difficult unless he tells us about those feelings.

But this cooperation in empathy is not yet being-in-relation. The difference between needing someone's help in order to have separate empathy and being genuinely empathic in-relation emerges when we reconsider Bly's story. Bly wants us to believe that John's father rebuffs his son because of who he is—the emotionally crippled, absent father. But should we not also wonder what John is really doing? Is he suddenly afraid that his father will die and wants reassurance that everything will be all right? Is he feeling guilty about not showing his father any gratitude in the past and is he now trying to make up for that? Were there years while John was a student that he showed disrespect for his unlettered father? Is the distance between them the result of old wounds long buried by both? And is John now trying to profess empathy in order to pretend that those wounds are not there? Perhaps his father's refusal is not quite as perverse as it may have seemed at first.

John cannot be empathic with his father because his father will not let him. But his father's refusal, at first a seeming example of archetypal male refusal to be emotional, may well have some justification: Perhaps John pretends, to himself and his father, to be empathic but really wants reassurances that his father has forgiven him. Perhaps he really wants to assuage some guilt. His pretended empathy is actually a very different emotion. This is an example of separate empathy that is mere pretense—a cover for feelings such as guilt or anger that are more difficult to bear consciously and more difficult to display.

Here we begin to approach an understanding of empathy in-relation. If empathy is separate, the person who is empathic can tell us that he or she feels empathy and we need to accept that claim. But we know of course that such an account of John, for instance, may well be mistaken. Empathy in-relation includes as one of its aspects the agreement of all concerned that they are in fact feeling empathy rather than guilt or fear. Empathy cannot even begin until both parties can come to agree that it is indeed empathy that is being shown. John's father may acknowledge that John is being genuinely affectionate but not accept it as empathy. Without his acknowledgment that John's reaching out is genuine empathy, it is not clear whether John is really feeling or practicing empathy. John's *saying* that he is feeling empathy with his father is not sufficiently reliable. There is too much false sympathy in the world and too much straight selfishness that masquerades as empathy to take his word for it.

There are two different senses of "empathy." There is the sense of empathy between people who act separate from one another. Here empathy is guessing what is going on inside the other. Such guesses cannot assume that my motives are similar to those of the other, because those frequently are quite different. Empathy, in this sense, involves reconstructing the other's emotions in the light of what we know about the other—primarily from what the other has told us in the past. To the extent that the other is steadily uncommunicative, empathy has little to go on. Even in this separate empathy, one needs some cooperation from the other. Claims to be empathic in that sense are not easily verified because only the person making that claim has direct access to his or her feelings and thoughts. Such empathy is often mere pretense. It also lacks many other aspects of empathy: the conviction that what happens to the other is undeserved and unjust and the readiness to come to the other's assistance, if only by bringing flowers or a meal.

A much richer empathy is in-relation. It is not a characteristic of one person but is some sort of shared activity, a joint project. In addition, this other kind of empathy is not a characteristic of one person at a particular moment but describes a certain process, a conversation between people with its tone, rhythm, flow of speech and response, and ambience. Jean Baker Miller describes this for us:

> A woman, Ann, has just heard from her friend and co-worker, Emily, that Emily may have a serious blood disease. Ann is telling her friend Beth about this. Let us say that Beth knows Emily but is not as close a friend as Ann. Beth says, "Oh, how sad." Beth's voice and expression are sad and there is also some fear in them. Ann then says, "Yes, sad, but I have this other awful feeling—like fear. Like I'm scared—as if it could hap-

pen to me." Beth replies, "Me too. It is frightening to hear this. Maybe we all feel as if it's happening to us." (Miller, 1986:6)

As the conversation continues, it becomes clear that Ann was ashamed of her fear for herself and that that made it difficult to open herself fully to Emily's troubles and made her afraid to be with Emily. Empathy on Beth's part consisted of reassuring Ann that she need not be ashamed of her fear; Beth shared that feeling and did not think that one need to deny or to hide it. But Beth could help Ann in this way only because she shared of herself and she could do that because Ann let her. Empathy here is mutual, and it is possible only because both partners in the conversation acknowledge and accept the other's empathy. This empathy for one another is something they share, something that they each contribute to, and something that most properly belongs to them jointly.

Notice also that in this conversation, each woman discovers something about herself and about the other. The fear that both women feel over their friend's illness—the thought "this may happen to me"—is at first not felt very clearly because each is ashamed to feel it and thus tries to push it aside. In the course of an empathic conversation, the two women gain a clearer appreciation of their own feelings about their friend. Empathy is not just this person's knowledge about another but rather a certain spirit of the conversation in which each gains clarity about her own feelings as well as those of the other person. Empathy is a route to discovery of self and other.

Self-knowledge is an essential ingredient in this sort of empathy. It plays a much less central role in separate empathy, which is directed exclusively toward the other who is happy or suffering. As we just saw in the case of John, such empathy may not be genuine. But since the other's feelings are in the spotlight, the genuineness or self-deception of this empathy is not so easily introduced into the conversation. The empathic person tries to understand the other whose problems or emotions currently demand attention. Whether the empathy is real or imagined, or pretended, is often not even considered. Separate empathy thus easily becomes a burden. John thinks he is empathic with his dying father. His father sees through that but since John's word suffices to stamp his feeling as empathy, any demurral on his father's part will appear ungrateful. He cannot, gracefully, get John to spare him his guilt and anxiety because they masquerade as empathy.

If, on the contrary, we understand empathy as a shared process, knowledge of self is as essential as knowledge of the other. For in that case my empathy for you also involves my openness to your perceptions of me and the possibility of my having to reconsider my conception of myself. In empathy in-relation, each comes to know himself or herself at the same time that they come to know the other. How one sees the other is not unrelated to what one thinks of oneself. If the other sees me differently, I may have to readjust my view of myself. But that may also lead to a revision of what I think of the other. There is continuity between understanding of self and of the other. John's pretended empathy is received with distrust by his father. Before they can be empathic with each other, a good deal of distrust must be removed, and that will require a very unaccustomed openness between the two. If the two were able to have the necessary conversations, each would change his view of himself and his relation to the other. Short of that, each will harbor his ancient resentments and guilt and look for affection from a person he does not understand very well because he also does not understand himself very well or how he appears to the other. There is little hope for genuine empathy here.

Empathy in-relation, where it does develop, is then also a road to change. Both Ann and Beth, having helped each other admit their fear for themselves and the shame they felt over that, are now ready to be much more open to Emily's pain and fear and help her in the best ways possible; they are not confused by their own half-conscious guilt or their fear for their own well-being.

But empathy is not always reciprocal, you say. Sometimes empathy goes mostly one way. You are bereft or troubled and I attempt to comfort. I can be empathic with you without your taking up a similar attitude toward me. Here we need to recall the earlier discussion of reciprocity. Empathy is not reciprocal as if it were a bargain or an exchange; empathy need not always reciprocate in kind. But empathy does need to be accepted. Separate empathy is often offered where it is not wanted—perhaps that is one element of the tension between John and his father—because whether someone is empathic depends only on the person having that attitude.[2] But empathy in-relation is something that two or more people share; it is a common project. That does not mean that each does what the other does. Common projects often involve different persons playing different parts or doing their own jobs. But the jobs must be elements of a larger whole that belongs to both.

What being-in-relation means in empathy depends on many factors: Are persons friends, lovers, or coworkers for extended periods or is this a short-lived, very limited episode in the life of each? Over long periods, there more likely needs to be some evenness in a relationship. There must be some return of concern. In a very limited episode, the person who is the recipient of empathy must accept it, perhaps by being forthcoming about his or her feelings and fears, but need not offer support in return. If empathy prevails between persons of different status, age, gender, or position of authority, reciprocity may take different forms again. If I ask a student about her plans after graduation, she may signal acceptance by talking about those plans. If we have known each other for a while, she may also ask about my children, whose pictures are on the walls of my office. In both ways she accepts my interest. We need not engage in a conversation of what I will do after I retire from teaching. But she may also indicate by very brief replies to my questions that she does not want to talk about plans for the future. Empathy then consists of dropping the subject unless there are very good reasons for persevering.

This last remark suggests that there is a kind of empathy that belongs to one person alone. Although that is true, reciprocity is still essential here. Empathy is reciprocal, but sometimes the offer of empathy is not accepted and then the empathic person will pull back. Empathy is relational, but relations must be established. One way of doing that is to offer to enter into a certain relationship. Thus empathic persons are those who are inclined to make those sorts of offers, who are aware of when their offers might be accepted and when it is wiser, and kinder, not even to offer. Thus there is a relational way of being empathic that is not actually in-relation because the relevant relationship has not yet been established or perhaps the offer of a relationship has been rejected. But this empathic person is nevertheless not a separate person in his empathy because he is trying to establish a relationship. He knows that to be empathic is to have a relationship to another person and he is therefore keenly aware of the times when offers of such relationships are appropriate and when they are not. People who are separately empathic are not worried about that. They are not aware of times when their inclinations to offer support or sympathy are not wanted. Nor do they care because they do not understand that empathy needs to be accepted, acknowledged, and supported by the other.

There are, then, clearly two very different senses of the word "empathy." One refers merely to one's attempt to guess what the other feels. The other names an atmosphere of open inquiry into feelings and thoughts that two or more people provide for themselves and others to know, and where necessary to heal, themselves and others. This open and shared inquiry may take many very different forms. These two very different ways of being empathic are part and parcel of very different ways of being a person. One can be a Mr. Ramsay and pretend to be separate, concealing as far as possible the ways in which one needs others and depends on them. Separate empathy is a part of that stance. But that separate stance often fails because it is not genuine empathy. But one also can be openly and actively in-relation and be in empathy with another by laying oneself open to scrutiny just as much as the other opens himself or herself up. Self-knowledge and knowledge of the other go hand in hand.

Whether to be separately empathic or in-relation depends on one's choice of what sort of person to be. We saw in the previous chapter that there are good reasons for not choosing to be separate. There are also good reasons for choosing to be empathic in-relation. Being empathic in-relation is more demanding. It requires a certain amount of courage to open oneself and one's feelings to the scrutiny of the other. It takes less courage to feel the other's feelings than to be prepared to feel one's own. Attempts at empathy may fail; one may be rebuffed or misunderstood. One may not be able to understand the other. Separate empathy, by contrast, is safe. I do not open myself to the other's scrutiny and, perhaps, judgment. I do not even have to inquire whether what I offer as empathy really is empathy or perhaps a different feeling disguised as empathy. Empathy in-relation requires a certain strength of character. It requires autonomy, not separate autonomy but autonomy in-relation.

AUTONOMY AND CONFORMITY

I showed earlier that autonomy, as it is usually understood, is the exclusive property of stereotypical men, that it is oppressive to women, and that it is, in most cases, quite disingenuous. The "autonomous man" of mainstream philosophy is a caricature. It is, therefore, tempting to reject autonomy as an ideal altogether (Hoagland, 1990). But the idea of autonomy is important. To begin with, the demand for greater self-determination for women would make no sense were feminism to reject the concept of autonomy (Grimshaw, 1986). What is more, the traditional concept of autonomy has played an important and, on the whole, salutary role in the defense of the individual and political liberties of various categories of people. Also, the traits of persons that we ordinarily (before we start doing philosophy) associate with autonomy still seem desirable: It is good to be able to take care of one's everyday needs rather than be forever leaning on others, which is a kind of autonomy Mr. Ramsay lacks. Everyone should have a mind of his or her own instead of following authority blindly. It is important to have principles that one sticks to even if that makes one unpopular or invites punishments. It is desirable to give a certain coherence to one's life or have a distinctive style in what one does. For all these reasons, it would be a serious error to surrender the concept of autonomy.

The prevailing philosophical discussions of autonomy are unacceptable. There are many reasons for this. One of them is that in spite of extended discussion of autonomy, the concept remains hazy. In the perspective of separateness, one opposite of autonomy is conformism. The autonomous person lives by his or her own standards; the conformist borrows ideas and values indiscriminately from others without subjecting those ideas to careful rational scrutiny. But that contrast between autonomy and conformism is not really as clear as is usually believed. Philosophers have written much about autonomy but have assumed that we all know what conformism is. It will prove useful to pause for a moment and consider conformism in more detail.

There are genuinely separate persons who make a major effort to consign human relationships to the margins of their lives and for whom what they do by themselves is what matters most. Such lives are not easy to lead and are therefore rare. Quite clearly someone who chooses genuine separateness is extremely unlikely to be a conformist: The whole project here is not to be indebted to and dependent on others except in very minor ways—ways that embellish life and make it more pleasant but are not central to the separate person's existence. Genuine, deliberate separateness and conformism do not go together. The real conformist is most likely to be found among the covertly in-relation. But in their case, the distinction between autonomy and conformism is obscure and difficult to draw.

Think once again about Mr. Ramsay. He prizes clearheaded rational thought above all. Truth is so important to him that he is willing to disappoint his son, who wants to go to the lighthouse the next day, by assuring him that the weather will not permit it. When Mrs. Ramsay tries to comfort the boy by saying that the weather might change, her husband is enraged at her lack of truthfulness. But that does not stop him from indulging in all the prevailing prejudices against women. He keeps repeating that "women can't write, can't paint." The truth of that very serious accusation does not need to be subjected to as careful scrutiny as her doubts about the weather forecast. Truthfulness also does not prevent him from being utterly self-deceived about his autonomy and his independent role in the family. Mr. Ramsay is, in certain respects, a quite ordinary conformist. But that conformism is part and parcel of a shared project. He shares his misogyny with other men; it is one of the bonds that tie him to the others. The inferiority of women is the belief that unites them as members of a master race.

In the same way, Ramsay's academic demeanor is conformist. He happily gossips about colleagues and judges some "able" and others "brilliant but fundamentally unsound." What drives his work is the desire to be accepted as an outstanding philosopher by the other dons. Philosophy, his intellectual work, is not a solitary project. It is a web of continuing conversations in which the members of a complex group participate. Each takes part in a competitive game that follows precise rules as to who counts as a participant, what one must do to be allowed into the game, what one must do to win points, how one loses points, and how one gets to be one of the judges. It is also an intricate shared inquiry into questions inherited from previous generations. Both the questions and the rules by which questions are formulated and answers attempted are inherited but are also reconsidered and changed by each generation, as is the history of the entire enterprise.

Participation in this enterprise requires an odd mixture of conformism and originality. Just repeating what others say, summarizing the insights of others, or writing minor footnotes does not earn fame and power. But even those whose ideas are novel and provocative must obey certain sets of rules; they must be insiders to the whole project. Originality and autonomy are acceptable only from those who are accepted by others as genuine participants in the common project. Autonomy in intellectual work presupposes conformism in the way one does that work, specifically in the methods, the vocabulary, and the manner of writing. Often political views matter, as does keeping up the academic relationships to others—to continue the gossip, to maintain the scholarly style of jocularity, to show one's face at the occasions the profession regards as particularly solemn and momentous. To remain in the game one must continue to excoriate the common enemies, whether those be "analytic philosophers," "continental philosophers," "Marxists," or "feminists." Only those properly socialized in their graduate training can, afterward, afford to be different and to strike out on their own. Even their departures from accepted views and positions are always risky and must be rendered legitimate by remaining a loyal member of the group.[3]

Autonomy is carefully regulated. Not everyone who departs from the currently accepted beliefs and practices will be respected as autonomous; many will be ostracized. Some unconventional ideas will be taken very seriously and examined with care; others will be rejected out of hand because they are "beyond the pale" or their authors have not maintained their standing in the profession. They are thought not to be autonomous but rather to have succumbed to political ideology or the laziness that overcomes some of us (we are told) as we get older or to sheer eccentricity. There are rules governing what one may do as an autonomous thinker and what will no longer count as autonomy. Some of these rules are no doubt defensible. Others probably are not. But they are rarely discussed let alone defended.

One can draw several conclusions from all of this. One might say that philosophers who defend autonomy are, in fact, much less autonomous and more conformist than they think. A more interesting conclusion is that the distinction between autonomy and comformism is not best drawn as a distinction between what is all one's own and what one borrows from or shares with others because that distinction is too fuzzy to be of much use. One does not engage in an intellectual project, like philosophy, except as a member of a group that has defined and keeps redefining the project and thereby the standards by which accomplishment is measured. To participate in the project one must conform to most of the standards. One of the standards demands that one make a contribution, say something new, and think for oneself. Being an academic in general and a philosopher in particular demands that one be autonomous, but autonomous only within the limits that the project as currently practiced allows. If one is conformist insofar as one takes ideas and values, including standards of behavior and adequate performance, without examining them by oneself and subjecting them to rational scrutiny, then we are all conformists when we participate in a group project such as being an academic philosopher. Only as a conformist can one be autonomous. Autonomy is possible only according to prevailing standards in the joint project of a (large) group of people. The opposition between conformism and autonomy becomes very indefinite. It becomes relativized to a particular project. More important, it becomes very uncertain when we should call some behavior conformist rather than saying that a person who behaves that way is well socialized into certain roles.[4]

AUTONOMY IN-RELATION

The philosophical account of autonomy does not reproduce what we usually mean by autonomy. The prevailing account thinks of one's self as what is exclusively one's own. Surrendering something that is one's own is therefore always a threat to one's autonomy. One is, if autonomous in that sense, hesitant to give up one's own ideas, plans, values, and knowledge to accept someone else's instead. When you insist on separateness, your autonomy is constantly haunted by the fear of losing what is yours, being deprived of or letting go of what belongs to your self. Since actions exclusively one's own are rare, this separate account of autonomy retreats to a concept of "procedural" autonomy, where only one's internal mental states are relevant to the question whether one is autonomous. Actions cease being relevant to autonomy. But being autonomous in thought but not in action is so very minimal an autonomy that we may well wonder whether we should call it "autonomy" at all. Such a concept of autonomy neither captures why we believe that autonomy is morally admirable nor supplies us with good reasons for defending political liberalism. We need to begin by reminding ourselves what we think autonomy is when we are not under the spell of separateness and philosophical debates that take it to be self-evident.

Autonomy, as we usually understand it, consists of a certain strength of character in the face of people who disapprove or disagree, who are different or are outright enemies. In an earlier chapter I mentioned Nietzsche's insistence that the strong, autonomous person has his or her specific enemies. I pointed out that one can, under some conditions, be in-relation with an enemy. Autonomous persons have adversaries and do not shrink from that. They do not constantly attempt to have everyone like them, to avoid hurting others' feelings, or to get along with everyone. Mr. Ramsay, by contrast, is totally bowled over and made needy when his last book was not as great a success as he had hoped. He is very thin-skinned, but he is also quite oblivious to the feelings of others when they do not directly threaten him. Truly autonomous persons, in contrast, because they are not constantly worried about their own and separate selves, are much more likely to be aware of others. If they are not moved by every whisper of disapproval, it is because their autonomy consists of resting in themselves, being confident and feeling that they have their place in the world.

The autonomous think for themselves and have confidence in their own intellectual abilities (Govier, 1993). But that confidence is not so easily shaken that they cannot concede errors or consider openly the possibility that another has a better idea. The truly autonomous person is willing to examine the ideas of others with an open mind and will not feel threatened by disagreements but instead be ready to yield to better ideas cheerfully and with grace. The autonomous person eschews conformism but is also eager to learn and is not defensive about finding another's ideas superior. In valuing one's thinking for oneself, the emphasis is on the "thinking" more than on the "for oneself." Thinking requires open-minded reexamination of one's past beliefs and generous appreciation of the insights of others.

It is true that autonomy includes a certain independence, but does it not also include the ability to ask for help when necessary and the ability to accept help gladly?[5] Is it not precisely a mark of the autonomous person not to fear a loss of self at the slightest hint of dependence? Being able to ask for and accept help and still remain oneself requires autonomy of a much sturdier sort than that which cannot bear to acknowledge dependencies. Separate autonomy has trouble with all of these. It does not see that there is a difference "between depending on someone and being dependent on her" (Hoagland, 1990:146). You depend on another who gives you what is very important to you and you trust that he or she will give you what you want. But you are not thereby dependent. If I am not available when you need me, you do not collapse. If I am away, ill, or distracted you may be troubled, but your life goes on as before. You miss me but you carry on. Thus we depend on friends, lovers, and coworkers. If the relationship to them is broken, we are poorer but not destitute. We can re-create our lives, allow the wounds to heal, and perhaps find other sources of strength and inspiration. Connected with that, the autonomous are able to hold their own in intense and demanding human relationships. They have no need to preserve a sphere of their own by secreting thoughts and feelings in their interior. Genuine autonomy does not need to distance itself from love for fear of being overcome by it (Yanay and Birns, 1990). Autonomy is much more complex than is acknowledged by most philosophers.

Autonomy requires certain character traits: a realistic confidence in one's own abilities, confidence that one can solve some of the problems that open engagements with other persons sometimes create, the ability to be alone (which I will return to below), and willingness to trust others because one knows that one may be disappointed (and disappoint) but that one will not be devastated. All of these and other traits are characteristic of autonomy as usually understood. Autonomy requires strength of character. The procedural account of autonomy has omitted all those traits from its description of the autonomous person; what remains is the ability to weigh choices punctiliously. That does not reproduce the notion of autonomy outside of philosophical analysis. It does not tell us why we believe that autonomy is morally admirable or allow us to argue for political liberalism. All of these are captured by autonomy that is a form of openly chosen being-in-relation.

To understand this more complex autonomy in-relation we need to see clearly that we are distinct—that our bodies are not connected. But that does not necessitate, as we saw in the preceding chapter, that our decisions, thoughts, beliefs, values, actions, and so on be exclusively our own. Bodily distinctness makes it more difficult to make decisions jointly with others because we do not always know what others want, what others are thinking, what they are afraid of. (Since others often do not know that either before they start talking to us, that difficulty should not be exaggerated). A more adequate understanding of autonomy must take bodily distinctness very seriously. But it must not confuse it with the claim that there are no joint acts, no joint decisions, no joint beliefs.

There are several reasons for taking distinctness very seriously. I cannot know what you think or feel unless you tell me. For that reason I am in no position to define for others what is good for them without paying a great deal of attention to their perception of the world and their feelings and experiences of it. For those reasons the motives of others are not easily transparent to me; nor can I fully appreciate experiences if I have not had similar ones.

We are to a considerable extent the creatures of our own history. Even those persons to whom I am most intimately linked have not shared my entire life. Even if they had shared it, their experiences would not have been the same as mine, and the cumulative effects of those experiences would have shaped each of us in different ways. Being thus distinct, each of us has (potentially) a perspective all our own on the world and on events. It makes it easier to see what others may miss or see values and strengths where others see none. It allows one to invent solutions to problems that would not have occurred to others. These others, in turn, have their own perspectives, which allow insights as well as blind them.[6]

Once we choose openly to be in-relation, we can envisage a much richer conception of autonomy than we find in prevailing philosophical accounts. One can still continue to think of being autonomous as "being one's own person," but being one's own person is no longer something one does all by oneself, anxiously excluding help from or dependence on others, jealously guarding one's thinking against external influence, or avoiding at all costs the need to admit that one owes insights to others. Once I choose to be openly in-relation, I am my own person in particular contexts and in particular relationships to others. In these contexts and relationships, reciprocity is a goal, and joint projects are striven for. In projects that I share with others, all are expected to make a contribution. They can do that to the extent that their particular strengths, and weaknesses, are openly acknowledged by all. Each is seen to be distinct. Each is seen to be different. Each gets the attention and respect deserved and each does for the common project what he or she can or wants to do.

Parroting what everyone else says or thinks makes no contribution to a group that is trying to come to a decision or is trying to understand its situation. But being stiff-necked and defending one's own ideas because they are one's own is not being helpful either. My autonomy in-relation depends on having a position in the group—being acknowledged in the group as playing a particular role and as having particular strengths and weaknesses. (It consists, at best, also of being encouraged to play new and different roles and to learn to make new contributions.) That position is not enhanced by stubbornness in being unwilling to learn for fear of losing what is one's own. Sometimes, of course, stubbornness is needed anyway. It depends on who I am, what group I am in, and what is at issue to determine whether holding on to my own view is an exercise of autonomy in-relation or, instead, the old separate autonomy that cannot be flexible for fear of losing its identity.

I gain this autonomy in-relation through my own conduct in the group but just as much through the recognition, attention, and respect of the others in the group for my particular perspective, which is shaped by my history, inherited inclinations and character traits, race, gender, religious background, and many other factors. Thus autonomy in-relation is not all under my control. In some groups I am out of place. What respect I get is always grudging, as is my respect for the others. Here my difference may be recognized, but it does not earn me a place as a valued participant. My difference may make it impossible for me to participate actively and constructively in the efforts of the group. There is no autonomy for me in this group.

Many work groups are like that. One finds oneself working with others whom perhaps one likes, and even grudgingly respects, but whose conception of the work is too different from one's own to be able to work with the others for a joint end. One is and remains an outsider. One gains no autonomy within that group because one's opposition is ineffective. It is, of course, possible to be in a group in which one is always the one to disagree, to bring up new considerations and perspectives. The other members of the group may find that annoying and inconvenient but may, nevertheless, acknowledge in case after case that one's opposition is worthwhile and important. Even if in some respects one is an outsider, when one makes an important contribution that contribution is accepted and, however grudgingly, acknowledged by the group. One is autonomous in that group. Not so the person whose permanent opposition merely leads to isolation, ridicule, or being ignored. If your opposition makes you one of the common enemies who bind the members of that group together, you are excluded but not, in relation to that group, autonomous.

Autonomy, to the extent that it is in-relation, is therefore also relative. One is autonomous in some relations and not in others. One is more autonomous in some relations than in others. In some relations one is more autonomous at some times of one's life than in others. One can put this point in the terminology of "worlds" (Lugones, 1987). Most persons live in more than one world. The black woman as a maid in a household of whites lives in a very different world and is in many ways a very different person from when she is in her own home, church, and community (Gwaltney, 1980). In the first world she is not autonomous because she is not even perceived as a full person. In her own world(s) life and autonomy are very different. This clears up what was puzzling about Mrs. Ramsay. I asked earlier whether she was not also autonomous. In many ways she appears to be the autonomous one in her marriage, not he. She is a strong woman who has her own ideas and life plan, which she follows. She is powerful and leaves the impress of her personality on all persons around her. She has what it takes to be autonomous: She thinks for herself, she is reflective and critical, she is decisive, and she does not hesitate to follow her beliefs in running her house and in arranging dinners and making sure that the conversations do not stagnate. What is more, she is better able than her husband to share, to learn from others, to listen closely, and to open herself to others. She attends to her children in all those ways without having that impair her autonomy. She is, we must say, autonomous in some of her worlds but not in others.

For what is missing precisely is the acknowledgment by others, specifically by Mr. Ramsay and the other men who come to visit, that she is an autonomous person. Yes, he loves her, but he does not make a serious effort to see her for who she is, to acknowledge her strengths—to do so would require that he acknowledge his weakness, and the separately autonomous man cannot do that. To that extent she cannot be autonomous. Whatever autonomy she does have is in relations to children and to other women, where she is not misread and dominated in order to shore up male, separate autonomy. As a woman she is excluded from the world of men—the world of education, intellectual work, and activity in the public sphere, where men negotiate treaties, control finance, and rule India. She is not excluded for who she is, in all her particular concreteness, but because she is *a woman.* As a woman, her relations to men are always shaped by male privilege. No joint projects are possible there and thus no autonomy in-relation.

Once we understand autonomy in this perspective, we distinguish between dependencies that are fruitful, which promote growth and enrichment and empowerment, and dependencies that are restrictive, which impoverish and stunt persons. If we are openly in-relation, we ask not what is true of each separately autonomous person but what sorts of relationships autonomous persons have as they engage in joint projects. Borrowing ideas from others is fine if it promotes the development of one's own view of the world. *Thinking for myself is not thinking by myself.* Thinking for myself is participating in a collective thinking process, making one's contributions, accepting criticisms, and going along or not as one sees fit. But thinking for oneself also includes being listened to, being taken seriously, and being allowed to make a contribution. Autonomous persons count for something in a group. They make themselves felt, and they are respected. Their opinion is heard, even if not finally accepted. In thinking for oneself one is eager for conversation. One lays out differences for joint examination. A person who thinks by himself or herself but is not taken seriously by anyone may be thinking independently but does so ineffectively. Even seers and prophets need their audiences and disciples. The voice crying in the wilderness will get hoarse to no avail.

Autonomy in this richer and more complex sense involves, among other things, letting others be autonomous. In the perspective of separateness, "letting the other be" means leaving the other alone. Leaving others alone means letting them make their own choices and decisions, letting them formulate their own life plans by themselves, and letting them live according to them. In that perspective letting the others be autonomous means letting them run their lives by themselves and letting them bear full, and often exclusive, responsibility for how their lives turn out. (And it often means, in the end, blaming them for their misfortunes.) But that is not the same as letting them have their autonomy. On the contrary, letting others be autonomous is to have the sort of relationship to them that I have been describing. I let others be autonomous, to begin with, by taking their distinctness very seriously in the ways already indicated. I begin by paying close attention to who the other person is, what and how they think and feel. Letting others be, I do not leave them alone but let them be who they are. But that calls for paying close attention to the other. Paying close attention is the opposite of leaving someone alone. Paying attention is hearing what a person says, even what that person does not say in so many words. Paying attention is, of course, also asking others about themselves. Paying close attention is one aspect of being-in-relation.

But more than that, letting others be autonomous is encouraging them to be who they are by being appreciative of their particular perspectives on the world, being grateful for their being particularly good at some things, and providing an outlet for those particular talents. If people choose to be openly in-relation, their groups will be aware of differences and make an effort to encourage differences— differences in outlook, differences in what one is good at, differences in likes and dislikes—because this diversity enriches the group if only no one feels impelled to claim that his or her particular ways are normative for all the others. The distinct-ness of persons is an important ingredient in their autonomy precisely because in a well-functioning group the distinct differences are going to be valued and their owner encouraged to be different. One's difference is a part of one's contribution to the group.[7]

Paying attention is focusing not merely on who you are but also on who you are in relation to me. Parents must allow children certain of their wishes and choices, even if they are not the best wishes and choices, just because it is important for children to get their way some of the time. They must do so in part because of who the parents are in relation to the children—because of their looming pres-ence in the child's life, especially in the life of small children. A more distant per-son can be much more demanding without impairing the child's growth toward self-identity because their demands are not as serious a threat to the child's sense of self. If you don't do what your parent wants there might be serious conflict, an-ger, punishment. Those threaten selfhood much more than the anger of a more distant person. Doing what the parent wants, however, brings to light the most basic dependencies. This is not so in complying with the wishes of more distant persons.

Persons—not only children—are always in transition. They are learning, or failing to learn, the next lesson. They acquire new skills, try and fail, or pull back from new skills for fear of how they will change if they do learn them. Paying at-tention is being in a relationship with the other, and we have relationships to per-sons whose changes alter the relationships we have to them. In paying attention to the other, one notices changes and perhaps participates in them. One notices changes that would be good but have encountered obstacles. Paying attention means noticing the changes that move toward greater autonomy and those that seem to move away from it. Paying attention enables one in the relationship to help foster the autonomy of each in the relationship (Miller, 1976; Hoagland, 1990: 121). Autonomy in-relation involves each helping the other to be more autono-mous by helping transform the relationship in suitable ways.

For true autonomy, attention and helping must be in some sense reciprocal. That is true even in relations to small children. The parent does not just make the child be more autonomous: The two of them must work out ways in which there will be greater autonomy for both of them in the relationship. (Or sometimes people work out ways of reducing autonomy. Not everyone shares the view that autonomy is important.) This has often been read to mean that there must be equality between the partners. But obviously that cannot be because in many of our important relations we are not equal. We are not equal as children in-relation to parents, we are not equal as students in-relation to teachers. If we were, we would not be able to learn from them. But that only suggests that one is not the equal of one's friends and "peers" either. They are different: Some things they do better than I, some things they do differently from me. Difference does not always amount to inequality, but it does too often for us to demand simply that we be equal to those to whom we have relationships.

It is tempting to say that autonomy in-relation requires that the participants in a group, of any kind, be equal in power. But that also is too strong a requirement. I will return to that issue in the final chapter when I dicuss different conceptions of power.

DOUBTS

But, someone will say, the description given of autonomy as a way of being-in-re-lation seems to obscure forms of autonomy in which one is separate, where being separate, remaining separate, and insisting on one's separateness are the essence of autonomy. Consider the ability to be alone. That is surely a form of autonomy. It also appears to be a form of separateness. bell hooks talks about the importance of being alone.

> One of the things that is very different in my life from the life of my siblings is this ability to be alone, to be with my inner self. When we talk about becoming an intel-lectual, in the real life-enhancing sense of that word, we're really talking about what it is to sit with one's ideas, where one's mind becomes a workplace, where one really takes enormous amounts of time to contemplate and critically reflect on things. That experience of aloneness undergirds my intellectual practice and it is rooted in spiri-tual discipline where I have sought aloneness with God and listened to the inner voice of God as it speaks in my life.
> ... when you are truly able to be alone in that sense of Christ going into the garden of Gethsemane or going into the desert, of Buddha sitting under the Boti tree, it actu-ally enables you to re-enter community more fully. (hooks and West, 1991:81–82)

Being alone, being by oneself, thinking one's own thoughts, and putting one's own words on paper are important elements in being a writer and an intellectual. It is also, surely, a form of autonomy to be able to be alone, to work in the privacy of one's own inner space, to follow one's own thoughts without guidance by others. But that autonomy seems very separate. Must we then not recognize that autonomy is, after all, also being separate? bell hooks clearly treasures being-in-relation when she talks about "reentering community." But it seems that one can only be in-relation fruitfully and productively if one has something to contribute; that is, if one has gathered together one's thoughts in solitude and if one is separate. Being-in-relation ("reentering community") seems possible only if we are able to be alone.

The ability to be alone is, without any doubt, very important. But does that not show either that we must be separate or that being separate is a necessary condition for being-in-relation? Yes, to be sure, in being autonomous-in-relation one's difference from others must be acknowledged in the group. One must have something to contribute that is one's own and is acknowledged and accepted as such by the group. But none of that means that what I contribute, that the role I play in the group, is "all my own" or is all of my own making. On the contrary, one plays a role in a group that is shaped by the demands and the dynamics of this group. The self I have in this group is a function not only of my abilities and interests but also of the nature of the group. The thoughts and ideas I contribute do not need to be exclusively mine. What I took into my solitude to work out before I brought it back to the group may well draw on previous conversations and discussions in the group. It is, in fact, much more likely to be useful in the group if it has a certain familiar ring to it because it is not *all* my own but is my reflection on or elaboration of what the group has been thinking about for a while. To be in-relation one needs to be able to be alone. But it does not require that one be separate. Being-in-relation openly does not mean that one spend all one's time with others or that whatever one does, one does collectively. We are distinct. Thinking goes on in groups, but it also goes on in the privacy of one's own mind. For some, what matters most is thinking by themselves; for others the thinking in groups is essential.[8]

I am not merely saying that all intellectual work is done within a tradition and within a social network of other persons. That scholars publish books and papers, read each other's work, and learn from one another is only weak evidence for their being-in-relation. But in the vast majority of cases intellectual work is not only communicated to impersonal others and commented on by others whom one has perhaps never met, but it is also shared more intimately in ongoing conversations. One's friends are often colleagues, and one's colleagues are sometimes friends. These conversations move in an atmosphere of shared assumptions and values that are indispensable to the joint work. Earlier in this chapter I described some of the ways in which doing intellectual work is not only a collective project but also one where the participants are at least covertly in-relation because the rules governing the projects are shared and developed by the participants. There is a shared understanding of what they are doing. One's good standing in the profession depends greatly on one's writings; also important are one's participation in a number of joint activities such as conventions, reading and writing recommendations, and lobbying private and public authorities for money and power.

But our critic is not yet satisfied: You overlook, she says, that there are persons like Alice Koller or Barbara McClintock who seem to have chosen a very extensive separateness. For them the ability to be alone is not an adjunct of their relationships but is the essence of their lives. Their work is all their own. Their periods of withdrawal are not intervals between periods of intense involvement with other persons—the work that they do alone is only loosely connected with the work of others. But these are women one would certainly want to call "autonomous" and so it does seem, after all, that there are some instances where autonomy is very intimately connected with being separate.

One must grant that objection. There are instances of autonomy for which separateness is of the essence. But notice that this is separateness openly and deliberately chosen. It is not a pretended separateness that is propped up by the lack of separateness of others. It is not a separateness that is partly pretense and is, for that reason, so very precarious that it must constantly be reaffirmed by insisting on what is one's own, by withholding oneself from others, by being sparing with one's feelings and one's affection, and by reaffirming one's independence by wielding power over others and thus showing that they are dependent. That is the only separateness that most of us are capable of. There are some persons of exceptional fortitude who are able to lead their lives in separate autonomy, which they have chosen. They are willing to pay the price of considerable isolation. Most people are not willing or able to do that. Their autonomy is either openly or covertly in-relation.

To decide to what extent I am autonomous I need to know not only whether my life is my own but also *why* it is. Do I live my life essentially alone because relations to other persons are difficult and unsatisfying to me? Or do I live mostly by myself because the relationships I have are rich and nuanced and full of generous sharing, giving, and getting but I am happiest by myself? Do I refrain from sharing projects because I am afraid to lose my own perspective or that my own voice will be stilled if I am too free in allowing others access to my work? Or do I do my work mostly by myself because I have not found anyone who understands it or is interested in it? What one does alone, and how much, are not indications of one's autonomy. What matters is whether one is alone because one's hold on oneself is so tenuous that one must protect oneself by seeking solitude. Such a person is separate but barely autonomous. But if solitude merely strengthens a self richly engaged in activities and conversations and relationships with others, solitude perfects autonomy but is not its center.

But the critic is still not quite persuaded: Consider the many people whose lives are constrained by poverty and racism. They work for and under people who look down on them, who do not know them, and who make no effort to know them. "Now they [namely, whites] are great ones for begging you to tell them what you really think. But only a fool would really do that. Because whites don't really give a damn about what something really is" (Gwaltney, 1980:102). Many of the blacks John Gwaltney interviewed expressed similar views: Whites do not know them because they do not care to. Blacks work in situations where none of the relational interchange described above takes place. One party is willfully blind to the other. But, so the critic continues, does that prevent those blacks from being autonomous? Gwaltney's book elaborately documents their autonomy: their pride, their insistence on being honest, clean, and respectful of others and themselves, and their tendency to be cautious and to confide only in persons they know very well indeed. I agree, the critic might continue, that autonomy is relative to particular persons. Blacks have always tried to maintain their autonomy vis-à-vis whites. That involved two very different strategies: On the one hand, being a respected member of one's own black community was essential to autonomy. One tried to maintain a life and a self away from whites and white oppression. This was, no doubt, autonomy in-relation. On the other hand, there was a struggle for autonomy of some sort in relation to whites. That autonomy was not in-relation but required being uncommunicative, withdrawn, and, if necessary, deceptive and manipulative (hooks, 1993:20). Are those not also strategies of autonomy, and are they not forms of separateness? (The experience of many white women has been very similar in their relationships to men.)

Yes, there is a form of autonomy that consists of maintaining one's pride and integrity in relation to persons who deny one's integrity and try to suppress one's pride. Sometimes the defense of autonomy takes the form of constant struggle, of open refusal and resistance. Irina Ratushinskaya's memoirs about her years as a political prisoner in Soviet camps document that autonomy in struggle. Ratushinskaya and several other women political prisoners refused to wear the identification tags required by regulations. A major, protracted struggle ensued in which the autonomy of the prisoners, not the identification tags, was the issue. The prisoners suffered much harassment and serious deprivation in solitary confinement in order to maintain their stance (Ratushinskaya, 1989). But this is merely one more example of ambivalent relations that are instances of being-in-relation. The prison guards, from fear of the consequences and perhaps from grudging respect for their recalcitrant prisoners, continued the struggle rather than using their full power against them. Everyone participating was shaped by the continuing conflict.

In other cases, autonomy is maintained by devious means. Such autonomy is, however, very different from the anemic autonomy of philosophers. It does not consist just of *reflecting* about the structure of one's desires or about one's moral principles or life plan. Here one presents oneself to others as a certain sort of person. The problem is precisely that the camp guard, and the white employer, do not want to see one as one presents oneself. Least of all do they want to see one as an autonomous person. They deny one's autonomy, through coercion, or they deny it by sheer inattention. They assert their own complete separateness in order to deny the other's autonomy. The prisoner or servant, on the other side, continues to struggle for some, however minimal, relationship in which each acknowledges the presence of the other. The prisoner pushes the guard to ask for the prisoner's cooperation. In that way the guard admits a mutual need and a relationship. The servant may deliberately fail in some task to force the employer to concede that he needs his servant. Autonomy here is autonomy on the defensive, and that too is a relation that is constitutive of one's person and one's life. This is not a separate autonomy in the sense of an autonomy that is all my own. On the contrary, it is autonomy that one is constantly defending or even flaunting in the face of those who are unwilling to see it.

I must end by reminding the reader that whether we are in-relation or not is a matter of choice, but it is not a private choice: It is one that is offered to us to varying extents and in very specific contexts by our society. It could therefore also be a collective choice to broaden the range of situations in which being-in-relation is one of the options.

SEPARATENESS, LANGUAGE, AND PHILOSOPHY

We have by now encountered a series of cases in which the ordinary understanding of ourselves and our ways of being with others unquestioningly accepts separateness. Autonomy is thought of as a characteristic of separate persons, and so is empathy. The alternative, to choose to be openly in-relation, is completely overlaid by separateness. These examples, and others that follow in later chapters, show that we cannot trust ordinary meanings of words to represent accurately what we want to say when we talk about being-in-relation. Ordinary language is itself infected with the assumption of separateness. Language is likely to insinuate traditional perspectives into our efforts to put our understanding of being-in-relation into words. At the very moment that we are trying to clarify our understanding of being-in-relation by putting it into words, language will deform that understanding unless we reflect very carefully about the meanings of the words we are using. The words we utter will not express what we set out to say.

The previous discussion of empathy may help to make this clearer. When feminist theorists tell us that being-in-relation is empathy, they are trying to say that it is not being remote from the other, that being-in-relation involves really listening to others, really seeing them, rather than imposing stereotypical images on them. They are trying to say that being-in-relation is being alive to the emotions of others but also to one's own, that it involves an open exchange and sharing of feelings and thoughts. But most of all they are trying to say that genuine being-in-relation is not oppressive: It respects the other person as a person in his or her own right.

Most of that is lost if we interpret empathy with the metaphor of separateness in the background. Empathy, from the point of view of separate persons, consists of guessing the other's feelings. The person I am in empathy with becomes an object whose internal state I reconstruct from the available evidence. As we saw, even in its own separate terms that is hardly adequate: There is no mention of talking to the other, let alone being prepared to help, listen, or comfort. Here all attention is focused on the other. You have the problem, the pain, the passion, or the anger. I am detachedly, impartially trying to reconstruct what that feels like. Empathy does not, on that view, involve you also sharing my feelings or making myself vulnerable to you. My claim of being empathic is never challenged. If you reject my attempts you are at fault. I need not explain my motivations or defend them. Thus in the story of John and his father, the common understanding is that his father is at fault for not accepting John's approach to him. The father is not allowed his feelings and resentments. Seen from the perspective of separateness, the power belongs to the person who has empathy. Such a view of empathy in the hands of a therapist or a teacher is bound to be oppressive. It is the very opposite of being-in-relation.

If we identify being-in-relation as empathy without explaining that there is a separate sense of empathy and a being-in-relation sense, then we fail to make ourselves clear because readers and listeners will understand "empathy" in the ordinary, separate sense and will not understand all we had wanted to convey about being-in-relation as genuine listening—as relations that are not oppressive and involve mutual empowerment. For empathy in the ordinary, separate sense does little or nothing of that.

This is only one instance of a more general phenomenon. We had the same problem trying to explain being-in-relation as caring. If we take that word "caring" in its ordinary sense it refers to what women do for men who are largely absent and separate. "Being-in-relation" is liable to be misunderstood if identified with a relation in which separateness plays a major role. Hence we moved on to saying that being-in-relation is "reciprocal" or "mutual" but soon saw that those terms too are usually understood in a separate sense in which reciprocity connects two persons who are quite separate but are involved in some exchange where equals are traded for equals. Had we stopped there the real meaning of being-in-relation would have remained hidden. It was necessary to distinguish between a separate and a being-in-relation sense of "reciprocity" before we could make some headway.

We see here one of the ways in which dominant outlooks maintain themselves and co-opt thoughts that are intended as a challenge to prevailing ideas even before anyone begins to manipulate language or images deliberately. A good deal of work in feminist ethics and epistemology about caring, about different ways of being a person, and correspondingly about different ways of thinking about ourselves and doing philosophy is explicitly meant to challenge and eventually replace mainstream modes of thinking and philosophizing. But once these insights are expressed in our usual language they are obscured by the inappropriate verbal associations language supplies.

Thus language can be used to obscure genuinely novel departures. Revolution turns out to be reform after all, and the wisdom of the fathers stands. At the same time, we can also see that although language can easily be used to obscure challenges by ignoring that familiar terms may be used in new ways, and by evading the considerable effort of understanding required by these changed meanings of familiar terms, language is rich and flexible and allows us to shift meanings. It allows us to say what has not been said before and to think in ways that are new.

The widespread paranoia that language is "constitutive," that is, that it *makes* us think in ways we might not want to think, is misplaced. Language makes co-optation possible, but it also allows us to unmask it. Language allows us to talk, but it does not put words in our mouths.

This has direct bearing on the practice of philosophy. According to a familiar self-description, philosophers articulate common and shared understandings of the world. Human beings find their way around the world and function in it because they know many things that they are not always able to put into words. We know, for instance, that human beings are like but also different from animals and that both differ from plants and rocks. Early along children acquire an understanding of causality and learn that some actions are good and others bad. But ask anyone to formulate clearly the differences between humans and animals, to define causal relations, or to formulate criteria for good actions, and they will fail. Plato's Socratic dialogues traded on that fact that we know many things that we cannot talk about easily, if at all, and philosophers still think of themselves as making explicit what most of us know only implicitly. The effort at articulation is sufficiently difficult that there are extended controversies about the relative merits of very different ways of giving voice to this common sense of humanity that is embodied in philosophical writings. Much that divides philosophers are different expressions of commonsense understandings of the world.

Our commonsense understandings of the world are reflected in our language. The lines we draw, for instance, between animals and humans are evidenced by the ways in which we use the relevant words. Hence in their attempt to articulate the common sense of humankind, philosophers pay a good deal of careful attention to words. But language is not the unambiguous repository of the common sense of humankind: More likely it is a battleground where conflicts are kept alive and skirmishes are fought. Often the combatants are not fully aware of the battles they are engaged in. Separateness is deeply entrenched in language, but it is not a universal common sense of humankind. It is a stance perpetuated by some to maintain their superiority over others. In clarifying the meanings of important words, such as "autonomy" or "empathy," philosophers have not told us what autonomy or empathy are like. They have, more often, told us the myth that men have perpetuated of their own fearless independence, which entitled them to be the "masters of creation."

This has interesting implications for our understanding of the prevailing practice of philosophy. Many philosophers think of their work as a purely intellectual enterprise, removed from political or personal parti pris. As scholars, they think of themselves as neutral. But now it appears that their "common sense" is not beyond criticism but itself requires critical scrutiny because it is not entirely neutral and often distorts our understanding of the world. Dominant philosophy is interested; it defends a way of life (Alcoff, 1993). It does not reveal reality as it is in itself but often reflects the practices of the people in power. It conceals or mislabels many important experiences and conceals the unfair advantages that mislabeling allows dominant groups.

What philosophers call common sense is often partisan but conceals its partisanship behind unsupported claims of fact or logical necessity. We cannot end discussions by appealing to "common sense" or to our "intuitions." On the contrary, common sense is where philosophy should begin, by being critical of conceptions—such as separateness—that appear well-nigh self-evident to many but seem very strange to others. Clearly, philosophy at its best is critical of common sense. That does not deny, of course, that in its criticism of some commonsense views it appeals to others. Language, I said earlier, shapes what we say but does not put words in our mouths. Similarly, common sense affects our thinking but is not imune to criticism. Common sense can and must criticize itself. One is not above partisanship because one appeals to common sense. The contrary is true.

Philosophers in a being-in-relation perspective understand that and therefore advocate openly. They acknowledge that their being-in-relation stance is chosen and thus the views implicit in that stance are also chosen. They put those views forward to get others to make similar choices. But they advocate these views in a style different from that dominant among philosophers. They do not try to win arguments. They do not try to win competitions against different views in the "marketplace of ideas." They eschew overpowering the other by the sheer force of argument—the ambiguity of that metaphor is intended—but try to elicit a free decision on the part of others to freely acknowledge that they, too, are in-relation. Philosophy in the being-in-relation perspective may provide an opening for a philosophy less complicit in oppression than philsophy has been heretofore.

Love and Anger

BEING-IN-RELATION IS OFTEN thought to be closely associated with love or caring, but we just saw, once again, that that is not accurate: Some cases of love and friendship are in-relation, but so are some cases of ambivalence or protracted and irresolvable conflict. Nor is all loving in-relation. There is separate loving that is, more likely than not, covertly in-relation and there is love that is openly in-relation. Covertly in-relation love is always in danger of becoming mere fantasy love or of being, paradoxically, impersonal. It is not to be recommended. I shall move toward that conclusion by examining prevailing conceptions of love, most of them assuming that persons are separate. These conceptions of love cannot explain to us what makes love personal or what makes this person a lover of that other person and no other. The difficulties in the conceptions of separate loving reflect the realities of separate lovers: They are often seriously misinformed about the other and the others' view of them—the relation is, in important ways, not personal at all.

However, being-in-relation prevails not only in warm and positive relationships. In this chapter I want to continue to explore the ways in which even anger may be a form of being-in-relation.

CURRENT VIEWS OF LOVE

Love takes many different forms. It sweeps us away with the tempestuous force of passion or lightens our days with gentle affection. It disrupts carefully crafted and regulated lives or provides stability through the steady presence of friends. Some loves overpower; others are carefully nurtured by us. Some are short-lived; others last as long as we do. Love is desire, or love effaces itself. Love showers the beloved with gifts, or it is insatiable in its demands. Love is knowledge and illumination, or it is the most powerful of deceptions.

Love differs from context to context. In different contexts we have different expectations of those who love and those who are loved. In each, the lovers have different obligations toward each other. We think of the relations between romantic lovers—Abelard and Héloise or Tristram and Iseult—in one way, and in a way different from the love between husband and wife. The love between parents and children is different again, and more specifically, the relations between children and fathers differ from those between mothers and children. Different again is love between friends, between persons working on the same job or playing on the same team, between teacher and student, doctor and patient, therapist and client, and so on. In each of these settings we have different expectations and we make different demands. What is permitted in some situations is prohibited in others and is in others again almost obligatory. Sexual relations are an integral part of marriage, permissible between friends under some conditions, and wrong in many others. Nurturing is expected from parental love but is out of place between great romantic lovers. The varieties of love are overwhelming, for in each of these contexts we recognize further subdivisions: There is more than one legitimate way of being a teacher, a father, or a friend. Collegial relations take many different forms, as do the relations on a sports team.

However different from each other, all these forms of love are personal: They connect very specific persons to one another. No one can replace a lover or be-loved without changing the relationship. That is as true of the love between friends, teammates, or those sharing work as it is in romantic or family love. If real affection connects the members of a team or a work group, anyone who leaves will be missed. The new person may, in time, also become a genuine friend of the other members of the group. But in taking over someone's job one does not inherit that person's loves. That love goes with the person who has left.

What makes love personal? What connects me to you and to no one else in quite the same way? There are many different answers to this question. Not sur-prisingly, a large number of answers presuppose that persons are separate. Love, on that assumption, must be understood as the emotions, thoughts, desires, and actions of each person separately, the lover and the beloved. But here, as in the earlier chapters, it is not too difficult to see that separateness of persons is not an acceptable assumption. If separateness is assumed, love becomes unintelligible. I will argue this for some representative accounts of love.[1]

What makes love personal, it is often thought, are the real characteristics of the other and how they affect me. We love each other for reasons, for particular quali-ties that endear us to the other. "In the complete intimacy of love, a partner knows us as we are, fully" (Nozick, 1991:421). Of course, love is often blind and lovers are often deceived about each other, but in that case their love is in some way deficient. Love that involves serious error, deception, or self-deception is not love at its best, precisely because it does not establish a genuine but only a fanta-sied connection between two persons. Such an imaginary connection may be very strong and it may last for a long time, but it is not the model of love we hold up for ourselves (Soble, 1990; Taylor, 1986; Newton-Smith, 1973).

This view is quite common but is, for all that, not persuasive. If I love you for your good qualities, will I love everyone that has the same qualities? And will all the persons who are like me, in that they love the qualities for which I love you, also be your lovers? Well, you say, every person is unique—like snowflakes, no two are alike. But persons certainly are similar. What is more, I don't love another for all his or her qualities but only for some. There is certainly more than one person that has a particular configuration of qualities that I love in another. It is not uncommon, after all, for one and the same person to marry, live with, and love a number of persons in succession who are all very much alike. But that does not mean that those similar lovers are interchangeable. Nor does it mean that the relationship to each is not personal or quite unlike any other. But it does mean that what makes these relationships personal and unique are not the loved characteristics of the other. If my love for the other depended only on a particular configuration of particular qualities, love would cease being personal. We cannot elucidate what is unique about your and my relation by appealing to your or my qualities that are not unique.

There are additional difficulties: What if the person I love is very different from what I think he is, or what if he does not in fact deserve respect? Well, Taylor replies, in that case my love is not justified but it is still love, albeit misguided. But if I can love even if I am totally mistaken about the object of my love, then must we not agree with Stendhal and Proust that loving has nothing to do with who the other person really is, that it only has to do with me? Stendhal and Proust insist that love is always blind. What the lover sees in the beloved no one else sees—for good reason because we do not love the other person as she or he really is, only our image of the beloved. It is quite unimportant who that other person really is. It matters not who my beloved is, for I love him or her only for characteristics imputed by me (Soble, 1990). Love is not a connection with another person but homage to our own imaginings.

How can one take this view seriously? The paeans to love that fill our literature would be plain silly if love for fantasy beings were no less love than love for a real person. More important, were this view correct, we could say to the persons we love that we do not care to know who they really are. They are loved not for who they are but for qualities we think they have. Lovers might even resent discovering who their beloved is, for the actual human being may not be as perfect and ravishing as their fantasy love. So far from being a virtue, truthfulness would be a vice among lovers because it might tear the web of fantasies that each has spun over the other. With the view of Stendhal or Proust, we have not explained what makes love personal but have explained personal love away. Love ends up not being a connection between persons at all.

This is obviously one extreme consequence of considering persons separate: What matters are only one person's emotions or thoughts or actions. Love becomes entirely internal to this separate person.[2] But with that, love as a personal connection between two or more persons disappears also. To that Newton-Smith and others reply that we often do know the person we love. But that fact is beside the point. When love is described as my attachment to another's fine qualities, no matter whether that person possesses that quality or not, then it is a happy accident when I love another for the qualities that person actually possesses—it is not necessary for loving. Love is just as much love when it idolizes an unknown as when it cherishes a real person who is well known and understood. We may prefer love of a person we know, but if we turn out to have been completely mistaken, we may say that it was not a desirable kind of love that tied us to that other person but we need not deny that we loved. We are back with a view we already saw to have been unacceptable.

To meet these difficulties, some authors insist that it is not the lovers' knowledge of the other but their actions that make the love of separate persons personal. They describe those actions in different ways. Some writers remind us that lovers see each other very differently from how the rest of the world sees them. I want to spend the rest of my life with you, but few if any others see you as such an important or desirable person. Others do not see what I see in you. I am connected to you through your inestimable qualities that only I see to their full extent. How do you acquire these exquisite qualities for me? Irving Singer tells us that by loving them we "bestow" value on the persons we love. It is not that we love persons for their excellent qualities that are there for anyone to see, but that in loving them we make these persons supremely endowed. "Love bestows value no matter *what* the object is worth" (Singer, 1984:10). Our love is not pure fantasy; the beloved is worth loving because we have bestowed value on her or him. Piper (1972) offers a similar view.

In these accounts what makes our relation so personal is some act of mine, my "bestowal" of value. But something is missing here, namely, the actions, emotions, and thoughts of the person loved. Suppose I believe with Singer that loving is bestowing value on another. But the person I love responds: "No one can bestow value unless valuable themselves. Your bestowal of value depends on my bestowing value on you. But I don't like you; I have no respect for you. You can't bestow anything on me!" What happens to my love? Do I still love or has it become impossible? Singer has no answer for that question.[3]

An even more serious difficulty parallels that raised with respect to earlier explications of love: Are there any limits to this "bestowal"? What shall we say if I bestow love on a person who bears no resemblance to the way I see him or her? Lovers find their beloved beautiful, brave, or wise. But what if the beloved is none of these? To bestow value on lovers does not make them more beautiful, courageous, or wise than they are. My bestowal cannot make the person other than she is. There are two roads to take here: If we say that who a person is matters not for the value I bestow on her or him, then one's love, once again, is independent of who that other person is. The alternative would be to say that I can bestow value only on a person who has the requisite qualities (Tov-Ruach, 1980:469). But then my love is love of specific qualities, and we have already seen the problems that view has: It makes it impossible to explain the personal connection between lovers.

At this point we may try Brown's suggestion that love involves a commitment to the other and to the relationship to the other (Brown, 1987:106). Such a commitment implies not only that I love the person you are today but also that I will love you even if one or both of us change. But are there limits to this change, or am I committed to you regardless of who you turn out to be? If the commitment is utterly unconditional, the characteristics of the other person are not relevant to love. If the other's characteristics do set limits to one's commitment, then the problem of loving another for his or her qualities returns.

Some writers attempt to evade this difficulty by adding an additional condition to their definition of love: Whatever the beliefs, emotions, desires, or commitments of one, they must also be those of the other. Love is personal insofar as both partners have the requisite qualities, thoughts, desires, dispositions to act, and commitments. Love is personal insofar as it is reciprocal. Reciprocity, in its turn, is defined as two persons having more or less the same feelings and attitudes toward each other *at about the same time.* A loves and desires B; B loves and desires A. But that does not really advance our understanding of love and what makes it personal. Reciprocity need not be characteristic of love at all: Often lovers play very different roles in the relationships—think of parents and small children—and what each feels, thinks, or does is quite different from what the other feels, thinks, or does. Loving means different things for each.[4]

More important, we have been unable, so far, to make clear why my love for you is personal, why you are irreplaceable to me. That difficulty is not alleviated by adding that I must be irreplaceable to you at the same time that you are irreplaceable to me. Our problem was to understand what made each of us irreplaceable to the other. Insisting that two irreplaceabilities be simultaneous does not clear up what makes each one of us separately irreplaceable. As long as the connection between lovers is that of two separate persons, reciprocity means no more than what A feels for B and B feels for A at the same time. If we cannot understand A's love for B, reciprocity will not help us.

A number of thinkers have been aware of that problem and have therefore insisted from the beginning that love is a connection *between* persons. The question should not be, What is true of single persons who love? Rather, it should be, What connects lovers to one another? Hegel tells us that love means "the consciousness of my unity with another," (Hegel, 1949:261) and his view is echoed by Fromm (1970) and Buber (1958). Love is described as a "union"; men and women are said to "united" or "joined" in marriage. They are not separate persons with a reciprocal relation; they are united or joined to one another.

This view is not easily articulated. Its defenders take refuge in obscurity and self-contradiction when they discuss it. That should alert us that something is amiss, because strong love that binds persons to each other and makes them "one" in a variety of ways is the most ordinary thing, and we should be able to use ordinary words, in ordinary ways, to speak of it. We should not need to strain the resources of language to talk about our connections to parents, to friends, to relatives we have known all our lives, and to teachers who have wished us well and nourished us. Aristotle, as we shall see below, speaks of friends as "living jointly" and describes that in quite ordinary terms. But Fromm and Buber lapse into inarticulateness when they want to describe the ways in which love joins us to others. The reasons for this inarticulateness will prove instructive.

Love, Fromm tells us, involves care, respect, and knowledge. Knowledge between lovers is, however, not the ordinary sort of knowledge that is assembled bit by bit, tested, refined, reconsidered, and formulated anew:

> Love is active penetration of the other person, in which my desire to know is stilled by union. In the act of fusion, I know you, I know myself, I know everybody—and I "know" nothing. I know in the only way knowledge of that which is alive is possible for man—by experience of union—not by any knowledge our thought can give. (Fromm, 1970:31)

In love we know the other not in the way in which we know all other persons, and know the rest of the world, but through direct awareness that does not involve thought. The knowledge one has of those one loves is of a different kind from the knowledge we have of all other things in the world. It is not discursive; it is not put into words. It seems neither testable nor corrigible. Ordinary knowledge does not come to us in a blinding flash but is gathered slowly and carefully. We get to know other persons by paying close attention to, by thinking about, by talking to them. It requires an extended process and some effort to get to know another person. But the knowledge that comes with union does not seem to require any of that. This claim is clearly pernicious because it is a convenient doctrine for those unwilling to listen carefully and thoughtfully to their friends. All I need is the experience of union and I know you.

In addition, this view abandons Fromm's central insight that loving is learned and needs to be perfected in practice. Fromm begins his book with a criticism of romantic love, of love that one just "falls" into and cannot do anything about. Instead, he tells us that loving is an art that one learns and perfects. But now he adopts that very same view he set out to demolish: Lovers do not need to think about each other because their knowledge is direct and unmediated by thought. Knowing those we love, as he explains it, is not an art. Direct communication is not learned. It comes with "union."

Why does Fromm end up in this contradiction? He starts from the assumption that human beings are separate: "The deepest need of man is the need to overcome his separateness, to leave the prison of his aloneness" (Fromm, 1970:9). Human beings are separate, but love overcomes that separateness. But if human beings are separate, then they are separate also as knowers. I have my knowledge; you have yours. We are as separate from one another as knowers as we are in all other respects. But knowing the other is, of course, an important element in love, and if love overcomes separateness, then it must also overcome separate knowing. If one assumes, as Fromm clearly does, that all ordinary knowing is separate, then to overcome separateness one must leave ordinary knowing behind. Hence the claim that lovers do not know each other through thought, that is, separate know-ing.[5]

At the same time, these different views of love rest on important observations about our experiences of love. Of course, the qualities of the other matter in love. One does love other persons because they have specific characteristics. Of course, being loved gives the other a certain value they do not have in other relationships. Love does bestow value. Of course, one difference between love and, say, strong sexual attraction is precisely that the former involves a commitment for a long time. At the same time, if we think of persons as separate, all of these observations about love become opaque and lead into the sorts of conundrums I have been sketching out. If love consists of feelings, beliefs, and emotions that two separate persons have about each other, then we are faced with a dilemma: Either the char-acteristics of my beloved are of no consequence at all and love is not personal be-cause I love a creature of my imagination or the qualities of the other do matter but then the relation is not personal because I love everyone possessing the same set of qualities. In neither case is love a personal relation.

Nor are these only intellectual puzzles. Separate love does exist and exists, in fact, quite commonly. The marriage of Ned and Anna, discussed later, is an exam-ple of that. Such love is covertly in-relation. There is a joint project, at some time, but then everyone crawls back into his or her separate shell. The initial openness and rush of sharing secrets is replaced by each hiding thoughts, not saying what gets the other upset, withholding information, and pretending to the other. That relationship does then become fairly impersonal. The other does become more nearly replaceable by another with similar qualities, and what animates the affec-tion of each may well be fantasy as much as a genuine knowledge. There is really no way of telling. The intellectual problem of giving a plausible account of love, on the assumption that human beings are separate, reflects the actual problems of lovers who want to maintain their separateness.

The alternative—love that is openly in-relation—is better understood by con-sidering a very different way of thinking about love. It is interesting because it does not follow the path laid out by Fromm, Buber, and Nozick of regarding hu-man beings as separate in all but their loving. Instead, this view acknowledges that in love, as in many other things, we act, we choose, we deliberate, we do all sorts of ordinary things. However, we do not always do them as separate persons but jointly: Some of our choices, actions, and beliefs are neither only mine nor only yours but are genuinely ours.

LOVE IN-RELATION

This is Aristotle's general characterization of friendship: "To be friends ... [per-sons] must be mutually recognized as bearing goodwill and wishing well to each other ..." (Aristotle, 1941:1156a3–5). In addition, friendship involves "living with each other" and "companionship" (1156a28), and that means "living together and sharing in discussion and thought." Just eating together is appropriate to cattle but not to humans (1170b13).

It is, at first, not very clear what we should make of these generalities, but then we find Aristotle saying that the relations one has to one's friend are the same as the relations one has to oneself (1166a10). No devotee of separateness would ever say that: On the view that human beings are separate it is axiomatic that my relations to myself are totally different from those I have to others. I have my attributes, but I do not have the attributes of others. My attributes are mine and no one else's. We have seen a number of important implications of that:

- Empathy is the effort to reconstruct the feelings of the other. Mine are directly accessible to me. Those of the others need to be guessed at. My relation to my feelings is quite different from my relations to yours.
- Decisions are always made by separate individuals. Joint decisions are no more than the same decision arrived at by different persons at about the same time, perhaps after consultation with one another. Your relation to my decisions is not at all the same as your relation to yours. The same is true for me.
- Autonomy consists of having one's own values, life plan, and moral standards. These are exclusively mine, just as yours are exclusively yours. My relationship to mine is that of exclusive ownership. My relationship to yours is the relationship to someone else's exclusive property. My relationship to your values and life plan is quite different from my relationship to mine.
- The autonomous person is not dependent on others but does for himself or herself. The relation to self is quite different from that to others. That is also true when we lack autonomy, for then we have the relation to others— dependency—which we fail to have to ourselves. In chapters that follow I will also argue that in the perspective of separateness.
- Knowledge is mine or it is yours. I can claim to *know* what I believe only if I myself have the evidence that supports those beliefs. Hence Descartes had to start reexamining the foundations of human knowledge for himself and recommend to all of us that we do the same, each for himself or herself. Without such an independent testing done by every one of us, we cannot claim to know anything because we are taking someone else's word for it. Your knowledge is not evidence to support my beliefs. Thus my relation to my knowledge is very different from my relation to yours.
- My power is mine; yours is yours and a threat to mine. My relation to your power is the opposite of my relation to mine.

Aristotle is never very explicit about this, but it certainly looks as if he were denying these claims of separateness when he tells us that my relations to my friends are the same as my relations to myself. This impression is strengthened by another passage, in which we hear that friends know themselves better through knowing their friends. Because who I am is shaped by who my friend is and by our friendship, we get to be the same person in certain respects after we have lived, thought and deliberated, and chosen and acted together for a long time. Some of the thoughts each of us has are not strictly speaking mine or my friend's but ours. The same is true of decisions, choices, and even character traits we acquire in the course of the friendship. Thus there is a good deal of importance in our lives that is no longer separately owned but is simply ours. Since it is easier to see who another person is than to see oneself clearly, in seeing my friend I see myself because we are, in some way, the same person (1169b28).[6] Here is a description of friendship as union that does not take refuge in obscure talk about nondiscursive knowledge that comes to us in a flash: It explains that many ordinary activities such as conversation, thinking, choosing, and acting are, for friends, not separate but joint activities. The union of friends, or lovers, consists in nothing more mysterious than having feelings, desires, thoughts, choices, and actions in common. Separateness disappears to be replaced by being-in-relation.[7]

But, you may say, talking about friends being one person is still pretty obscure. They still don't feel each other's feelings, think each other's thoughts, or, for that matter, sneeze each other's sneezes. More important, their differences are important to the relationship. Friends are the same person, in some ways, but that is remarkable only because they are, even in their friendship, distinct. Their feelings about the friendship and about one another may well not be the same. One is perfectly happy about the friendship; the other has some uneasiness. Each may well see the other differently from the way that other sees himself or herself; each may have a different view of the relationship. All of this is true and very important. Friends and lovers are not the "same person" in the sense in which each of them is self-identical; they are not numerically one person. What is more, they are distinct, different, and in many respects separate. Not all of their acts, beliefs, and values are joint acts, beliefs, and values.

We can agree to that without taking refuge in "I-thou" talk à la Buber or Fromm. Being the same person turns out to be the complex project of two persons in which they talk and act and feel together. The joint project involves doing many things together. There is conversation and making love, but there is also buying groceries and paying bills. There may be children and friends, civic associations and subversive activities. These two persons develop ways in which they go about each of these activities: who does what, how things are planned or done on the spur of the moment, and where disagreements are liable to come up and how they will be resolved, concealed, or evaded. The two come to know each other insofar as they know what they have done in the past about, say, birthdays and what each can expect to do in the future. They know themselves by knowing the other insofar as they know the established ways in which 10,000 mundane daily details, as well as deep convictions about what is right and good, are shared or are under extended discussion. This knowledge is not separate empathy—guessing what the other thinks or will do. I know what you will do because we agreed on ways to bring up our children and arrange household chores or what bills to pay first. If your actions or mine depart from the other's expectations, we may have to sit down and think about it together. As time goes on that gets to be easier because we know how to think about problems jointly. We are one person in those projects and activities that are shared, where what each of us does is part of a project we take on, plan, and oversee together.

BUT WHAT ABOUT UNREQUITED LOVE?

Let's grant, you say, that the happy love that binds two persons together is a form of being-in-relation. But what about young Werther, about love that is not shared? Is such love not separate, exclusively a state of the unhappy one? Let's look at that.

It is surely true that there are early stirrings of love—which may or may not come to fruition—that are merely internal. I meet Eric and I like him. But I do not know him at all and therefore also do not know what it is about him I like and whether he actually is the sort of person I think he is—whether I like him for who he is or for reasons all my own. After a while, I may make overtures to him and say that I want to be friends, but my efforts are rebuffed. He does not like me. Now the story may unfold in many different ways: I can withdraw and be done with him. I can also withdraw and regret that we could not be friends but know better than to keep offering my friendship. I am left with some regrets, and those, most likely, are quite private.

But I could also persevere. I might become a generally acknowledged, unsuccessful suitor. Eric's friends may tease me or make fun of me behind my back; Eric himself may be tolerantly discouraging or may angrily avoid me. There are suitors, successful and unsuccessful, and there are secret lovers who conceal their love while they play a more mundane role in relation to the beloved. In most cases these different relationships are negotiated in some way by the participants. Eric accepts me as an unsuccessful suitor. I accept that role, always hoping, of course, to change it. After a while, Eric may relent, at least occasionally, and I become a slightly more plausible suitor. My hopeless love for him is a common construct. It is not mine alone. Even unrequited love may well be something shared by the lover, the beloved, and their friends.

But what if no one takes me seriously. Eric may say, You don't really love me. It flatters your vanity to be seen with me and to have people think that you are my lover because I am so beautiful. Alternatively, Eric may tell me that I am too old, too poor, too ugly to be his friend. The very idea is absurd. Everyone agrees. I am not regarded as an unhappy lover but am laughed at for my unrealistic expectations. Can I still maintain that I love Eric? I am getting to be very much like the person who loves a movie star whom she or he has never seen and has no hope of seeing, let alone of making friends with. Or I am like the persons who love Elvis Presley even though they never knew him when he was still alive.

There are different possible situations here. If my unsuccessful suit is public knowledge, we may well regard it as a collective effort. My role depends on what I do but also on how others respond and support my stance of an unsuccessful suitor. This does not show that we are in-relation. There are, as we have seen repeatedly, collective activities in which the participants are quite separate from one another. I have used playing tennis as an example before. But my relation to Eric may also be in-relation, to varying degrees. Ambivalence can, I said earlier, be in-relation and so can the suitor who is not wanted. What if I nourish my love in private, carefully concealing my feelings and thoughts and my hopes that Eric may still change his mind? There is no reason to deny that that may well happen. Nor do we need to deny that this secret passion is genuine love, even though it is clearly not shared with anyone. There may well be instances of love that are private, that belong exclusively to persons who are separate. Not all kinds of love are forms of being-in-relation. In previous examples of being-in-relation, we saw that there is separate autonomy and autonomy in-relation, that there is separate empathy and empathy in-relation. We can draw the same distinctions with respect to love: There is a loving that is very private and very separate. It often is love that is unrequited and unconsummated.

But often, even if love is requited and consummated, lovers in a relationship are separate. Then their relationship is susceptible to all the difficulties mentioned: Do they love each other or only a fantasy of each other? Is their relation truly personal or is it a relation to anyone who has a given set of characteristics?

Separate love is very common. It is startling to think of all the men who have shared their lives with a woman, and who have thought that they loved that woman, without ever owning up to the pervasive misogyny in which they participated. They were systematically misinformed about their own feelings and their attitudes toward their partners. Nor did they have a true sense of the resentment that women have felt against men and the ridicule to which they held up their life partners in their conversations with their women friends. Mr. Ramsey has no idea how much his wife feels burdened by his neediness or how silly she thinks his conversations are with his friends and students. He does not know that she is angry at the ways in which he is useless around the house, useless as a father, useless even as a companion. Yet he thinks he loves her, and in a way he does. But he also thinks that women are incompetent when it comes to the things that really matter in the world. Does he understand how much condescension and contempt are mixed with his love? And who *is* that person he loves? It is not really anyone he knows, even though they have been intimates for years and have eight children. True love among separate persons has been as self-deceived as has been the separate autonomy of the men in those relationships. When lovers are separate, the other often is as much a creature of fantasy as a real flesh-and-blood person. Separate love is not to be recommended.

The philosophical conceptions of love between separate persons reflect the practice of philosophers who assume that human beings (read "man") are sepa-

rate. If we assume that persons are separate we find that love tends to be impersonal. The reality of the beloved is as elusive as the reality of the object of knowledge in traditional epistemology. We have seen that at some length in this chapter.
But that elusiveness of the other in the theory of love only mirrors the elusiveness
of the other in actual relationships in which at least one of the partners chooses or
pretends to be very separate. But what is worse, separate love is not only very distant and faintly connected love but is also frequently oppressive to women. Separateness is not of the human essence at all but belongs primarily to men. Women
are not supposed to be separate, as men are. Separateness not only misconstrues
love and anger and thus leads us into intellectual error, but it also contributes to
the oppression of stereotypical women by stereotypical men.

Ann Ferguson invented the term "sex/affective production" to enable her to
speak about exploitation in the family, where "women have less control over the
process of production (e.g., control of human reproductive decisions) and the exchange of services; and men characteristically get more than they give in the exchange of those services" (Ferguson, 1991:70). Women have less decisionmaking
power over the sex/affective production process not only with respect to child-
bearing, abortion, and so on. They also have little power to resist when men want
sex, love, nurturing, and support, such as Mr. Ramsay's demands on Mrs. Ramsay
for reassurance. What Mrs. Ramsay gets in return is Mr. Ramsay's repeated decla-
ration that "women can't write, can't paint." To herself, Mrs. Ramsay returns the
compliment. She thinks that men's conversations are arid and that men are really
inept at the things that matter most, namely, to make things "merge and flow."
But she can't say so. She can't go around ridiculing men for their abstract, impersonal, and childishly competitive dinner conversation. She has to keep all of that
to herself. Men are allowed to be separate and not care about the feelings and
needs of others when they don't feel like caring for them. Women cannot be separate in that way. They must be available whenever they are wanted, and they are
not free to vent their feelings about men and their incapacities.

Male separateness incapacitates men. To be a separate man one must be strong,
impervious, in control, autonomous. Since that is not an easy stance for human
beings, to say the least, men are early along taught to ignore their feelings and,
rather than feel and speak of them, express them in aggressive action (Miller
1983). Men grow up being very ignorant about themselves. Mr. Ramsay cannot
talk about his disappointment with his last book. He—the articulate philosopher—is mute when it comes to talking about his own inner life. The way of becoming an autonomous person in control of himself involves becoming disabled
in self-knowledge and thus to lack in real self-determination with respect to his
feelings. He must give his inner life, such as it is, into the hands of his wife because he is utterly incompetent to deal with it himself. The autonomous man pays
for that separate autonomy with emotional impotence. Ned, whom we are about
to meet in the next section, is thus, in part, unable to talk about his feelings for
Anna because he is unaccustomed to put his feelings into words. To say "I love

you" is, he thinks, to report certain private facts. For married persons such reports are redundant because their mutual love is institutionalized in their marriage. Or so Ned argues. He has no sense of the wide variety of emotional expressions and their uses because, as a proper man, he is totally unskilled in them. He has no sense that talk about feelings is a response to the other—that sometimes for him to avow his love is a way of touching Anna, sharing of himself, making himself vulnerable, giving gifts, and expressing admiration or even gratitude and that all of those, at the right moments, are acts of love, of being-in-relation.

Men's separateness not only incapacitates them for the very autonomy they are claiming so vociferously for themselves, but it also deprives their partners, from whom they demand love and support, and makes the exchanges so unequal. Separateness makes stereotypical men emotionally impotent, and they compensate for this by dominating their partners. In the process of sex/affective production men get more than they give. That does not mean that men do not love women. It means that the love they give is very different from the love they demand and get in return. Male love, being crippled in the expression of emotions and hidden behind the pretense of separateness, is often oblivious to the person, the world, the experience, and the feelings of the other. When women do express their needs, or make demands not yet fulfilled, even the men who love those women at first tend to react with anger. "In order to pursue their prescribed male identity, [men] had learned to close off large areas of their own sensibilities; one important area is precisely that of responsiveness to the needs of others" (Miller, 1976:68). Because men love their wives but are insensitive to their needs, their anger flares up when their wives express new needs: That makes the men feel that they have failed in some project that is important to them. Here separateness makes everyone lose. Men are incapacitated for love; women do not get what they need and deserve. Separateness once again shows itself to be a bad choice.

Loving relationships have their histories. They begin inevitably as rather separate—the partners do not know each other and there has not been time to build a joint relationship. Many relationships remain separate. But good relationships slowly move toward being-in-relation. In the example examined in the next section, being-in-relation replaces separateness—but not without a great deal of anger and struggle. But those too, it turns out, are forms of being-in-relation. Love, at its best, is a form of being-in-relation. I argued earlier, in Chapter 4, that ambivalence was also a form of being-in-relation. We shall see now that we must say the same about anger.

LOVE AND ANGER AS FORMS OF BEING-IN-RELATION

Love is a gift but it is also an accomplishment. In May Sarton's *Anger* (1982), Ned, a banker, and Anna, a singer, battle over each other's divergent expectations of love and marriage. They meet when both are no longer young. He is successful in his business, she a rising star as a singer. They are immediately drawn to each other and marry not too soon after. But after the first heady weeks, they begin to fight and soon they live in battle with interludes of armed truce, angry, withdrawn, and resentful. What divides them are different expectations of intimacy. His is wordless. There are no avowals of love, even in the heat of sexual passion. Demonstrations of affection belong, he thinks, exclusively in courtship. Once the lovers are joined, all demonstrations of love are superfluous. Why would you say "I love you" unless your love were somehow in doubt? She wants emotional displays and wants to talk about her feelings and his. Battles are not to be fought and then forgotten or avoided by avoiding each other. Conflicts should be discussed. But such conversations would, and would be meant to, uncover feelings—something that he abhors. He refers to her attempts at talking as "scenes" because she is trying to share feelings in conversations about their differences. But feelings are shared by feeling them. The conversations she attempts are "scenes" because they are emotional.

In some respects, their differences are stereotypical. He is a typical male who eschews emotion; she a typical woman who seeks openness about emotions. The novel also suggests ethnic and cultural differences: He is a Boston Brahmin and her mother is of Italian extraction, and Anna has inherited her mother's Mediterranean temperament. He is a banker and very proper. She an artist whose power depends on her ability to feel and express emotion.

But stereotypes do not explain their problem. What drew them to one another in the first place were aspects of each that departed from the stereotype. He loves music and is, as a music lover, sensitive to emotional nuances in ways that are not at all stereotypical. That love of music was a powerful bond between them from the beginning. She is a strong woman, independent and ambitious in her career, and that suited him well. But they lack a common ground on which they can stand to fight out the different expectations and needs that divide them. Their disagreements soon become repetitive. No one moves, no one learns. She demands affirmations of love from him and openness about his feelings. He withdraws further into his silences. Each, not getting what he or she wants, feels rejected and responds with anger.

Love involves trust. It requires trust so that anger can be expressed, differences be defined, and disappointments aired without threatening the connection. But trust must be established. In the first burst of love, Ned and Anna trust one another, but as they begin to live together, trust is shaken because conflicts seem so deep and constant. At the center of their conflicts is anger. As Anna realizes after a while, even though she is strong and independent in some ways, she is insecure and in need of persistent affirmation. When that affirmation is withheld in moments when she needs it, her anger bursts out abruptly. In Ned's family, however, it was considered supremely important to be controlled and to maintain decorum. Yet contrary to her constant admonitions to maintain a smooth and sunny surface, his mother made his life miserable with constant complaints and tears. Having been admonished over and over to be controlled, and by a person who seemed to have no control over herself at all, he grew up unable to show emotion. Displays of feelings enraged him; he was afraid of them. So when Anna demands open shows of affection he shrinks deeper into his shell. That unresponsiveness on his part is what Anna fears most of all; she needs the proximity of a warm emotional person to reassure her. But her demands for emotion, which are so frightening to him, also make him very angry. Since he cannot express that anger openly, he responds to her anger with cold, punishing withdrawal. What he perceives and presents to her as his immunity to anger is in reality anger in a different form from hers. Their struggle for trust is a struggle over anger and a struggle over the form it takes.

Anna begins to see, in reflecting about her failing relationship to Ned, that his actions, and her own, can be seen and understood in more than one way. What she first sees as Ned's rejection of her she then begins to see as anger. Is it only anger at her? It is clear that she provokes it. But why? What is it that Ned is so angry about? Why, she then continues to ask herself, is her own life so full of angry outbursts? There she encounters the line from Rainer Maria Rilke: "Perhaps everything terrible in us is at its deepest being something helpless that wants help from us." What does she want from Ned, and what does he want from her? First his actions seemed rejections, then anger, then a cry for help. In turn, her anger, she begins to see, springs from a need for affirmation, to help her through times of self-distrust. So far all of that is purely intellectual and makes little difference in the actual skirmishes that punctuate their lives. But it prepares her to see his actual anger, once it bursts out into the open, not so much as an attack on her but as an expression of his own pain. That is what she hears, and that is what she reflects back to Ned. And thus he sees himself in a different light. He actually can begin to talk about his past. He can name his fear of emotion and where it is directed. They are beginning to *reinterpret* each other's anger, by perceiving it differently from how they perceived it at first. Thus their anger changes; they change and so does their relationship.

We get the first indication that they will succeed in establishing trust when she gets him so angry that he shouts at her. He actually allows himself and her to feel his open fury. He acknowledges that showing love is terribly frightening to him. His anger is transformed from withdrawn to open anger. That anger is easier for her to bear than his withdrawn, withheld, concealed anger, and thus she can continue to push him toward openness. He, in turn, having once expressed deep emotion without incurring terrible punishment, begins to feel a bit safer with her. Trust is growing as his anger changes character. Her anger becomes more articulate and focused as she sees that it is his pretended coldness that so infuriates her. So each changes in very specific ways in reaction to each other: He opens up to her a bit, and that makes it easier for her to feel her own needs more clearly. As time goes on they learn to accept love in the form in which it is offered, not only in the precise form in which they ask for it. The new trust, the new anger, the new latitude in accepting gifts of affection—all are elements of their love. All are possible only between these two persons; they are their joint achievements and thus genuine examples of being-in-relation.

Love and anger are intimately connected. They are not opposites. For Ned to be openly angry at Anna is, paradoxically, an act of love—it is groping his way into trust. On the road toward love, anger is not banished. On the contrary, it is let out in his case and transformed in hers. There are many sorts of angers, and part of love is for two persons to transform their angers so that they will not destroy love.

Here we see clearly the difference between saying that love is reciprocal and that it is a form of being-in-relation. Love is said to be reciprocal if A feels for and believes about B what B feels for and thinks about A. But that, as we have just seen, is much too abstract: Anna's anger at Ned is very different from Ned's anger at Anna, and so of course is their love. One thing they need to learn is the variety and complexity of angers and loves and how hers is not at all like his. But then these angers and loves change, though not in the direction of reciprocity: Ned's anger does not become more like Anna's, but they each take forms that are more acceptable to the other. The angers of each become parts of the joint relation they are building. They are not reciprocal but become forms of being-in-relation.

Of course, anger in other situations may well be separate. The bureaucrat at the tax office is being unfriendly and patronizing and my anger flares but I keep it to myself. Here anger is not in obvious ways a form of being-in-relation. Anger is often distinct; it is only mine, it is hidden away inside of me. But it is interesting to observe that anger expressed does not seem to be just mine. However carried away by rage, people are very careful in their expressions of anger. We express anger with very little restraint to children or animals but are usually very cautious in the presence of judges, military superiors, or the boss from whom we expect a raise (Miller, 1983). It is not entirely clear that even anger that is all my own does not, once expressed, take on more the appearance of something that I share with the object of my anger. The lines between separate and in-relation anger are not easily drawn.

LOVE AND ANGER AS OPENLY CHOSEN FORMS OF BEING-IN-RELATION

Once we distance ourselves from separateness we can understand why some of the views of love, discussed in the first section, are plausible. Yes, I do love you for some of your qualities, but they are qualities that are enhanced or even created in our relationship. They are qualities that are not privately owned by you but are ours. Aristotle expressed that by saying that in knowing the other I know myself. We have this close connection of knowledge of each because some of the qualities I love in you are qualities I share, that we have developed together over the course of our relationship.

But don't I love you just for the ways in which you are different from me? To be sure, but those differences are often still a joint project of ours. Love and friendship are not reciprocal because the friends play different roles and in friendship that is in-relation those assignments are jointly made. You are the decisive one, the one who organizes our social life. I am the steady one who does routine maintenance of things and relationships. We come to the relationship as persons who are suited for those roles. We play the roles in the relationship only if the other does his or her part: I let you organize, I let myself be organized. You rely on me to see that what needs maintenance is attended to. Even where we differ we are in-relation.

Hence there is no problem about my knowing what your qualities are. This knowledge is integral to how we are with each other, day by day. Similarly, love is affirmation of the other. One does "bestow" value on the other by loving, but only if that bestowal is something we do together, with each of us giving and receiving, so that giving and receiving become indistinguishable (Gregory, 1986). Most important of all, once we surrender separateness, we can see clearly why love is personal—one loves this particular person who is irreplaceable. For love is what two persons have together. It is a joint accomplishment, and with any other person love would not be the same. What is personal about any love is not anything pertaining to each partner separately but what they have and make together. A good deal of what is commonly said about love is accurate—but once explicated in the language of separateness it leads to hopeless confusion and insoluble problems.

If we try to love but still remain separate, the intellectual problems about love become bitter realities. Both partners have their emotions, needs, expectations. The relation need not be as inhibited as that of Ned and Anna. The partners may well talk a great deal about how each of them feels, what their needs are, how each sees the other, and how each understands his or her own history that produced and explains their feelings and needs. If there are conflicts in such a relation, each partner can stand pat and hasten the inevitable breakup or they can give in by surrendering some feelings and accepting that some of their needs will never be met in this relation or perhaps in any. Or they can make more limited adjustments by keeping some of their feelings and needs to themselves or by expressing them only in ways that the other finds acceptable. These compromises may be made by both. It is more common, of course, that women make most of them. May Sarton provides a variety of instances of that in her novel. As Anna talks to other women about their marriages and her own, she hears again and again that women simply gave up on those projects or sides of themselves that threatened their marriages.

As separate persons we believe that each of us, separately, is the ultimate arbiter of what we are doing. "You are attacking me!" says my partner. "No," I reply, "I am just being tired and irritable. You are being neurotic about people raising their voice in your presence." The precise character of my action, I assume, depends on my intentions and motives. What is in my mind when I begin to raise my voice? As long as I adhere to separateness I also must insist that my motives and intentions are mine in a particularly intimate sense, namely, that I can, perhaps with an effort, know them directly.[8] Your different interpretation may well make me pause and reexamine myself, but in the end it is I who knows what I feel, what is in my mind, and what I am doing when I begin shouting.

But if I accept being-in-relation openly I also accept that actions, such as expressing emotions by shouting at each other, are public events and that, as Aristotle remarks, one is not always in the best position to see what one is doing because one does not see oneself doing it. I do not hear my precise tone of voice because I do not hear my speech as others hear it. (It is only when I listen to my voice recorded that I hear my German accent.) I do not see my facial expressions, the tension of my body, my changed posture as I begin to get angry. More important, actions do not have an unambiguous meaning. There is no impersonal, neutral objective identity of actions: You and I must negotiate what I am doing when I raise my voice. The meaning of my actions is again a joint accomplishment. In establishing a strong relation, the partners not only change how they act but they also change what each other's actions mean.

Once I do acknowledge that my actions are public and that therefore I am not the exclusive arbiter of what I am doing when I begin to raise my voice, my conversation with the other becomes much more complicated. I must now take seriously the other's claim that I am indeed angry and aggressive. That will lead me back to a new scrutiny of motivations. I become more finely attuned to the ambivalence of almost all our actions. Even the most straightforward expression of irritation is now to be looked at more carefully, to be questioned about its implicit meanings. Am I merely tired and irritated? Have I been angry about something else for a while? Who is it that I am angry at?

But at the same time, of course, corresponding questions are to be asked about my partner. Is my friend merely recording, as only a neutral observer can, what my actions are? That is not very likely. So as we begin to talk about my outburst of what she calls "anger" and I call "fatigue and irritability" we also think about her perceptions and the different meanings one might find in them. More important, as I begin to accept her perception of my anger and modify my behavior, her perceptions change because she too is able to see her own reactions differently and modify them. We both change in-relation to one another.

In these ways, persons openly in-relation work out the difficulties in love. In similar ways, when they celebrate their accomplishments they will see how each contributes in specific ways made possible only by the other. What they gain and enjoy is not to be taken apart as the contributions of the one to which are added those of the other. The love they celebrate is theirs in common. Openly chosen being-in-relation allows us to acknowledge and live out fully our relations to others. These relations are formative; they make us be who we are. In these openly chosen relationships, we can become autonomous persons without false separateness and the pretense of being the exclusive owners of ourselves.

EROS AND AGAPE

The tradition distinguishes between eros, the love between persons for which sexual love is a central example, and agape, the love of neighbor that Christianity regards as a moral obligation. This distinction is not merely of antiquarian interest. I pointed out at the beginning of this book that the difference between separateness and being-in-relation is important for liberatory theory. Separateness is oppressive, whereas the various forms of being-in-relation promise to make a world of freedom and community more accessible to us. In the movement toward liberation the distinction between separateness and being-in-relation is of central importance. But so is the distinction between eros and agape. The command that we love our neighbor is, after all, one of the earliest explicit responses in Western tradition to oppression of the poor, of the less able, and, more ambiguously, of women. But love is selective; it connects us with specific persons for specific reasons. I love you because you are just the sort of person you are; it is love for this unique person. Neighbor love is not so selective. It is love for any person with whom I have dealings, however indirect. Neighbor love, as has often been pointed out, appears to be a contradiction in terms.

But equipped with the distinction between being separate and being-in-relation, we can now see the point of speaking of neighbor love: It is being-in-relation that is not selective, not sexual, and not necessarily erotic. Unlike love and friendship, these examples of being-in-relation may be quite limited in scope and have very specific and limited goals. But they have other characteristics of being-in-relation. They are jointly brought into existence and maintained. Caring in-relation as well as empathy in-relation are of central importance. So may be knowing in-relation. But of overwhelming importance is the fact that such relationships empower. The use of separate power, power over the other, or power that dominates is replaced by relationships in which each is empowered by the relationship and each empowers the other. Neighbor love does not overpower, does not coerce, does not use compulsion. It is not separate but in joint projects empowers all the participants. I will return to the idea of empowerment in Chapter 8.

◄ 7 ►

Knowledge: Separate or in-Relation?

KNOWING HAS ALREADY made its appearance in these chapters. Caring, empathy, and love involve knowing another person. It is now time to examine knowing directly. Like the other concepts examined earlier—autonomy, empathy, love, and anger—there is separate knowing and there is knowing in-relation. Separate knowing has been studied assiduously by philosophers since the time of Descartes and is assumed to be the only kind of knowing, even by those philosophers who regard knowledge as a collective product. Separate knowing is subject to serious failures: It is unable to still the worries about skepticism, it is weak when it comes to objectivity, and it is oppressive of women, people of color, and all those whose work is not purely theoretical. Separate knowers have managed to certify themselves as the only knowers, all the while allowing others to keep the world patched together.

Knowing is a complex relation. There is always a person who knows, there is what that person knows, and there is what that knowledge is about. In knowing, understood as separate, all three elements of knowing are affected; separate knowing is vulnerable in all three respects. The separateness from other knowers leads to skeptical problems for which philosophers have not found answers acceptable to a significant number of other philosophers. The assumption that knowledge is propositional serves to deny the honorific title of "knowledge" to most of what we know and reserves for people with academic credentials a special status and prestige. The separation from knowledge, from the known, as well as from other knowers has created problems of objectivity for science. Examples abound of social and medical science viciously distorted by race and gender prejudice.

All of these problems are very familiar. I do not need to discuss them at length. I merely need to show that separateness gives rise to the problem of skepticism as well as to the scandals of lack in objectivity. Those are intensified by separateness groundlessly inflating the prestige of theoretical knowledge. In addition, that inflation is to the disadvantage of most people whose knowledge raises children, makes sick theoreticians well, and manages to keep populations alive in famine, war, and deprivations often brought upon us by theoretical knowers.

An adequate account of knowing in-relation is not at present available. In this chapter I will concentrate on one aspect of knowing in-relation, the requirement that no one be excluded from inquiry. Knowing in-relation cannot exclude different points of view; in fact, it needs to seek out and actively try to incorporate points of view different from and in opposition to any given ruling consensus. Other aspects of knowing in-relation have been discussed by a range of feminist theorists and will require a great deal more discussion elsewhere.

THE PROBLEMS OF SEPARATE KNOWING

Separate Knowing Leads to Skepticism

Skeptics deny that we can know anything. There are skeptics with respect to the existence of an "external" world, with respect to the existence of other minds, and with respect to the existence of a past or a future. There are also skeptics about induction. Generations of philosophers have discussed these problems with impressive ingenuity. They have not seen until rather recently, however, that skepticism follows directly from the assumption of separateness, and even today most of them do not see that.

The connection between skepticism and the assumption of human separateness is obvious, though. If we are separate, each of us separately bears the entire burden of establishing human knowledge claims. The beliefs and knowledge claims of others are not irrelevant to mine but can never be decisive. I can claim to know only what I, myself, have very strong evidence for. Philosophers often express this by demanding that knowers be autonomous (in the sense of separate autonomy)—that they not take on beliefs merely on the say-so of another but accept as knowledge only what they, each separately, can show to be true. As knowers we are separate from one another. Each of us must lay the foundation of knowledge of the world alone.

.But if I am thus separate as a knower, I do not have the requisite evidence that there are minds other than my own. Since we are all distinct in our bodies, I have my sensations but know of yours only because you tell me about them. I do not have direct access to them. As separate knower I can never know that you do indeed have that inner life because the relevant evidence is not available to me. To accept that you have a mind, and that means in part that you have an inner life like mine, I have to believe your account of your inner life. To accept that you have a mind I must give up my separate autonomy as a knower and believe that your account of your inner life is trustworthy. As long as I hold to my autonomy I must remain a skeptic with respect to other minds.

Similarly, I do not have the evidence that a world exists when I do not perceive it. Other persons' perceptions of things that are not at this moment perceived by me are, at least, a necessary condition for the existence of an external world. I would not be in a position to know that there exists a world independent of my perceptions if others could not observe what I am not observing. But, according to the assumption of separateness, the perceptions of others cannot count as evidence for me until I have satisfied myself that the others "perceive" in the sense in which I perceive. That requires, minimally, that I satisfy myself that the other has a mind. Since I cannot know that, I also cannot know that the other perceives as I do, and hence I cannot know that there is an "external world." I must remain a skeptic in that respect also as long as I hold to my separate autonomy as knower.

The issue here is not that it would take too much time to answer all these questions but that *as a separate person,* I do not have the resources to answer them. I am separate—philosophers assume—and can know only what I have assembled the evidence for. But what sort of evidence do I have for the existence of other minds? for the existence of a real world outside my mind or in the past, which is behind us forever? I can rely only on my own experiences and my own thoughts. The knowledge claims made by the separate knower always rest on what is evident for this separate person: Thus the Cartesian project comes into existence, that of founding all of human knowledge on the evidence available to a single, separate person. But that foundation is too restricted. Knowledge requires multiple perspectives, a shared language, a common methodology, a universal logic. By myself, as separate knower, I do not have the evidence to support this entire edifice.

Many solutions have been offered to the problem of skepticism. But the skeptic is only encouraged by them, because each solution is earnestly embraced by its author and rejected by most other experts. Nothing suggests more strongly that the skeptic may well be right than the continuing proliferation of "solutions" to the problem of skepticism. This has induced a significant number of philosophers to hold that we can escape the problem of skepticism only if we surrender the picture of separate knowers; that is, those assembling evidence for their beliefs all alone and relying on others for suggestions but being themselves exclusively responsible for the truth of their knowledge claims. It is widely believed that once we recognize that knowledge is a social product, we can put the skeptical anxieties behind us. I will return to this conception of knowledge as a collective product below.

The debate over skepticism may waste time and resources, but otherwise it does not do harm. Not so the companion claims that knowers are separate from what they know or that knowledge takes the form of propositions. These claims have allowed knowers flagrant lapses of objectivity. They allow academically trained knowers to maintain that they alone have genuine knowledge. In both of these manifestations, separateness has been, and remains, oppressive.

Separate Knowing Lacks Objectivity

In the past twenty years, feminist scientists and scholars have documented in painful detail the pervasive misogyny in science and scholarship that has excluded women from being respected practitioners in different disciplines (Rossiter, 1982), has ignored the experiences and contributions of women (Dalmiya and Alcoff,

1993), and has given a distorted and pejorative account of women (Fausto-Sterling, 1985). Even in areas of study not directly connected to men and women, male misogyny has distorted scientific and scholarly work (Keller, 1983). Corresponding aberrations are easily documented with respect to people of color (Gould, 1981; Haller, 1971; hooks, 1989; Sales, 1990; Harding, 1993b). Scientists and scholars have been sadly lacking in objectivity.

Persistent beliefs in eugenics are another example of this lack of objectivity. From the 1890s until World War II, eugenics was very popular among biologists and social scientists, as well as in the general public, both in Europe and the United States. Eugenicists believed that the capabilities of human beings were genetically transmitted. Any progress for the human race, or portions of it, required that inferior genetic material be eliminated by carefully supervised human reproduction. The major tool of eugenics was "compulsory sterilization of the criminally insane and other people considered genetically inferior" (Lifton, 1986:22). By 1920, twenty-five states in the United States had passed laws for compulsory sterilization. German eugenicists complained bitterly at the time that Germany was lagging behind the United States in sterilization programs. In the period between 1907 and 1963, "more than sixty thousand persons" were sterilized without their consent in the United States. The rise of Nazism with its eugenics programs did not lessen the enthusiasm for involuntary sterilization in the United States: "American advocates pointed to Germany to illustrate how an enlightened sterilization program might quickly reach its goal" (Reilly, 1991:94–95). The involuntary sterilization program had solid support from physicians and was promoted in articles in medical journals, including the prestigious *New England Journal of Medicine* (Reilly, 1991:89).

In Germany many eminent anthropologists and psychiatrists held eugenicist beliefs that made them look with favor on the Nazi party because it supported such programs (Harding, 1993b:344ff.). In 1932, even before the Nazis came to power, members of the Kaiser Wilhelm Institut for biology—one of the very prestigious research institutes—drafted a eugenics statute. The Nazis took over that draft and made it into law in July 1933. The members of the KWI welcomed the projects for sterilizing various classes of "mental defectives" and actively participated by evaluating large numbers of inmates of various institutions prior to sterilization. As a consequence of this law about 200,000 people were sterilized in 1934, 1935, and 1936. Three hundred sixty-seven women and 70 men died as a result of the operations (Mueller-Hill, 1988:32). This sterilization program subsequently evolved into a euthanasia program in German mental institutions and eventually turned into full-fledged genocide.

The prevailing understanding of genetics was Mendelian. Human traits were passed along by mechanisms only slightly more complex than those that determined the color or skin texture of peas. Thus it seemed to follow that if traits like insanity were purely hereditary, and passed on from generation to generation, it would not be desirable for insane persons to have children because their "bad" genes were going to be passed on to do damage in future generations.

But it does not require a great deal of thought to see that the actual research and sterilization programs were shaped by more than a primitive understanding of genetics, for we must surely ask how it was decided *which traits* required compulsory sterilization and which did not. Compulsory sterilization was imposed on persons in prisons and other institutions. It was not applied to businessmen who went bankrupt through lack of judgment or diligence, to politicians who took bribes, to bankers who embezzled money, to judges who were corruptible, to financiers who watered stock or defrauded the public by other unscrupulous means, to art dealers who mislabeled works of art, to ministers who fell away from the path of righteousness, to husbands who beat their wives and children. We can extend the list indefinitely. But the point is clear: Only certain sorts of failures were regarded as a threat to the well-being of the country sufficient to warrant compulsory sterilization.[1]

Pervasive racism was manifested not only in some scientific results and theories but also in experimentation that was useless from the scientific point of view and utterly repugnant from a moral point of view. Such was the Tuskeegee study in which the U.S. Public Health Service studied several hundred black men with end-stage syphilis while withholding treatment (Thomas and Quinn, 1991). Most important for our present purposes was the fact that the "experiment was never kept secret ... the Tuskeegee study had been the subject of numerous reports in medical journals and had been openly discussed in conferences at professional meetings" (Jones, 1993:279). The scientific community was well aware of the Tuskeegee project, but there was little objection to it until newspapers uncovered the story in 1972, forty year after the study was begun. Neither were Mengele's twin studies in Auschwitz a secret. Mengele kept sending body parts obtained in autopsies to Professor Otmar Von Verschuer, one of the very respected members of the Institute of Anthropology (Mueller-Hill, 1988:72; Annas and Grodin, 1992). Neither would have been possible except for widespread and shared racism in the scientific community.

These glaring failures of objectivity are directly connected with separateness. It is widely assumed that each of us, as knower, is separate whereas what we strive for, namely, knowledge, is the same for all. Separate knowers are paradigmatic knowers. Objectivity therefore consists of distancing oneself from all that is personal and idiosyncratic about oneself—from everything one does not share with all other members of the community of inquiry. It consists of, in the words of John Dewey, discounting and eliminating "merely personal factors" in the pursuit of knowledge (Dewey, 1938:44). Others use the familiar metaphor of a standpoint and characterize objective knowledge as knowledge that is not tied to a particular standpoint. It is, in Nagel's phrase, "the view from nowhere."

A view or form of thought is more objective than another if it relies less on the specifics of the individual's makeup and position in the world, or on the character of the particular type of creature he is. (Nagel, 1986:5)

From that absolute point of reference come truths that are independent of contingent human affairs and of natural language's role in concrete human experiences of interaction and intercourse. (Nye, 1990:174)

Knowing is done by persons who have left behind their specificity as this person or that—man or woman, white or black, old or young, speakers of this or that language. Others, again, stress that to be objective, science and scholarship must be value free, that the only values by which one may be guided in one's intellectual work are those that are intrinsic to the work itself: the importance of truth and impartiality and the need for full public disclosure of one's data and the procedures by which one has gathered them (Longino, 1990). Values or political stances must be kept out of scientific work. Slightly different again is the formulation according to which objective knowledge is remote from feelings: "... objectivity, the separation of observation and reporting from the researcher's wishes, which is so essential for the development of science, becomes ... [the] separation of thinking from feeling" (Levins and Lewontin, 1993:43). With these conceptions of objectivity—all variants of the same general view that in striving for objectivity the separate knower must distance himself or herself from all that is personal and idiosyncratic about himself or herself—come corresponding explanations of the widespread and glaring failures of objectivity in the work of accredited scholars and scientists. They all continue the underlying assumption of separateness. Objectivity is the task of the separate researcher. Failures to be objective are to be blamed on individual investigators. The particular researchers are thought to have failed to eliminate all that was personal, thus falling victim to partiality or prejudice. They were simply doing bad science (Antony, 1993). At work here is a very traditional conception of science as a self-correcting enterprise: "At any rate we can say ... that science is capable of learning. ... Any assumption can in principle be criticized. ... And that anybody may criticize constitutes scientific objectivity" (Popper, 1971:221).

But separateness leads us astray once again. On the one hand, the defense of "science" as self-correcting fails on factual grounds. These racist or misogynist errors were often committed by scientists or scholars who were very well respected and rightly so. These were not practitioners who did "bad" science (Fausto-Sterling, 1985). On the other hand, the distinction between "good" and "bad" science is neither clear-cut nor judged by universal and invariable criteria. Sometimes politically motivated work in science is good science; sometimes it is not. Each case must be examined and evaluated individually (Nelson, 1990:205). Neither on factual nor on conceptual grounds can we be confident that racist or misogynist science is bad science in all cases.

More generally, we should notice that the separate conceptions of objectivity—whether they demand that we distance ourselves from feelings, from values, from our individual points of view, or from political commitments—are too vague to be of any use. My ideas are not clearly identified as "personal" or "impersonal." Simple introspection will not tell me which of my mental states are "thinking" and which are "feeling." They do not present themselves to my inner eye with those labels attached. Neither does what I speak or write bear clear identifiers as thoughts, on the one hand, and feelings, on the other. Thus the injunction to strive for objectivity by eschewing the personal and emotional is extremely difficult to follow, and it is not at all clear how one can tell that someone has observed it scrupulously. The same applies to the recommendations that we stay away from irrelevant value judgments. Not only sentences that have words like "good" or "right" in them are evaluative, and sometimes value judgments are well disguised or blend into the background of our thinking so as to be invisible to ourselves. (I will give an example of that later in this chapter.) It is enormously difficult for any individual person to identify beliefs that are tinged by moral values, political stances, and unargued-for beliefs.

Instead, prejudices come to light when one's views are challenged by others who find them improbable. When we rise to defend them we discover that we did not question assumptions that, when they are questioned, lose their previous plausibility. Thus researchers have been enabled to discover some lapses of objectivity when the opinions of individual researchers departed sharply from established opinions. But prejudices, such as racial and gender prejudice, that were shared by virtually all researchers were happily assumed to be self-evident truths and distorted scientific work over many generations (Harding, 1993a:57).

In some cases, individual prejudices are spotted and eradicated by the scientific community. But that does not vindicate Popper's claim that science is always self-correcting. To be sure, Nazi science is dead, and the blatant sexism and racism of past social science has all but disappeared. Sexists and racists must be more circumspect these days. Science is no doubt self-correcting to some extent (and that is no mean accomplishment), but it is also clear that there are prejudices like antisemitism, racism, and sexism shared so universally in a community of inquirers that no one will ever succeed in challenging it from within that community. *Grossly prejudiced science was not refuted by the members of the scientific community itself.* It took wars and major social and political upheavals to put an end to the prejudices. Antisemitic science was not subjected to experimental criticism but came to an end in the wake of World War II and the Nuremberg doctors' trials. Science experienced a *political* correction. The critique of misogynist and racist science did not come from within the ranks of the existing scientific community: It became possible when, because of *political* upheavals, outsiders subjected current scientific consensus to an essentially political critique. Science is only partially self-correcting.

The conception of knowers as separate from one another brings with it a view of objectivity that is not helpful because it presupposes that we are each, by ourselves, able to distinguish thinking from feeling, descriptive from evaluative judgments, and political from politically neutral beliefs and to separate out clearly what belongs exclusively to us and what is neutral, impartial, and not dependent on the idiosyncracies of each of us separately. In practice, the idiosyncratic is not discovered by each of us separately but only in discussions within a group of researchers. That method has severe limits: Prejudices shared by all will never be challenged. When Popper claims that "anyone may criticize," he is simply mistaken. The range of those whose criticisms will be taken seriously is severely limited, and separateness plays a role in imposing those restrictions.

Prejudices shared among wide strata of the educated cannot be challenged because researchers, as a group, have erected barriers against other groups and thus have made challenges impossible. Separate knowers have systematically insulated themselves as a consequence of two other aspects of separate knowing. They have defined knowledge as a relation to a separate entity, such as a proposition, and thereby excluded all those from the domain of science whose knowledge is not only propositional. They have thereby protected themselves against possible criticisms of their work by all those who lack university credentials. The knowledge of the uncredentialed has been uniformly disparaged; their criticism of the intellectual work of intellectuals therefore has not been heard. Separateness has, in addition, also been extended to the relation between knowers and what they are studying. Knowing is not a joint accomplishment of the inquirer and the subjects of a given study, but the accomplishment of the knower alone in which the subjects are more or less passive. Their views of their own lives, as well as of the knower and the knower's work, have been suppressed.

Separate Knowing Is Exclusive

Lucius Outlaw has remarked on the tension confronting traditional Western liberal thought:

> The political philosophy that gave primacy to the *individual,* supposedly without regard to race, creed, or national origin since all men are created *equal* and to the rule of law with *universal* force, had also to rationalize social distinctions, ultimately group-based in terms of race (ethnicity or gender), to curb its own egalitarianism, ... (Outlaw, 1991:24)

Liberalism has been committed to deep-seated equality, but the practitioners of liberalism—liberals—have never been radical egalitarians. They have therefore always needed justifications for inequality that would not undermine the basic assumption of an original and "natural" equality. One modern strategy for solving that problem was to link political with cognitive authority: Power, all natural equality to the contrary notwithstanding, belonged to those who *know*—the experts, technocrats, professors, doctors, engineers. The equality that we were supposedly all born to could be maintained in a society stratified by class, race, and gender if we could persuade our citizens that the large majority of them did not have the requisite knowledge to govern. Thus political power would be of two sorts: (1) the pervasive electoral power that would belong, in theory if not always in practice, to every adult citizen and (2) the actual power to govern reserved for a small elite of the educated.

The claim that knowing is separate has made an important contribution to this project of justifying actual inequalities by means of its conception of knowledge. Here separateness has to do with the nature of knowledge itself rather than with the relationships between knowers or between the knower and what is known. Separate knowers are separate not only from one another, and from what their knowledge is about, but also from what they know. That assumption has determined the characterization of knowledge as something that is separate from all knowers; it has a substantial identity of its own. It is something that different knowers may have, or have a relationship to, without it being in anyway affected. Knowledge must be something public and accessible, in principle, to anyone; it is something to be grasped by anyone and to be transmitted by some persons to others. Knowledge, or ideas, can therefore be likened to economic values and be said to be traded in a "marketplace of ideas" where things have their characteristics and price regardless of who produced or who owns them at the moment. This conception of knowledge has taken many different forms: Platonic ideas, Aristotelian universals, laws of nature, states of affairs, eternal truths of reason, and, lately, propositions. All are different pictures that philosophers have invoked as descriptions of this knowledge. The most recent version of that conception of knowledge is the claim that all knowledge is propositional (Code, 1993).[2] Knowing is having a particular relationship to a proposition.

Propositions are expressed in language. All knowledge can be formulated in language. What a person knows can be expressed in sentences beginning with "that." If you can't put into words what you believe, then you certainly do not know it. You cannot know what you cannot articulate. Propositions are, moreover, true or false, and their truth or falsehood can and must be argued for. Propositions require evidence before they can claim to be true. Thus knowledge, if it is propositional, must be supported by evidence.

Philosophers regard that view of "knowledge" as self-evident, but others may well wonder about it. Is there not knowledge that is not easily put into words, such as that of my mechanic, who listens to my car and knows that it needs a new right tie-rod? There seems to be knowledge that does not readily fit into the propositional schema of the epistemologists. There is also knowledge that does not seem to rest on evidence, as in the example that follows. Philosophers are not daunted by these difficulties but instead draw a distinction. What my mechanic has is not properly speaking knowledge, they tell us, but is a kind of "competence" or "knowing how." An example of knowledge that does not centrally demand evidence is my knowledge of other persons. But that again is not knowledge strictly speaking, we are told, but merely "acquaintance." Thus knowledge, properly speaking, remains propositional. What appears to be knowledge but does not fit the standard propositional mold is then called something else, either "competence" or "acquaintance" (Lehrer, 1974). Knowledge is knowledge that some proposition or another is true. Although there has been a complex debate about the difference between knowledge and true belief in the past twenty years, mainstream philosophers have no doubt that knowledge is, at least, true belief—that it is propositional, can be put in words, and rests on evidence. This also brings with it the additional idea that knowledge—*real* knowledge—is theoretical. It does not just consist of collections of propositions, for those could be random beliefs not connected with each other, but knowledge consists of theories, that is, propositions arranged in complex logical webs.

But consider this example of knowing: Love involves knowing. Love is not instantaneous but grows. There may be times before love has fully unfolded in which one or the other does not know that he or she loves the other. But once a relationship is established, lovers, friends, companions, parents, and children all know that they love and are loved and that is an essential ingredient in their love. But how do I know that I am loved? Drawing on a story by Ann Beattie, Martha Nussbaum has argued that knowing that one loves is of a piece with allowing oneself to feel and to trust the love of the other. Knowing that one is loved involves accepting the other's love. But that acceptance is frightening, for in loving one makes oneself vulnerable: What if one is mistaken, what if the other's love is not right, and what if the other is too demanding or too withholding? But then the other, through a sentence or a gesture, responds to my reluctance. She or he has seen me as I am—that is love—and now is not urging me to surrender, or is scolding me for being fearful, but with a tender gesture accepts me for who I am—that is love also. That acceptance by the other gives me new strength and courage, and I can now accept the love that I could not accept before. In accepting the other's love, I also accept for myself that I love in return. I discover my loving as I open myself to the other's love in the course of a complex exchange of words, looks, gestures. Loving, and the knowledge of it, issue from the conversation about everything but love, from the reaching out and holding back. The love I discover is not just mine but ours. "Is this discovery or creation? Both, we must say" (Nussbaum, 1988:504). Is it my creation or the other's? Clearly, we must say that it is a joint creation. Knowing that one loves or is loved rises up in the actions of lovers; it is neither mere belief, nor mere feeling, nor both of those, but is how they are with one another.

Knowing that I am loved is not propositional. The jealous man—Othello, Robert Browning's duke—mistakenly demands evidence that he is loved. But the knowledge that you are loved cannot be forced on you by evidence and proof; you must accept the other's love. It is one more instance of the perversity of a separate love that asking for "proofs" of the other's love appears appropriate. But these demands for evidence only demonstrate the man's own failure of loving, and Desdemona or the last duchess fall victim to that. You cannot prove that someone loves you. Nor is proof what you need. That is one of the points of the Beattie story. You need to learn to accept the other person's love.

Knowing that one is loved is not propositional; it is not separate. Now philosophers may well recognize that but then continue to say that knowing that you are loved is not knowing, properly speaking. Knowledge that is propositional, and theoretical, and separate, they say, "is fundamental for human cognition" (Lehrer, 1974:3). The conception of knowledge as separate, and propositional, encourages the assumption that propositional knowledge, preeminently knowledge of physics or of mathematical disciplines, is knowledge in the best sense and knowledge of the most important kind. All other kinds of knowing are, in some way, derivative from knowing propositionally. In some way, never made clear, propositional knowing is logically prior to all other kinds of knowing. Philosophers, not surprisingly, have believed that for a long time.

There are many other examples of knowing that by the light of epistemologists are not "real" knowing, but it is difficult to take this seriously. Is, to return for a moment to our original example, knowing the ins and outs of the Gettier paradoxes real knowledge and more fundamental than knowing that you are loved? Is knowing your duty a matter of knowing that a certain proposition is true or is it being ready, at a moment's notice, to do your duty? The person who knows his or her duty in the second sense will act right and we can depend on that. There is no way of telling what the first person will do. I have known a number of persons who could discourse eloquently about their moral duty as the preliminary to doing something really immoral. Is the former more "fundamental" than the latter? Is knowing what this child needs less fundamental than knowing a generalization about the needs of children of a certain age group? We can think of many more examples of knowing that are neither obviously propositional nor require evidence above all but which are essential for our daily lives, for raising our children, and for surviving in a society increasingly dangerous to everyone. It is difficult to take the claim seriously that these are not examples of knowing at least as central and important as the propositional knowledge of the academic. The philosopher will respond to that by arguing in a particular case that either this kind of knowing is not fundamental or that it is fundamental but that it is "really" propositional. But those arguments have not actually been made in the detail required. The assumption that propositional knowing is fundamental is no more than that—an assumption.

The conception of knowledge as propositional leads us very easily into a set of normative judgments: Theoretical science is the highest kind of knowledge, and only those who have scientific knowledge are genuine knowers. As a result, knowledge that is not propositional is denigrated. We can all agree that knowing is preferable to not knowing and that, therefore, knowers are preferable to those who do not have knowledge. Who could argue with that? But if we add the assumption that all knowledge is propositional, then we are forced to conclude that those who have propositional and theoretical knowledge are to be preferred to those who have "competences" or are "acquainted" with other persons but are not real knowers. We move from the sensible assumption that it is good to know to the pernicious conclusion that only the beliefs of those with academic credentials deserve serious attention. The error between premise and conclusion enters with the assumption that knowing is separate.

But that view, once put into words, is not persuasive. What is more, its consequences are oppressive[3] to many different groups of people. The different examples I will discuss can be read in two ways. They are counterexamples to the claim that only propositional knowing is genuine knowledge. They also show the devastating consequences of the fact that propositional knowledge does carry special, and undeserved, prestige.

The assumption that scientific knowledge that can be put in words, and printed in a book or journal, is the only knowledge there is and thus all that researchers need to take into account in their studies has serious effects in policy-making.

> A case study of World Bank sponsored social forestry in Kolar district of Karnataka is an illustration of reductionism and maldevelopment in forestry extended to farmland. Decentered agroforestry, based on multiple species and private and common treestands has been India's age-old strategy for maintaining farm productivity in arid and semi-arid zones. The *honga,* tamarind, jackfruit and mango, the *jola, gobli, kagli* and bamboo traditionally provided food and fodder, fertilizer and pesticide, fuel and small timber. The backyard of each rural home was a nursery, and each peasant woman a silviculturalist. ... Plans were made in national and international capitals by people who could not know the purpose of the *honge* and the *neem,* and saw them as weeds. *The experts decided that indigenous knowledge was worthless and "unscientific"* and proceeded to destroy the diversity of indigenous species by replacing with row after row of eucalyptus seedlings. (Shiva, 1993:311; my italics)

Eucalyptus, it turned out, was ill adapted to the semiarid conditions. The replacement of indigenous trees by eucalyptus proved an ecological disaster. In addition, the farms that supported the population before were replaced by pulpwood farms that supported "brokers and middlemen" but not the indigenous population. The mistaken belief that only propositional knowledge is genuine knowing brought with it a total disregard for the knowledge of the people who had made their living in this particular area for a long time. They were ignored, and their way of life and livelihood was destroyed without providing for them a comparable replacement. The results were environmental degradation and great suffering for the people of the region. Comparable disregard of the experiential knowledge of women who had been injected with Depo-Provera, a contraceptive, for a long time ignored the serious side effects of that drug: "The complaints of women on the drug were not taken as side-effects of the drug but, rather, reinforced the stereotype of women as 'complaining' or 'overanxious' (Bunkle, 1993: 294).

Counting only propositional knowledge as knowledge leads to discounting the experiences of local farmers when it comes to setting agricultural policy or of women patients when drugs are being tested on them. More generally, it disconnects knowing from action because the propositional knower only needs to be able to talk and those whose knowledge takes the form of acting in the world, like my mechanic, often can say only so much about what they are doing.

If only propositional knowledge is knowledge, and theories thus become the paradigm of what knowledge is, the knowledge of, for example, African Americans who have always struggled, as have white women, lesbians, and homosexuals, is denied its value and importance. These are groups who have not been able to afford the luxury of purely theoretical knowledge, for what they needed was knowledge for survival. The exclusive valuation of propositional and theoretical knowledge has treated that knowledge for survival as worthless. That leads to the further conclusion that outside observers, if equipped with the proper research tools, are in a position to know the lives and problems of people quite different from themselves better than the members of those groups themselves. The experience and the hard-won skills at surviving of different groups count for nothing; textbook knowledge is everything.

At issue here is not only the question, for instance, whether whites can speak about the lives and experiences of persons of color (and vice versa) but who has *authoritative* knowledge. As long as propositional knowing is the paradigm, authority goes to the person who has the graduate training, the research protocols, the statistical tools, the grants, the computers, the assistants, and the credentials. Persons who lack all that, who have "only" firsthand experience of their lives, have nothing to contribute: "Given the politics of domination—race, sex and class exploitation—the tendency in this society is to place more value on what white people are writing about black people, or non-white people, rather than what we are writing about ourselves" (hooks, 1989:42ff.).[4]

The claim that only theoretical knowledge is real knowledge has led to the overvaluation of theoretical knowledge and of those who claim to possess that knowledge and a denigration of those who are actually able to fix cars—those who make things work. This has been a denigration of manual workers as compared to engineers, of people who make the decisions of their bosses work as against the bosses who decide, of women who raise children as against the psychologists studying child development, of classroom teachers as against the educational theorists, of farmers as against agronomists. The assumption that real knowledge is propositional is intimately connected with prevailing class and gender prejudice and supports existing maldistribution of power and wealth (Dalmiya and Alcoff, 1993).

The results of these assumptions about knowing have done massive damage to populations whose carefully constructed ways of life were carelessly destroyed by the "experts." These same assumptions have also sowed self-distrust and thus sapped the powers of resistance of those who could not claim "expert" status. People are told that others—psychologists, therapists, all kinds of experts—know more about their persons and their lives than they know themselves. But there are few injuries as serious as denying the capacity of ordinary persons to understand their lives. If I cannot understand what is happening to me, if I cannot be confident that I can draw reasonable lessons from my experience, if I need to wait for another to tell me what just happened and what I should do in response, then I am completely powerless. I become dependent on another's wisdom and insight to tell me who I am, what my life has been like, and how I should run it. Denying me the power of self-understanding is to deny me full human agency. That is one theme in Charlotte Perkins Gilman's *The Yellow Wallpaper* (1973). Insofar as the separate conception of knowing denies ordinary people the ability to understand their lives, it threatens to deprive them of their full humanity as responsible adults.

But it has also made it much easier for academics and other professional intellectuals to exclude the views of persons outside their group from the deliberation. White scholars have been able to indulge their most virulent prejudices against African Americans without any objection from those they applied their "science" to because those were already ruled out of bounds—with few exceptions—for not possessing the education needed to have propositional knowledge. And most of those who did manage to get an education and to become scholars could be ignored because their scholarship was in the service of their community and thus lacked what white scholarship called "objectivity." "The activities of nineteenth-century Black women intellectuals such as Anna J. Cooper, Francis Ellen Watkins Harper, Ida B. Wells and Mary Church Terrell exemplify this tradition of merging intellectual work and activism" (Collins, 1991:29). In similar ways W.E.B. DuBois (R. C. Williams, 1983), Eugene C. Holmes (McClendon, 1983), and William T. Fontaine (1983) were "activist-scholars." In matters of race, of justice and equality, those African-American scholars did not share the prejudices of the dominant white intellectuals and that made it permissible to ignore them.

These activist-scholars were scholars who were at least as good as their white colleagues but were also activists. It was not defective scholarship but racism that excluded African-American scholars from white scholarly company. But separateness made it easier to conceal that racism behind standards of "objectivity" and knowledge that made sense if one assumed that human beings are separate. In comparable ways separateness concealed gender prejudice behind demands for scholarly standards and objectivity. The demand that those few women or African Americans who managed to get an education be "impartial" or "objective" and that they study the world "from nowhere" served to mask the real reason for excluding them from access to white institutions and resources. That did irreparable damage to those excluded. But it also deprived white scholars of an essential corrective to their work, without which it could trumpet its scientific objectivity while being blatantly racist and sexist.

Objectivity demands, I said earlier, that one leave irrelevant value judgments aside. But one's value judgments are not always easily brought to light. We have just seen an example of that: The apparently descriptive claim that all knowledge is propositional defends itself against many counterexamples by taking refuge in a value judgment; namely, that only propositional knowledge is "real" knowledge. The entire apparently dispassionate conception of objectivity, separateness, and knowledge as propositional rests on the passionate belief that one's own intellectual practices and those of one's friends and colleagues are better than those, of, say, intellectuals of color or women scholars whose intellectual work proceeds from the premise that racism and sexism must be rooted out. That is not easy to see for those white male scholars who move in the intellectual world of separateness. But it is perfectly obvious to those intellectuals of color or those women scholars excluded from white male science. It is therefore also obvious to those same dissident scholars that the objectivity of white male science and scholarship is often extremely questionable. By silencing those critics, those same white male scholars made sure that inconvenient critics would not be heard and thus racist "objectivity" could prevail unchallenged.

SOCIAL KNOWLEDGE

Separate knowing is oppressive; it cannot avoid or correct gross lapses of objectivity; and it gives rise to the apparently insoluble problem of skepticism. It is this last problem that has moved many philosophers to give up the claim that we are separate as knowers. But as we saw in earlier chapters, one can reject separateness in quite different ways. One can claim that certain actions are collective actions, such as playing tennis, without denying that the players are quite separate agents. One can also be minimally in-relation, whether covertly or not makes little difference here, where there is an initial shared understanding about a joint project and then all go their separate ways. Or one can choose to be openly in-relation. Most of the philosophers who insist that knowing is not separate are only minimally in-relation. Their stance is no more objective or less oppressive than separate knowledge.

The futile search for "solutions" to the problem of skepticism has moved many philosophers to surrender the separate conception of knowing. We should substitute, they think, a view of science in which the knower is no longer a separate person but the scientific community as a whole is the subject of knowing (Nelson, 1993).

In the earlier discussion of conceptions of autonomy that do not assume that we are separate, I pointed out the ways in which philosophy is a collective project where members are minimally in-relation. To be a philosopher is to meet a series of unstated social criteria and to subscribe to mostly unstated and usually unargued-for standards that are the common property of the community of philosophical scholars. Philosophers are engaged in a project for which they have devised complex and very specific requirements. These requirements tend to change over time but are not often subjected to rational scrutiny. Philosophers of science who reject the conception of the separate knower make very similar points about science and its practitioners.

Quine attacks foundationalist epistemology by his claim that language and theories are wholes and that the meaning of particular words depends on their place in that whole. He complains that philosophers in the Cartesian tradition thought that we could compare sentences to reality one by one. Instead he thinks it is only entire theories or languages that are supported by observations as a whole. What decides a given scientific community in favor of one set of theories rather than another? Quine's answer is very much like that given by Kuhn.

Kuhn examines the ways in which scientists adopt new theories. He shows that in case after case, new theories are adopted before much of the evidence is in that will later support it. Often it made sense to collect the relevant evidence only after the new theory had already been adopted (Kuhn, 1977:323). It is adopted before being adequately supported by evidence. Many of the "crucial experiments" that we learn about in science class, he argues, are done long after the new theory ceased to be controversial. Their role is not to justify the adoption of the new theory (Kuhn, 1977:328).

Foundationalist philosophy of science, Kuhn points out, assumed that for any given scientific claim there is a unique collection of evidence that renders that claim more reliable than its competitors. But suppose, Kuhn says, that theory choice is not as definite. In many cases there are good reasons for adopting a certain theory, but there are also often quite good reasons for adopting a rival theory. Like Quine, Kuhn claims that often there is more than one theory that we have considerable reasons to adopt, and there is no decisive reason in favor of one rather than the other (Kuhn, 1977:329). Theory choice is indeterminate; there is "no fact in the matter."

Kuhn echoes Quine's conclusion that

> The hopelessness of grounding natural science upon immediate experience in a firmly logical way was acknowledged [by Carnap and others]. The Cartesian quest for certainty had been the remote motivation of epistemology, both on its conceptual and its doctrinal side; but that quest was seen as a lost cause. (Quine, 1969:74)

For the claims made by the Cartesians that they had found unshakable foundations of knowledge we substitute an appeal to our common language. The best we can do by way of providing foundations for our knowledge claims is to appeal to shared languages. Kuhn adds to that that scientists, in ordinary times, can appeal to shared paradigms, that is, to shared symbolic generalizations, models, and exemplars (Kuhn, 1977:297). Shared intellectual resources take the place of a benevolent God as guarantors of our knowledge.

Rorty begins an argument much like Quine's with an extended polemic against the traditional conceptions of mind as the private space in which we find ideas or meanings. "Justification [of scientific theories] is not a matter of a special relation between ideas (or words) and objects, but of conversation, of social practice"

(Rorty, 1979:170). "Nothing counts as justification unless by reference to what we already accept" (Rorty, 1979:178). Whatever justifications we provide for our beliefs, they are always partial. At a certain point, the search for foundations ends and we appeal simply to what we all believe, to the way all of us think or talk about something.

As long as we think of knowers as separate, each one must provide all the required support for any knowledge claim. Thus whatever supports a knowledge claim is, potentially, in the possession of and under the control of the separate knower. But the Quineans say: No, knowing is a social process; to be a knower is a social role. Now whether you are a knower does no longer depend exclusively on you and the evidence that you possess. Your knowledge claim must be accepted by others. They accept it in the light of the empirical evidence. But they also accept it insofar as it is couched in the language that is used for claims of this sort or insofar as it draws on theories that are thought to be the best science has to offer. Steve Fuller formulates this claim starkly: "My having knowledge may involve an interpreter crediting me with a certain range of possible utterances and actions ... the brain scientist would find my knowledge in the brains of those who credit me with knowledge" (Fuller, 1989:82). Is this social effort "collective" and minimally in-relation or is being-in-relation chosen openly?

The scientific effort must be minimally in-relation such that there are certain shared procedures, metaphors, and so on that function until they are called into question for some reason or another and are then examined carefully and either retained or rejected. The skeptic has nothing to say here because the Quineans do not claim that these methods are proven valid; nor do they deny that methods currently in use may be open to objection. Quineans do not, in other words, claim that a certain premise or procedure is true or correct simply because it is widely used. Their claim is much more modest: Certain premises and procedures are used because they have not been challenged. They are, of course, open to challenges but those must be motivated. The blanket challenges that are the staple of skeptical arguments are not acceptable.

Here knowers are, at least, minimally in-relation. But with that view separateness is not completely abandoned. Knowers are no longer separate with respect to each other. There is a modicum of being-in-relation at least with respect to the basic presuppositions of their shared enterprise. Researchers do cite each others' results and depend on the other to have done good work (Lehrer, 1977; Trout, 1992). In theory scientific results are replicable and one tests them by, in fact, trying to replicate them. But not everyone does everyone else's experiments over. Science is done in a community of credentialed workers who have established their reliability by means of earning credentials, publishing, working in prestigious institutions, and so on. One can freely borrow the results of those other workers. What is more, many scientific results are produced even though each worker does not really understand fully what the other is doing. Each separate researcher knows only a piece of the whole, and the final result is not known by any separate researcher (Hardwig, 1985; Latour and Woolgar, 1979:54–55, 140). But at the same time, researchers are fiercely competitive with each other and, like Mr. Ramsay, imagine themselves riding with the Light Brigade. Napoleon's campaigns were the inspiration for one researcher quoted by Latour and Woolgar (1979:130). The imagery is martial: A researcher in neuroendocrinology, cited by Latour and Woolgar, described his scientific work as like "fighting Hitler. You have to cut him [namely, the scientific problem] down. It's no choice" (Latour and Woolgar, 1979: 118). About himself he wrote, "Guillemin and I fought our way to the top" in the field of neuroendocrinology (Latour and Woolgar, 1979:119). In quote after quote it is clear that the different researchers are fiercely competing with one another.[5]

But with all this surrender of separateness between knowers, knowledge itself remains propositional, and the relation of knowers to what is known is as separate as ever. As a result, the old exclusions can remain in force: Knowledge is still the privileged domain of people with academic credentials and therefore so is a great deal of economic and political power (Nelson, 1990:277). Although the scientific *community* now plays a role in epistemology, its membership remains as restricted as it always has been. Thus Quine insists that there is a continuity between science and common sense. That suggests that there is only one kind of common sense. We can guess whose common sense that is. We can be sure that it is not the common sense of feminists, African-American men, or other "nonstandard" thinkers. Similarly, Rorty recommends to us a general "conversation" in which we all participate. But it is quite clear that this "we" is a collection of intellectuals, professors, and white middle-class males for the most part (Comay, 1987). When new groups are allowed into the privileged halls of the academy they are easily tempted and molded into maintaining traditional exclusions.

Most surprisingly these sorts of exclusions are replicated among feminist theorists. White middle-class women had some difficulty seeing the narrowness of their own perspective (Spelman, 1988). The development of feminist theory has been disturbed by the class and racial prejudices of some women against others. (Lâm, 1994).[6] That case is enormously instructive: It is tempting, even to those who want to be more inclusive, to extend being-in-relation only to those closest to oneself (Tronto, 1987). Here the criticism often raised against making "caring" or "mothering" or even "friendship" the paradigm of ethical discourse comes into its own: What we expect of ourselves as moral agents is that we deal fairly and humanely even with people who are not friends, who are very different, and even whom we dislike. Caring, mothering, and friendship are too limited to serve as models of all ethical relationships.[7] The same reasons serve to raise doubts about knowing that is shared only with friends or those who are like us. There is an easy way of being-in-relation that extends only to friends and lovers. I have tried to show that that is too narrow a conception. We can also be in-relation with enemies, with those with whom we struggle. But for the sake of knowing, we must insist that everyone possible be included into our researches. The time is past when credentialed men can decide what women are like, and what they want, without consulting women actively or when whites can claim to understand the problems of persons of color, and come up with solutions, without giving the persons studied a central role in the study. (That is not to say that that is not going on all the time—witness the talk about "family values.") In our knowing we need to be in-relation not merely haphazardly but systematically, with those closest to us and particularly with those who are distant. If knowing is to be in-relation our exclusions must be extensively and scrupulously justified. That is a very difficult demand, but it is unavoidable.

KNOWING IN-RELATION

Separate knowing fails in objectivity and is oppressive to all those who do not have the narrow range of skills of middle-class intellectuals. Openly in-relation knowing aims to do justice to the knowledge of everyone. Everyone's perspective deserves a hearing. Everyone must be heard when articulations of their experience are under scrutiny. Openly in-relation knowing aims at a much more democratic epistemology (Alcoff, 1993).

bell hooks has observed that as a black woman intellectual, she is bilingual. She speaks the language of the working-class blacks who gave birth to and raised her and among whom she grew up. She also speaks the rather different language of middle-class intellectuals, most of whom are white and many of whom know the working class only as employees (hooks, 1989:78). These differences in language are very real. When an alternative epistemology commits itself to a more democratic process of coming to know the world, it is not aiming at democracy with formal equality, that is, a kind of democracy that overlooks the real differences between citizens. On the contrary, openly in-relation knowing is knowing across differences, such as differences in language. That requires, as hooks points out, the willingness to be bilingual and to the extent that that is not completely possible to make major efforts in that direction. Taking the other and the other's experience seriously also means taking seriously the way the other talks. Different persons talk very differently, not only in their vocabulary and syntax but in that they tell stories in different ways. They have a very different sense of what should follow what and of what is relevant to what. Some stories go right to the heart of the matter; others gingerly circle around and around. Where some people want elaborate detail, others are silent. What some describe cursorily, others relate in minute detail. Some people are in a hurry when they talk: They say it all quickly and then they are done. Others are slow in their speech and in their telling of stories (Riessman, 1987).

The difficulties of this inclusive inquiry must not be underestimated: How can I take others seriously if I do not understand them? We need to find ways of taking everyone's experience as seriously as possible and yet be able to say that the lessons some draw from their experiences are not as important or worth remembering as the lessons drawn by others. But we need to be able to respect the other's world and life and person and thus the very different way in which he or she talks to another and yet to be able to say: But what you say here appears to me not to be right—it is one-sided, deceived or self-deceived, or just not as clear as it might be.

There are other difficulties: There surely are people who are sufficiently irrational, ignorant, and frivolous that it would be wasting time and energy to try to talk to them at length and make the effort to understand them. Must we really argue with advocates of the flat earth theory or with creationists? The objection is important only to remind us that we cannot confidently say that this alternative way of knowing will not allow us to exclude anyone from conversations. We could not possibly commit ourselves to that standard—at least not in the world as we know it. At the same time, we can commit ourselves to being extremely reluctant to exclude anyone. It remains for future work to develop detailed standards for exclusion, but in the preceding we have encountered some of the general concepts that would serve to formulate those standards.

The concept of reciprocity discussed earlier will be important here. We cannot exclude anyone from conversations as long as they are trying to participate in a reciprocal conversation. The concept of reciprocity is itself not easily articulated. But we saw in Chapter 4 that it is essential to the requisite sort of reciprocity that both partners choose to be openly in-relation, that each is fully aware that what his or her conversation yields is a joint product. In the same spirit, all participants in a conversation must not only be willing to change but they must also be willing to acknowledge that they will change in-relation to the others.

Examples of this democratic inquiry can be found in feminist research projects. Separateness demands that the researchers draw clear boundaries between themselves and the people they interview. Ann Oakley quotes from a textbook about social science research:

> Regarded as an information gathering tool, the interview is designed to minimise the local, concrete, immediate circumstances of the particular encounter—including the respective personalities of the participants—and to emphasise only those aspects that can be kept general enough and demonstrable enough to be counted. (Oakley, 1981: 309)

It is the interviewer's separate and solitary responsibility to see to it that the interview produce objective results that are useful for social science research ("can be counted"), and hence the interviewers must distance themselves from the persons interviewed and treat them as interchangeable objects of study rather than as this or that specific person. The research is not a joint project between scholar and the persons interviewed—it can be that, as we shall see below—but, on the contrary, objectivity demands that interviewers keep their distance and make sure that the persons interviewed keep theirs. What they think about the project, its premises, and its possible usefulness thus cannot come into the open, and if this is allowed to slip out, the questioning cannot count as legitimate for the researchers. Thus separate isolation from often essential critical views is once more maintained.

Not so in feminist research projects. Here an effort is made to have the person(s) studied participate as fully as possible in the project. The goal is to reduce the differences between the researchers and their "subjects" as much as possible. The first step in that is to formulate questions that are important to the persons studied so that they can see that answers to these questions may be of real use to them and their community (Collins, 1991:29). One does not approach a community with questions and hypotheses firmly in hand but consults the persons whom one will study in the process of formulating one's questions, just as one will later consult them when the data are to be analyzed. That would tend to assure, also, that the people studied will work along more eagerly and will be more forthcoming with answers researchers raise. When observations are made, preference is given to observing people in their everyday interactions and everyday settings rather than having them respond exclusively to questions formulated by the researchers or on the researcher's terrain (Reinharz, 1983). In interviewing persons one does not treat them as passive but develops genuine human relationships with them, of the sort possible under the circumstances (Billson, 1991).

The women whom Ann Oakley interviewed about the changes motherhood brought overwhelmingly thought that being interviewed in a nonhierarchical style enabled them to "reflect on their experiences more than they had otherwise done" (Oakley, 1981:50). The interviewer gained much more extensive and reliable information because she followed the maxim of "no intimacy without reciprocity" (Oakley, 1981:49). This may mean, in some cases, understanding why subjects do not tell the truth and respecting their reticence as a legitimate defense on the part of persons who have found survival difficult (Duelli-Klein, 1983:95).

If inquiry is to be democratic, seeking knowledge must be a conversation across differences. But that is not sufficient. These differences are liable to be very difficult and very emotional. They are conversations in which each side may well make claims that the other barely understands and at first has no way of evaluating. Trust is therefore of the essence. The participants in such a conversation must have found ways of establishing that the other is to be trusted, that his or her stories are believable, and that each participant is an "epistemically responsible" participant.[8]

One aspect of being epistemically responsible is that one stands one's ground and reacts critically to the stories and insights of the other. Talking across differences requires that one give an account of one's view of the world as strongly and elaborately as one can, and that involves that one be as honest and articulate about one's doubts about the other's stories and insights. Being at the same time respectful and sympathetic of the other's views is very different from caving in to the other's criticisms too readily, being unwilling to brave the strong winds of conflict that are inevitable in the conversations across differences. One wins the trust of the other by being critical in this way. I cannot trust a conversational partner who has no stand of his or her own, who agrees too readily because conflict is frightening.[9] But what is the line between just knuckling under and really critically examining and accepting the point of view of the other?

In this process of joint inquiry, each learns. But learning takes many different forms. In traditional epistemology with its propositional conception of knowledge, acquiring new propositions together with the evidence for them is what learning consists of. In learning, one changes by getting to know propositions that were previously unknown or not understood or for which one did not possess the requisite evidence. Clearly in knowing in-relation the knowers are more intimately connected, and the changes that are evidence of learning must be more fundamental. Each changes in ways more significant than merely acquiring new propositions. Persons change in learning not only by acquiring new truths but by becoming different persons in other ways.

Much more work on the changes in persons that are involved in learning is needed, but some really interesting suggestions are available: One learns, as a white, about one's own racism by changing, that is, by learning to act differently (Babbit, 1993). One's sense of oneself changes not only in that one talks differently about oneself but also in that one learns to stand differently in the world. One learns to hear what before one did not hear, including what one sounds like to others when one means well but is, in fact, very hurtful. One learns to distance oneself from one's own traditions so that one can perceive the traditions of others as rich and powerful in their own right.

Feminist epistemologists have insisted that women's consciousness-raising sessions should be taken as paradigms of inquiry. One of the reasons for this recommendation is that in those sessions persons changed, and the relevant changes were not merely intellectual but also in women learning to act in new ways. They learned to do what before they had found very difficult—too difficult to do it well. Thus one kind of personal transformation one would cite as evidence for learning is the acquisition of new ways of acting and of new skills without necessarily being able to talk very differently about oneself or about the world. That may come later, but it need not. Thus one example cited repeatedly is of women who learn to accept their own anger at sexist oppression and the particular persons who have been oppressing them. Learning to accept one's anger is learning to express that anger without being reduced to tears, without overwhelming guilt, and without knuckling under and apologizing if that anger provokes anger in return (Scheman, 1980; Bernick, 1991).

I have repeatedly said in the preceding chapters that "really listening to others" is an important element in being in-relation. Although that is true it raises more questions than it answers. There is a lot of oppression that masquerades as "really listening." It is not enough to look into the other's eyes or say "I understand." What is needed is a willingness to change, to acquire new skills such as the ones mentioned. Taking the other seriously involves, among other things, the willingness to allow the relationship to the other person to make one into a different person.

This is, without doubt, a difficult task. The prospect of changing in response to the other's view of oneself comes uncomfortably close to invalidation by the other. Once I open myself to the perspective of the other I begin to see how, as a man, I have traded on my male privilege, how as a white person I have perpetuated the very racism I abhor. Those are painful realizations, and there is no point in deceiving oneself about how difficult it is to assimilate them. But here we return to the concept of autonomy in-relation discussed above. To be autonomous in-relation is to be able to assimilate such changes because one's self is to a significant extent defined by one's relationships. As someone who attempts to move away from the prevailing racist and sexist practices of our society, I am affirmed by my partners in those efforts. And my failures, as pointed out to me by them, are as much part of my relationships and who I am as my successes. Autonomy in-relation is eagerness to learn to change and being sufficiently resilient to do so even if, at the moment, the requisite insights are painful.

DIFFERENT KINDS OF KNOWLEDGE

But is it not downright silly to think that knowledge emerges only from openly in-relation conversations? To gain new knowledge, I do not always need to change. Learning Latin does not empower; neither does research in particle physics. The description of inquiry offered in the preceding section may be appropriate in some areas of our lives, but by and large knowledge is arrived at in much less emotional or convoluted ways. How do you know your friend's telephone number? You look it up. How do you know the property line of your garden? You get it surveyed or look it up on a map at the Registry of Deeds. Most of what we know are matters of ordinary information gathered in ordinary and familiar ways. It may be true that some knowledge is not best thought of as propositional, but surely a good deal of what we know is just that. We know that it is Wednesday, that water freezes at thirty-two degrees Fahrenheit, or that the square of the hypotenuse in a right-angled triangle is equal to the sum of the squares of the other two sides. The traditional reply to this sort of observation is that *all* knowledge is propositional. We have seen ample reason in the preceding chapter for rejecting that idea. We are therefore also committed to claiming that physics could not possibly be the paradigm of all knowing.

There are different directions one can go after that. One can assert that a different sort of knowledge, namely knowledge of persons, should be regarded as paradigmatic of knowledge (Code, 1993:32). But what shall we then say of physics? Is it knowledge at all, or knowledge of a lesser sort, in the way in which today knowing about persons is regarded as a lesser sort of knowledge because it tends not to be quantitative? One proposal is simply to reverse priorities: Whereas currently the "hard" sciences are regarded as paradigms of knowledge and knowledge of person is thought of only as knowledge in a lesser sense, the proposal is now to regard knowledge of persons as paradigmatic and the natural sciences only as knowledge in an inferior sense. A more conciliatory stance revives the old distinction between *Naturwissenschaften* and *Geisteswissenschaften,* sometimes also put as the difference between science and hermeneutics, which assigns separate domains to each and refuses to make one of them the paradigm of knowledge.

These distinctions are, however, misleading insofar as they suggest that different kinds of knowing can be distinguished by their subject matter: Here knowledge of material objects, there knowledge of persons. That does not do justice to the central insight in the polemic against propositional knowledge, namely, that it obscures the kind of knowing that requires a particular kind of *relationship between persons.* Knowing in-relation is not just a relation to a quasi-substantive entity we call "knowledge" but is to be in-relation to other persons. I have, to be sure, many relations to propositions. I have facts and figures, say, about the incidence of poverty in our society, about the distribution of poverty between city and countryside and among different ethnic, racial, and gender groups, and so on. I may even have more sophisticated information about the sorts of places poor people often live in, about their consumption of food and other goods, as well as about their medical and other services. But having all that information does not amount to *knowing* what poverty is, what it means to be poor, how one tends to think about oneself and one's problems when one is poor. To know about poverty I must be poor or know poor people; I must know what their lives are like, what they think about their lives, and what they think about me, who is not poor. Such knowledge comes from the sort of being-in-relation I have been discussing.

Once we distinguish knowing propositions from knowing in-relation, there is still the question of which is better knowledge. The tradition has been to say that knowing propositions is the only "real" kind of knowledge. We have seen good reasons for rejecting that normative claim. Shall we refuse to express preferences? That seems tempting since, having turned our backs on the quite groundless claim that knowing propositions is the best kind of knowledge, we do not want to make an equally groundless claim for the superiority of knowing in-relation. There seems no conceivable argument for saying that a certain kind of knowing is *the* all-time best kind of knowing. The absurdity of such a claim must be obvious once we ask ourselves how one could possibly justify it.

But more modest claims are defensible. In our world, professional intellectuals ride high, but in spite (if not because) of that, the number of unsolved practical problems increases every day. It is therefore plausible to say that we need more knowledge in-relation—knowledge of how to tend to the matters at hand, which arises from hardworking relationships between different sorts of persons—and less propositional knowledge.

Knowing in-relation denies that knowledge is propositional in the ways sketched out. Knowing involves change of the participants, learning to be new persons. A conversation across differences is likely to yield real advancement if the participants gain in power as a result of the conversation. They gain in power if they learn to respond more adequately to others, if they learn to complain loudly and effectively about injustices done to them, and if they learn to hear the complaints of others as said and not as translated and misinterpreted in the prevailing language of the powerful. Such change is centrally one of empowerment.

Empowerment has unfortunately become a cliché of those in power to reassure the powerless. It needs extensive rethinking. I will reexamine power and empowerment in the next chapter.

◀ 8 ▶

Power and Empowerment

AT THE END OF THE previous chapter we saw that openly chosen knowing in-relation transforms knowers, specifically by empowering them. But what does "empowerment" consist of? As we shall see in the early sections of this chapter, power is usually conceived with the assumption of human separateness in the background. Power, in that separate sense, is always power-over, that is, power to coerce, compel, determine, or materially affect the actions and choices of another in ways the other would not have freely chosen. The increase in power—empowerment—that knowing in-relation promises is of a very different kind. Before we can understand it, we need to develop an alternative understanding of the notion of power. I will take only a few first, tentative steps toward an elucidation of empowerment. A more complete account will have to wait for the work of other theorists and for changes in the social world that will make empowerment a more familiar and therefore more easily understood phenomenon.

The question of power has been in the background throughout this entire book. The search for a social order less coercive and destructive of human lives than ours is the context for the detailed discussions of separateness and being-in-relation. Central to such a search are reflections about power.

The mainstream view is that all power is power-over, or power to dominate. If that is true, then the search for liberation, for a society in which all can freely seek to be the best and most accomplished persons they are capable of being, is the search for a society in which differences in power-over, in the capacity to coerce or compel others, are not being used unjustly. This is the position of mainstream liberal theorists: They conceive their task as finding a social order in which people will not use their power over others unjustly. But radicals have always been suspicious of the hope that power to coerce and compel, if used justly, will produce a free society, that is, a society without coercion and compulsion. Instead they have looked, however hesitantly, for a society without power-over, or at least one where the differences in power-over were much reduced. Hence anarchists wanted to abolish the state, and Marx hoped and worked for a society without economic class distinctions. But those prescriptions for liberation were so global that they ended up being no more persuasive than the liberal project of sanitizing power-over, or domination, and making it into a tool of liberty.

The suggestion that we distinguish separateness from being-in-relation constitutes progress over the idea of a society without state or without classes, for it enables us to look for a kind of power that enhances persons but does not coerce. We can, then, tell a more concrete story about societies not based on coercion, where differences in power-over are set aside in favor of empowerment that springs from being-in-relation.

The concept of power was also implicit in the earlier discussions of specific manifestations of separateness and being-in-relation. The separate conception of autonomy stresses the importance of being independent. One can rephrase this: Separate autonomy consists of not being in the power of another who could then impose choices or sets of options on us or actually make decisions for us. I gave a series of reasons for rejecting that conception of autonomy and recommended instead a conception of autonomy in-relation, in which one's identity depended on being a respected and active member of a variety of groups. But suppose that it turned out that all power is separate power, that there is only power-over. In that case, our relations to others, however deeply committed to joint decision and joint action, to careful attention to the other, to empathy and caring in-relation, and to knowing that is in-relation, are forever threatened by the difference in power between the members of a group. The threat of being overpowered by another would always be there. In that case, it would be unreasonable to surrender separate autonomy with its attention to insulating oneself against coercive moves by others. The recommendation that we seek to be autonomous in-relation presupposed that there is a different kind of power that does not dominate, coerce, or compel but instead empowers.

In similar ways the conception of empowerment was in the background of the discussions of love, empathy, and caring. In all three concepts, the assumption was that being-in-relation is not always under the gun of separate power, that one's willingness to open oneself to the other is not always threatened with exploitation by others who single-mindedly pursue power to dominate. But in addition, when it came to discussing love, we were reminded that there is an ancient tradition of liberatory thought that recommends neighbor love as the cure for a world of violence and injustice. Such neighbor love is easier to understand if we understand the difference between separate power and power in-relation, or empowerment.

The power that oppresses is, as we shall see in this chapter, power that is covertly in-relation. This will emerge from a discussion of prevailing theories of power—theories that are shaped by the unquestioning assumption of separateness. These theories leave open important questions about power and are none of them satisfactory. Each is incomplete. As long as we maintain that persons are separate, a complete conception of power is not available. But these defects merely reflect our vacillating practices with respect to power—we are here once again covertly in-relation and thus alternately act as if we were completely separate and, then again, as if we were in-relation.

The alternative is power in-relation, or empowerment. Often this is not chosen explicitly and we are in empowering relationships with some, only to be able to be more destructive to others. I will end this chapter with a tentative explanation of what empowerment is and how we might go about choosing to empower one another, without excluding anyone.

TRADITIONAL CONCEPTIONS OF POWER

Ever since Voltaire, it has been thought that "power consists in making others act as I choose" (Arendt, 1970:36). Modern theorists echo that understanding, notably Robert Dahl: "A has power-over B to the extent that he can get B to do something that B would not otherwise do" (1957:203). This conception of power makes a number of assertions: Power is a form of causality that directly affects the behavior of another. Persons have power insofar as they directly affect the behavior of others. Power is power-over other persons. Such power is exercised only when the other would rather have done something else: Power comes into play where there is conflict (Lukes, 1974:14). The concept of power is, therefore, closely allied to notions such as force, coercion, and manipulation (Wrong, 1979). Such power is, finally, thought to be the possession of individual persons.

Dahl's conception of power is very persuasive. Arendt cites a number of classical texts that all put forward very similar formulations—namely, of power as the ability to make another do what I want: "To command and to be obeyed: without that there is no power. ..." Thus de Jouvenel and similar views may be found in the work of Mill, Weber, Clausewitz, and others (Arendt, 1970: 36–37). Contemporary authors continue to echo this conception of power (Elster, 1985a:125; Goldman, 1972:223; Martin, 1977)

POWER AND SEPARATENESS

The source of this conception of power is the assumption that persons are separate. Power in its most general sense refers to persons' ability to do what they want, to meet their needs, to achieve their goals. In a society in which humans act separate and think of themselves as separate, the central use of power is bound to be domination (Young, 1990:31). I shall argue below that separate power is a pretense, as are other forms of separateness. However, they are not, as noted much earlier, mere pretense but acquire a certain, if tenuous, reality of their own. To the extent that we consistently act separate, our power is, equally consistently, power-over.

If we are separate from one another, then so is not only our power but also our goals, needs, desires, and beliefs. Often the goals of two or more persons coincide. Often they have the same desires and each can meet those only if the desires of others are met also. It is very difficult, for instance, to provide sanitation and public safety for individuals without also providing these for a number of other persons. But it is at the same time easier to provide these goods for some citizens but not for all. It is, moreover, very difficult to provide them for some citizens without harming someone else: The public water supply is built across the land of some citizens. The police who protect some citizens terrorize others. The separate goals and needs of separate citizens are constant sources of conflict. Where conflict arises, compromises are often possible, but if you have more power than others the temptation is great to forge a compromise that favors you and does little for the other parties to a dispute. Separateness breeds a society of citizens who are always potentially in conflict. Power among such separate citizens is always on the verge of becoming coercive.

Separate persons, as we saw in Chapter 2, regard decisions as separate acts. As separate persons, we treasure our autonomy, which means that we are reluctant to allow another to make a decision for us. The skills, capacities, and resources of another—power in the broadest sense—are always a threat to my power as long as I insist on my separateness. For whatever I do, you may have skills that might help me do something better that I do now only with difficulty or do badly. Your powers present me here with a choice between compromising my independence and doing better or more easily what I can barely do alone. But as a separate person my independence is of central importance; give that up and I give up my identity as a separate person. Hence the other's powers and skills present me with unwelcome choices. They threaten my autonomy.

Your powers are a threat to me in another way. If your philosophical insights are deeper than mine, they make mine look humdrum and commonplace. Your skills at the stove overshadow my cooking, which, by comparison, lacks subtlety and panache. Your powers are a threat to my autonomy, but they also threaten my merit and accomplishments. The powers of others are first of all threats to mine. They threaten to diminish or devalue my powers.

Power in its more general sense refers to my capacities to do whatever I am able to do. But in a world where we act separate and where, therefore, autonomy is the ideal, your powers in this more general sense, that is, your abilities and capacities, threaten my autonomy and my accomplishments. Attention is thus constantly drawn to the threat your powers are to me. Your powers elicit my impulse to resist, to overpower you, or to flee. They prompt me to try to stop you from being a threat to my independence or to diminish my achievements. As a separate person my relations to others are therefore fundamentally conflictual. The ability to resist, or to coerce another, thus becomes the primary meaning of power, because all our powers, in all their different senses, provoke conflicts from which we must first extricate ourselves honorably before we can be powerful in any other ways.

PROBLEMS WITH THE PREVAILING CONCEPTION OF POWER

As we consider power in more detail we see that the separate conception of power is inadequate. A number of theorists have pointed to the severe shortcomings of the traditional conception of power as the power that one person exercises over the behavior of others. Once again, separateness turns out to be a very dubious assumption; once again it is unmasked as pretense.

The most obvious objection is, however, rarely if ever made. The conception of power as the ability to coerce another unduly and quite unjustifiably restricts the notion of power. In its most general sense, "power" refers to the ability to achieve an end. It is, as Hobbes said, the present means to "obtain some future apparent good" (Hobbes, n.d.:56). Power in that sense may belong to individuals or groups; it may be at work in conflictual situations; it may require overt action; or it may manifest itself in the willing cooperation of a group with its leaders. Power may grow out of the barrel of a gun or out of the smooth working together of the members of a group. Power may be used to dominate, but it may also serve to educate and to heal. Power destroys and power creates; it brings into being and maintains what exists already. Power may be power over, power to, power with, and just plain power (Emmett, 1953). "Power" is a very general term. It refers to one's ability to do something—to capacities, skills, ability, the options conferred by resources one disposes over, and strength of body, personality, and moral rectitude. Power over others—power to determine the actions of others regardless of what they might choose for themselves—is only one sense of power. Power-over, in fact, seems just one *use* of power. I can use my bodily strength, for instance, to coerce others. But I can also use it to carry a child across a swollen river. The unquestioning assumption that all power is power-over is wide of the mark. (The distinction between power and power-over will prove important in the discussion of the relation between empowerment and power-over.)

Power can also be used to affect another person's decisions indirectly by structuring the other's alternatives in such a way that certain decisions never come up for consideration and other decisions must be made. Luhmann cites an interesting example of that: A woman is planning to go to school. That is a simple desire that she is about to realize when a military induction notice arrives. Suddenly the straight course toward an education is complicated. New possibilities open up: complying with the military order, leaving the country, seeking a deferment, making an appeal, or resisting the order in other ways. The power of the military here has structured the situation and opened up a series of new possible courses of action. It has not decided for the student what course to take, but it has determined what the options are and, to a considerable extent, how to think about them (Luhmann, 1975:34).[1]

Other authors have pointed out that power is not owned by individuals but is rather a collective product. Normally power wielded by specific persons presupposes complex networks of cooperative and supportive activities and attitudes. The judge, as Wartenberg points out, can do his or her job only because there is an army of other functionaries—police, bailiffs, prosecutors, defenders, prison wardens and guards, record-keepers, and cleaners—who are essential parts of a complex web of actors. Without them the judge would be powerless. Once removed from this web of roles and actors, the judge has no power (Wartenberg, 1990:chapter 7).[2]

Parsons distinguishes between coercive and consensual power and insists that a well-functioning society must have both kinds. Power as commonly conceived, power-over, or power to dominate, is "coercive power." Consensual power consists of an "'acceptance' on the part of its members of their belonging together, in the sense of sharing, over a certain range, common interests" (Parsons, 1963:245).

The power of individuals or organizations needs legitimacy. That legitimacy is given to those in power by the groups that are governed. But the power that legitimates is not conflictual. The power manifest in the support a people gives to its leaders springs from harmonious social and political relations. Legitimacy consists precisely in the fact that there are only low levels of conflict between the governors and the governed. The people at large have the power to give or withhold legitimacy. But that is not a power evinced in conflict but rather in conditions of harmony. It consists of certain ways in which a group functions (Partridge, 1963).

Boulding observes that even armies, often cited as the most obvious example of organizations held together by the exercise of power-over, require good morale, camaraderie, and a wide range of symbolism to legitimate leadership. Medals, uniforms, and a complex set of rituals create an esprit de corps without which the power-over of superiors would be ineffective. The soldiers in a particular army are powerful as a result of the emotional and ideological ties between them of which uniforms and rituals are material manifestations (Boulding, 1989). This is not power presupposing conflict between the members of the military hierarchy but power that arises out of shared beliefs, team spirit, and pride in the organization.

This power does not belong to the soldiers separately, but to all of them together as soldiers in this particular army. Power often belongs to groups; it is not true that power always belongs (only or at all) to individuals. Once we think about that, it seems obvious: Nations are powerful, as are families or corporations. Thus power cannot be considered to be the sort of thing that only individuals possess. The legitimating power of communities and the morale of military, commercial, and athletic organizations are forms of being-in-relation. The members of a political community must have a shared understanding of what they are about, what the role of government ought to be, and whether their government accomplishes what is expected of it. Such a political community also needs to have shared conceptions of their accomplishments, of national pride, of their role in the larger world. These are conceptions that are not just held unconsciously but are also actively celebrated in political rhetoric, discussed in the media, and passed on to children in the schools. The power that legitimates, as well as the power that springs from morale, is not separate power.

AN ALTERNATIVE THEORY OF POWER

Power that legitimates—that makes societies flourish and organizations effective—has no clear individual owners. Neither does the power of groups to oppress other groups lodge in individual owners. There is not one person, or even an unmistakably identifiable group of persons, who imposes and maintains stereotypes, controls agendas, legitimates rulers, or shapes desires. Rather it is the complex network of assumptions and practices that shape our daily lives—assumptions about social roles, rights and duties, and so on—that constitute a power that rules over us and makes us be the sort of person we are (Cocks, 1989). Power, therefore, is not properly conceived as something belonging to individuals but is more correctly described as a "structure" (Isaac, 1987).

To do justice to that insight, several thinkers have proposed that we think of power not as the actions or properties of individual persons, or even of groups of persons, but as something that is not, properly speaking, possessed at all. It is, in Luhmann's words, "a medium of communication," analogous to a language. The central thought is this: Except in cases of using physical force to make someone do something, all power works through the understanding and the choices of the persons affected. The prospective student, who suddenly finds her range of alternatives unpleasantly extended by receiving a draft notice, is confronted with new and unwanted choices. If she chooses to heed the draft call, she makes a choice to join the military; she is not bodily abducted and awakens to find herself in uniform. The exercise of power results in choices that are not free but compelled. The person compelled needs to understand the situation, the threats made, what her options are, the costs and benefits of those options, and the likely consequences of different possible courses of action. Power is effective because it is communicated to others. The dominated are told, This is what you must do. They are told that in words and in symbols, such as the policeman's badge and revolver and the physical arrangement of the courtroom (Foucault, 1980). Power to dominate is therefore not something individual persons possess but is inherent in power as a communicative medium (Luhmann, 1975) or in a kind of shared social knowledge (Barnes, 1988). Such power is not exercised by individuals but is pervasive; it is a "regime without a master" (Cocks, 1989:186).

These are important suggestions. They seem very right. Power works, by and large, not through mere physical force but through the medium of human understanding, knowledge, and calculation. It is not the power of the individual judge that puts you behind bars but the complex set or roles, beliefs, and practices that makes it possible for one person saying "five years" to have the effect of putting you in prison for a long time. There are many acts of domination that cannot be understood as acts of one person coercing another. If a white man attacks a black man, or any man attacks any woman, those are not acts of domination between two individuals but are acts of domination between groups of persons, white over black, men over women. The outcome of such aggressions is determined by the fact that the aggressor is white or is a male. It is the aggressor's group membership that is decisive in this conflict. The power of white over black, of men over women, is a social fact. The conception of power as a quasi-language can make those sorts of observations more intelligible. The words we use to describe persons, such as "black" and "white," and the actions appropriate to persons so described are parts of that quasi-language of power. They convey and continue existing social practices and valuations. This particular man who dominates this particular woman is not exercising power that is his personal property. He is no more than the bearer of a role assigned to him by the language of power.

Thus the constraint that power exercises over individual lives becomes more intelligible. One of the objections, raised earlier, against the understanding of power as the action of one person or group against another person or group was precisely that power configured the spaces in which individuals or groups choose to comply or resist the commands of the powerful. Power thus does not merely command but also predetermines the setting in which commands are issued and obeyed. If we understand power as a quasi-language we come closer to understanding that form of power as domination: Power, as communicative medium, assigns places to us in the social world. It defines and assigns roles—what it means to be a woman or a man and who will fill each kind of role. Power shapes us very intimately: It forms our desires and constructs us as sexual beings of very particular sorts. It imbues stereotypical men with a fear of homosexuality that borders on hysteria; it leads them to identify sexuality with performance and domination. Power can do that if it is a quasi-language. It could not do it if power were only what enables a particular person to bring another to heel.

It is important to appreciate what an attractive view this is. For if there were particular individuals or groups that dominated us, we would have to be able to identify them. We would be able to name names and identify the actions by which the persons named perpetuated patriarchy on particular days and in particular places. But, the defenders of this view argue, we are not really able to make those sorts of identifications. Some people blame men for the domination of women, but such accusations are vague gesturings instead of carefully argued indictments of particular groups. Such gesturings have considerable rhetorical force and pedagogic value. But the power of the patriarchy remains diffuse and poorly understood. Are all men patriarchs or only some? Are they all equally involved in perpetuating patriarchal institutions or are some more guilty than others? Do men who perpetuate patriarchy do so all the time, or do they do it in some ways but not in others? Do some men fight patriarchy in some of their acts and further it in others? None of these questions have ready and easy answers. The patriarchy appears as an impersonal power in the same sense in which money as an institution is an impersonal power before anyone acquires it and in the same way that a language, like English, does not belong to anyone even though all speakers of English use it, though sometimes in very idiosyncratic ways.

POWER IS NOT A COMMUNICATIVE MEDIUM

But in spite of all that, one is left with an uncomfortable feeling about this view of power as a quasi-language rather than the capacity of particular persons to domi-

nate others. Part of that discomfort may be caused by a lack of clarity: The relations and exchanges in a society are immensely complex, and the theory of power
as a medium of communication does not, so far, match actual power relations in
complexity. (One is left with the suspicion, for instance, that the distinction between a language, its users, and its specific uses is blurred in this theory of power
as a medium of communication.)

But there is also a more serious problem: The theory of power as a medium of
communication is at pains to explain the nature of power, more specifically of
power that dominates. Power, like language or communicative media, the theory
asserts, is not individually owned. It follows that power-over, power that dominates, is not someone's—it is not the power of a person or a group. That is precisely what the theorists under discussion want to tell us. Foucault tells us that
"power is no longer substantially identified with an individual who possesses or
exercises it by right of birth; it becomes a machinery that no one owns" (Foucault,
1980:156). Patriarchy, Joan Cocks tells us, is a "regime without a master." We are
dominated by patriarchy, but there is no one who dominates—neither individual
men nor all men as a group.

But that is not satisfactory. The preceding argument overstates the extent to
which power is anonymous. Power as quasi-language becomes impersonal. Power
is not anyone's and hence, presumably, is not used by specific groups or individuals for their own benefit. But that overstates the point: Languages do not belong to
particular individuals but to groups. There is a group of English speakers. If they
all disappeared from the face of the earth overnight, English would become a dead
language. But as long as English is written and spoken, there is an identifiable
group of English speakers, even if the borders of this group are fuzzy. Similarly, we
can get into long arguments about this or that man's complicity in capitalism, in
patriarchy, in white supremacy. But those difficulties do not show that there are
no capitalists, patriarchs, or white supremacists who use their power to oppress.
Patriarchy is of advantage to men; white supremacy to whites. Capitalists not only
dominate workers all around the globe: They also lead lives of luxury at the ex-
pense of those who work for them. That tight connection between power and advantage is so uniform that it just cannot be accidental. Whites, men, and capitalists are better off than blacks, women, and workers because the former have
power-over the latter. That sort of unambiguous causal relation between having
power and drawing profit from its use is obscured, if not denied, by the idea of
power as a communicative medium, a regime without a master, or a machinery
that no one owns.

Thus there is a serious tension between these two kinds of theories of power:
One tells us that power is owned by individuals or by groups and is used, for the
most part, for the benefit of its owner(s). The other asserts, on the contrary, that
power is not the sort of thing that any one individual or group owns or uses. One

sees the power of some persons as the cause of the conditions of others; the other denies that power is properly considered a cause at all. The first kind of theory circumscribes the owner of power-over too narrowly; often it is not a particular, identifiable individual who wields power-over. But the second kind of theory exaggerates the anonymity of the owners of power. They are identifiable as a group even if the precise membership of the group remains indeterminate.[3]

Our conceptions of power are internally incoherent insofar as we have difficulties identifying the owner of power and thus the perpetrators of various forms of oppression. We act and talk, alternately, as if power was the power of this person or that over these other persons, and in the next moment, we speak vaguely of power as a social force, a structure, a medium, a quasi-language. How can we understand this tension in our different views about power?

HOW POWER CAME TO BE ANONYMOUS

The assumption and practice of separateness transforms power into power-over, power to ward off the threats of domination by seeking domination for oneself. Conflict and competition are the standard condition of separate persons because every other person's power is a threat to my autonomy. Every other person's virtues threaten to devalue mine. But then there are many instances of power that do not seem to fit that picture of one person using superior power to make the other do what he or she does not want to do. Theorists then develop another view of power, quite consistent with the separate conception of power, that says that power is not anyone's. Behind that theory stands an argument that goes as follows: Power, like all other human attributes, belongs exclusively to separate individuals because we are all separate from each other. But there are many cases in which power does not seem to have such a separate individual as owner. In those cases power is said not to be anyone's at all.[4] But that merely continues the prevailing misrepresentation of persons and of power. If we consider our actual practices we see that they are more complex. We pretend that we are separate and, in fact, make considerable efforts to conceal the fact that power is owned, created, and maintained by groups of persons in-relation.

Our practices with respect to power are in tension because we both insist on separateness and implicitly acknowledge relatedness. In fact relatedness is most clearly in evidence precisely when we deny it most strenuously by insisting on our separateness. In many situations, the job of subordinates is not just to maintain the power of the superior but also to make it appear that the superior has all the power. In the relation between doctors and nurses, for instance, "the nurse's dilemma ... [is] to make suggestions about patient care while appearing to be deferential and passive; the doctor's to ask for and receive recommendations without jeopardizing the appearance of omniscience and control" (Hoffman, 1991). The doctor's power has to be presented as the doctor's alone. That means that not only the doctor's power but also his separateness itself is a joint production. The doctor's dependence on the knowledge, expertise, and support of nurses needs to be hidden. The nurses' situation is paradoxical because they make the doctor who he is but they also are victims of coercion.

They are powerful and without power. The paradox flows from separateness. The nurses see the doctor's dependence on them and that the doctor's power is not only his alone. But they also see themselves as isolated power holders, and as separate they have no power because the power to make the doctor powerful belongs to all nurses *together*. Only because all or most nurses support the doctor's pretense of separate power can the doctor pretend to have all the knowledge and power. But in a separate world, that jointly owned power of the nurses that secretly supports the doctor's pretense disappears from view because power is seen only as what individuals own. What is effected by groups is invisible. Hence the nurses both know and do not know that the doctor's power is a joint creation of many persons.

The prevailing conception of power parallels the separate conception of autonomy. There, as we saw in Chapters 2 and 3, the official view is that each person is self-determining and independent. But when a rational, autonomous man like Mr. Ramsay decides to be a father, the actual work of making him a father and the work of fathering is, for the most part, done by others. As a father, Mr. Ramsay is anything but autonomous. He depends on the work and support of others. Similarly, the power of the doctors is not the power of separate persons. They have power only insofar as a complex network of other persons execute their decisions and support the pretense of autonomy. The autonomy of the Mr. Ramsays of this world is covertly in-relation. It presents itself as separate, but it depends for its existence on others whose job it is, in part, to make it seem as if they were not supporting this project of separate autonomy. Similarly, power-over that is thought to belong to separate persons is really covertly in-relation: The power of some depends on the actions of others, but this cooperation is not supposed to be mentioned.

The tensions in the prevailing conceptions of power have no resolution, because they do no more than reflect the actual incoherences of our power practices. On the one hand, everyone knows that those in power cannot do anything, and thus have no power, without the assistance of many other persons. But on the other hand, we all participate in the pretense that the power belongs to particular persons. Existing theories of power are torn by inner conflict. Even if sufficiently rich and comprehensive to make a place for a wide range of important instances of power, they cannot provide a coherent account of what power is. I do not think that that is the fault of the theorists. They, after all, do no more than capture the experienced world in the nets of their theories. If what they catch for us always turns out to be full of tensions and ambiguities, that is not surprising: The internal conflicts in theories reflect the ways in which our practices that have to do with power often seem to be at odds with one another. *It is power itself that is disrupted by internal tensions.*

COVERTLY IN-RELATION POWER IS OPPRESSIVE

We have talked so far of power-over that ostensibly belongs to particular social actors: judges, generals, doctors. All of these are examples of power that accompany a particular social position. There are social roles that are defined as seats of power, such as the roles of judges, generals, government officials, employers, and teachers. In the past much of the discussion of power focused on these examples, on power that is exercised in the public realm by persons who have generally acknowledged positions of power. But this is only one context in which domination occurs regularly. More frequently, domination occurs in informal settings where the different roles are not defined primarily in terms of different degrees of power. The family is usually thought of as a setting of love and mutual concern. Only rather recently have theorists acknowledged that power plays as much of a role in families, among friends, among schoolchildren, and in the informal relations in classrooms as they do in the realms of government, war, or the administration of justice. We do many injuries to each other not by virtue of the power attached to a particular social role or a job that we get paid for but by virtue of informal power relations. What follows is an example of that informal domination.

I live in a white neighborhood. Only whites live here, and not many blacks come down our street. One day as I am walking down the street, a pickup truck comes by slowly, driven by a middle-aged black man. A black woman, the same age, sits next to him. I stop him and inquire politely whether he is looking for someone. The houses on our street are numbered in erratic ways. People often have trouble finding the house they are looking for. I am just trying to be helpful.

But afterward I begin to worry. Would I have tried "to be helpful" if the couple in the truck had been white? These two people stuck out. Something in me said: They do not belong here. My response was conditioned by the difference between their skin color and mine. It is not so clear that I was being helpful. Perhaps I was responding to pervasive racist exclusions.

The example illustrates that actions are equivocal. What description is most adequate to them depends a good deal on the surrounding circumstances. Inquiring of a white couple whether they are looking for someone in a white neighborhood is a very different action from asking the same thing of a black couple. The actions are very different in a racially divided society, in which people of color are second-class citizens. The actions might be much more alike in a society that is less preoccupied with race or does not use racial classifications to oppress.

In this context of racial prejudice and oppression, my actions, which I at first congratulate myself for, thinking that I am really a pleasant person and a good neighbor, are clearly an offense to the person whom I ask where he is going. It is insulting because it as much as says, You do not belong in this neighborhood. My inquiry thus enforces pervasive exclusions. It denies this couple the ordinary rights we believe every citizen to have to move freely on public terrain. The city and its streets, we say, belong to everyone. Freedom of movement is one of our basic rights. But in practice, I am excluding these two persons from my neighborhood. The meaning of my action is clear: It is to enforce an exclusion of blacks from white neighborhoods. But it also, by implication, enforces a second-class position for these persons. They do not have the same rights as other citizens. The implication is either that they are not citizens at all or that their citizenship is under a cloud. It is not full citizenship.

I can do this only because I have the power to do so. This power is not given to me by some job I have. My social roles as parent, life partner, teacher, and even as property owner do not carry with them the power to control who travels on my street or drives around in my neighborhood. I get this power from my group, from all the other whites who would more likely than not back me up if there was any conflict. The judge's power depends on the support of all the other employees of the criminal justice system. It depends, in addition, on the legitimation conferred on various organs of the government by the citizenry. The individual white racist's power to exclude blacks from his neighborhood rests on the support of all the other like-minded whites.

This support is not openly manifested. My neighbors and I have never talked about excluding certain people from our neighborhood. I do not know, as a matter of fact, what they would say if I went door to door to ask them. I suspect that I would get a considerable range of responses. But neither have we come together to ferret out our prejudices or to decide on ways to make our neighborhood genuinely open to everyone. Pervasive racial prejudice is maintained by us as it is maintained by most other whites: by ignoring it, by overlooking the subtle racist messages in the newspapers—where pictures of criminals are usually shown only if they are men of color—and in horror movies, where the monsters are more likely to have negroid features than to look like blond Aryan types. To keep the peace, we do not respond firmly to racist comments of our neighbors even if we are pained by them. We let sleeping prejudices lie and thus maintain and perpetuate them.

I am able to exclude these two blacks on my street. The power to do that, informal though it may be, is power in-relation. But it is covertly so. I did not shout racial epithets or pursue the strangers with a baseball bat. I have always been a good liberal who believes in equal rights for all and live and let live. Considered out of context, my action is kind or, at worst, intrusive. It is racist only because it occurs in a silent, unspoken setting of prejudice, rejection, and denigration that is widely shared, even by those who do not believe they share it. It depends on a shared understanding between myself and my neighbors that is pretty well ignored, or even concealed, by the prevailing belief in separateness. That allows us to pin the racism on individual actors and ignore the fact that we are all partipating, supporting, and responsible. My action is implicitly oppressive. The power to exclude is not mine separately but depends on the prejudices all of us share.

This covertly in-relation power oppresses in two different ways. It oppresses openly when it is the power of the judge, the general, and the president or when it is the power of the father, the bully, or the drill sergeant. Here it appears as separate power belonging to someone whose role it is to dominate. It oppresses when used unjustly. That oppression is overt when it is there for all to see. The judge has power; if the judge uses that power unjustly the oppression is patent. Everyone can know what is being done. The domination is out in the open. But what is less obvious is that it is not the separately owned power of the government bureaucrat that oppresses—the bureaucrat is only a functionary, an executor of the power inhering in the government by virtue of the citzens' legitimation. The doctor's power is, in part, a theatrical performance on the part of the nurses and is a joint production of nurses, doctors, and administrators. But that is concealed behind the image of the doctor's separate power.

But then there is also the racism that is covertly in-relation but under the surface and thus not as overt as the actions of those endowed with social power of some sort. Thus the double message of the "good neighbor" who excludes African Americans from his white neighborhood. Oppression here is implicit but often only for the oppressors. In many cases the oppressed have no doubt about what is being done to them. Here again there is a clear parallel to the earlier discussion of autonomy. Many stereotypical men consider themselves autonomous, as self-determining masters of themselves. The women who support that pretense frequently are not fooled. Mr. Ramsay may have thought of himself as autonomous, but Mrs. Ramsay knew better. The same is true in covertly in-relation power. Many whites honestly think of themselves as unprejudiced, open and fair minded, and even helpful. They claim to be color blind. But blacks know better. They experience daily the distrust and the inclination not to take them seriously, to regard them as incompetent, or, worse, to deny them full citizenship and participation. Many men believe in equal rights and treatment for women, but their actions show that they mistake themselves to be much less patriarchal than they are. But women do not mistake them. They know when they are being ignored, patronized, or objectified.

It is in the interest of the oppressors to conceal from themselves the nature of their oppressive compact with one another. Sometimes it is also in the interest of the oppressed to overlook the precise lineaments of their oppression. At other times, they have no doubt about what is being done to them.

COVERTLY IN-RELATION POWER ALIENATES

But this discrepancy between the view of the powerful and those who are less so only intensifies the effect of separate power. Not only are some people oppressed, but the oppression is often hidden by the oppressors. Racial or gender oppression is made to look like a series of individual acts that flow from the prejudices of the actors. The complicity of the other whites in maintaining a racist culture is denied. What is more, since oppression is perceived as a series of separate acts, and since acts are equivocal—one can understand them in more than one way—it is easy to get into long arguments about each individual case as to whether it is really a case of prejudice or just a misunderstanding. The severity of racial oppression is denied and the pervasiveness of the oppression hidden.

As a consequence, racial and gender oppression are systematically misstated. They are represented as the acts of individual persons motivated by irrational prejudice. The exclusion of a black from a white neighborhood then becomes no more serious than any particular uncivil and disrespectful act. It may be hurtful and make one angry, but it does not imply a complete denial of one's full citizenship rights, one's claim to full humanity, and one's particular recognized excellence because it is, after all, an isolated act. Accosting a black in my neighborhood does all that only because what I am doing is not just an individual breach of etiquette but a representative act, one instance of rejections and disparagements that are the daily lot of the oppressed in a society segregated by race or gender.

To the extent that all of us not only share this exclusionary attitude but also deny its very existence, we heighten the injury we do. The oppressed complain about their oppression. They object to being excluded, to being assigned a lesser status as citizens or as humans. But the oppressors deny that that is what they are doing. Racial and gender prejudice is no more than rudeness or irrationality on the part of some individuals. Hence the complaints of the oppressed are rejected as exaggerations. The oppressed are perceived as complaining too much, as exaggerating, as being too demanding, as being excessively sensitive. To the complaints of the oppressed we reply that the rest of us have our problems too: When our grandparents came here as immigrants, they had the same problems. Men are oppressed too and do not get justice in divorce courts. To be sure, it is often said, there are individual whites who are racist, but as a group whites have made great strides in squelching them. To be sure there are individual men who are disrespectful or even violent to women, but greater sensitivity among police and legislators has made great strides to end that. By concealing the covert support we give one another to maintain existing power relations, the systemic nature of racial and gender oppression is obscured.

But that only means that added to all the other injuries inflicted on blacks by whites, on women by men, is the injury of not listening to their complaints in any serious way. They complain of being *systematically* excluded, belittled, ignored. The dominant groups deny those accusations and by that denial show that the complaints are justified—the oppressed *are* ignored. Now the individual injuries become instances of global oppression: the inability to get a good job, or any job, the inability to get a loan, the inability to get a taxi to stop for you, the doctor being mistaken for a maid, the academic whom everyone keeps asking about her credentials. As the systematic oppression becomes invisible so do the oppressed. They are not heard when they complain or when they describe their experiences. Their individual experiences become part of a general condition of being shut out from the rest of the world, of being invisible, inaudible, not understood. As a consequence, one finds oneself "animating" a world one has not helped create or chosen to live in (Lugones, 1987). One is seen as a certain sort of person and since one's protests are not heard, it is useless to try to rectify the mistake. One is compelled to be the person and play the part that is assigned one by the dominant society with its covertly in-relation power.

But this is alienation—finding oneself in a world not of one's own making and playing a role that one has not chosen and does not want to play because it presents one as a person one is not (Schmitt, 1993). We owe the use of the concept of alienation as a term of social and political criticism to Marx. But he used the term *alienation* in two senses. The more familiar sense is that of alienation that is "a crippling of body and mind" (Marx, 1967:363), of being less than fully human, of failing to develop fully. Persons are alienated if they lack fulfillment (Ollman, 1971; Olsen, 1978; Schaff, 1970).

But there exists in Marx a further, different understanding of alienation: He observes in the same set of notes that as a fully free and developed human being one "contemplates ... [one]self in a world that ... [one] has created" (Tucker, 1978: 76). Here alienation is no longer powerlessness in the economic or the political realm but finding oneself in a world that one has not created, in which one not only does not recognize oneself but is also constantly reminded that one does not really belong. This is the alienation of the victims of sexism, racism, ageism, and class prejudice. This concept of alienation is considerably broader than the previous ones. It is the condition of all those whose identities are constructed for them by other people and imposed on them with more or less overt coercion.

One is alienated when one's identity is imposed on one. But this condition takes many different concrete forms. Not all of them are as carefully concealed as the examples just given. At one end is the complete dehumanization forced on slaves or inmates of concentration camps. Here separate power is out in the open; oppression shows its horrible face. Mary Prince describes how she and her sisters stand weeping in the marketplace, being about to be sold away from their mother, who is standing next to them. The buyers come and inspect the weeping young black women and not a one has any human fellow feeling for their grief. The slaves are effectively excluded from the human race (Prince, 1988:4). Primo Levi reports on an interview with one of the managers of the artificial rubber plant at Auschwitz. When he enters the office the man was writing and did not look up. When he was finished "he raised his eyes and looked at me ... this look was not one between two men ... [it] ... came across as if the glass window of an aquarium between things that live in different worlds. ..." (Levi, 1961:96)

The extreme of alienation occurs when one treats the other as not a member of the same human species. In stereotyping, by contrast, one allows that others are human but sees their characteristics as fixed and known. We need not ask those others who they are, for we can see that she is a woman and that he is black (and we all know what they are like). Milder forms of alienation are imposed in situations where only certain questions are allowed; all others are ridiculed or simply punished with a bad grade. Only certain kinds of language are acceptable; all others are taken as a sign of ignorance (Nye, 1990:2). We encountered that kind of alienation before, without calling it by that name. In Chapter 7 I pointed out that the separate conception of knowledge denies that anyone except specially trained persons has knowledge. This debilitates most persons because it deprives them of the ability to understand and interpret their lives and to shape them in the light of their understanding of the world. They are excluded from the process of shaping the social world and of saying who they are—as Americans, as men, as women, as white, as black, and as the many different exemplifications of these groupings. Being cast out of the realm of knowing makes one a passive object of the defining activities of others.

These latter forms of alienation, as also the racial exclusions described earlier, function precisely because the exclusions are concealed. Behind a veneer of liberalism, of equal rights for all, hides a covertly in-relation compact to exclude, demean, and ridicule the target groups. Overt racism and overt sexism are becoming, fortunately, less acceptable at least in some segments of our society. They then go into hiding, doing their work surreptitiously through exclusions dressed up as neighborliness, exclusions from knowledge draped in the flag of science, and exclusions from academic conversations in the name of logic or rationality.

Each of the different versions of the condition of alienation has a wide range of different effects. Alienation fills some with rage and saps all energy to resist in others. Some become distrustful of their own abilities; others become sycophants of those in power. Each of those expresses alienation or adapts to it in ways characteristic of that particular person. In each case, we are obliged to act out parts assigned to us without getting our consent. We are made to don costumes and masks in which we barely recognize ourselves.

At the same time, it is important to understand that alienation is relative to context. One is always alienated in a particular setting. In the white world, persons of color are, more often than not, alienated, as women are in the world of men. But at home in their own world, the oppressed are in a world of their own making, in a world that they have participated in making and which they participate in maintaining or changing (McGary, 1993). Here they are not alienated but have genuine autonomy in-relation. They are alienated in some settings but empowered in other groups. We now need to clarify what this empowerment consists of.

EMPOWERMENT

Most of the discussions of empowerment take the separateness of persons for granted and, therefore, also assume that all power is power to dominate (Kreisberg, 1992). Thus Wartenberg talks about the uses of power in teaching and points out that the goal of the good teacher is to emancipate the student. Teaching should make itself unnecessary (Wartenberg, 1990). The picture here is of two separate persons, one of whom has power to dominate another and who uses that power to render the less powerful person more independent, thereby enhancing the other's power-over. In the political realm, Saul Alinsky provides a very similar picture. The organizer enters a disempowered community and provides for its members what they need to gain greater power-over their local government (Alinsky, 1972). Politicians like to talk about "empowering" groups and usually mean by that allowing that group to compete more effectively for limited resources. The empowered gain power to dominate others. Empowerment consists of gaining more power-over.

It is often true that power, especially power-over, is gained by groups when they have strong organizations run by the leadership with the rank and file no more than passive supporters. There empowerment is understood to mean "increasing one's power to dominate." Empowerment in that sense is often accomplished for people by their leaders. Examples from labor unions and elsewhere abound. But power to dominate gained by those means, namely, strong but very hierarchical organizations, does not empower people in other important ways. They still cannot do for themselves. The death of the important leader, or the collapse of the leadership, leaves the rank and file adrift and unable to put its energies to good use (Boyte, 1989). Their organization cannot survive the loss of the leaders because the people cannot provide new leadership. The strength of the organization never depended on the spontaneous and self-motivated activities of the membership. Thus people remain disempowered, if by that we mean that they are oppressed and are unable to resist, except in the small and stubborn ways in which they have always resisted. They may gain a small measure of usually very specific and limited power-over. City Hall may pay more attention to them. They may gain the vote, or access to new jobs, but they do not change. They remain mired in the misery of internalized oppression.

But the power one lacks when alienated is not power-over, or power to dominate and coerce. The power one needs to resist alienation or to create for oneself an identity of one's own is not power-over the oppressor. It is the power to hope, to continue to struggle to survive, to continue to think, to maintain some standards of personal probity, and to continue to some extent to be open to the pain and needs of others. It is the power to acknowledge who one is, what one stands for, and what matters most. It is the power to persevere and serve what matters most. Many victims of the Holocaust succumbed to the deprivation and the gas chambers. But many failed because the will to survive was no longer there. They lost the power to hope and to preserve their own being because they lost the sense that they deserved to live (Gill, 1988:123). Bettelheim reports that middle-class professionals who arrived in the concentration camp demanding to be addressed by their professional titles, whose entire sense of themselves revolved around their social status, collapsed quickly and died. Their sense of themselves depended on the respect of others. Without that they could not live (Bettelheim, 1960:119).[5] That power to maintain oneself, to be strong and dogged, and to refuse to be deprived of one's humanity and life came more easily to those who were in camps for a "reason," for example, the "political" prisoners, mostly communists. They were there, in some way, because they had made certain choices. They had defined themselves as certain sorts of persons: political beings, revolutionaries. Having defined themselves gave them incredible power of resistance (Gill, 1988:131).

This is the power that empowerment provides. In less extreme situations the power of empowerment is often called pride, the ability to stand one's ground and to stand up for oneself—"pride from knowing who you were," as one of John Gwaltney's informants calls it (Gwaltney, 1980:237). Closely related to that is power to know one's own mind, to know what one wants and hence what is good for one and what is in one's own interest. Lacking such power, women often lack "a sense of her self—or even a self at all—that would support a sense of her flourishing" (Babbit, 1993:248). For them to gain that sense of themselves, they need nothing less than a conversion experience. They have to become new persons.

One can certainly have power-over without being empowered. Physical strength and superior weapons give the most disempowered persons power-over others. Power-over others is a frequent substitute for empowerment in our society. But often the oppressed can only begin to resist the power others have over them, and begin to demand and to conquer more power-over for themselves, after they have empowered themselves. That empowerment requires that they resist and struggle against alienation, against others defining who they are. Empowerment here comes with "self-naming."

> The civil rights movement generated the capacity to speak—the ability to define oneself, to think, to talk and to take initiative. Indeed, as its first act, the movement challenged the very *definition* of being "Negro" in Southern society, the profound alienation that stemmed from being defined and dismissed by the other, by white society. (Boyte, 1993:236–237)

In an alienating society personal change is always central to empowerment. Empowerment changes the persons whose relationship to each other is empowering. It changes them by releasing them from bonds that previously reined in their capacities: "But in terms of what happened to me and what happened to other people I know about, it was a change in my concept of myself and how I stood. ... The Civil Rights Movement gave me the power to challenge any line that limits me" (Reagon, 1979:23). Persons are empowered when they are able to attempt what before they despaired of ever accomplishing. The change empowerment brings with it is a new sense of one's capacities. Since we tend to think of persons as separate, such changes tend to be thought of as changes experienced by separate individuals. They gain self-confidence, we say, or learn to feel better about themselves or increase their self-esteem. As long as we continue to think of persons as separate, empowerment is also thought of as a change that we undergo singly. It is therefore a change in something that is exclusively one's own, such as love of one self or one's opinion of oneself. All of these changes are internal to the person; they are changes in emotion, attitude, and beliefs about oneself.

Empowerment is, however, not just a new state of mind. Empowerment is *a change in relation to others*. Barbara Deming observes how women at the Seneca Women's Encampment "seemed to me to move with a lively independence of spirit ... each seeming to have learned, or to be learning, not to despise her body—as we all have been taught to ..." (Deming, 1985:201–202). Here women learn to overcome a particular hindrance that has reined in their power all along. Empowerment releases capacities hitherto restrained by external prohibitions adopted as one's own or enshrined in the implicit rules of the group. It might seem at first that these are changes internal to each woman. Her sense of herself changes; she gains new confidence. To be sure, that is what is going on. But it is going on *here* because she finds herself in a new context where it is possible to change, where she can be a new person. Change of consciousness is intricately tied into change of one's social situation. In a situation where there are no men, no whistles, no derogatory remarks about her body, no sexualizing of intellectual conversations, or casual encounters, it becomes possible to have the body one perceives for oneself and to have the body other women perceive. It becomes possible "not to despise her body" because she is in a situation where her body is not despised.

The early civil rights movement was a movement of blacks for their own liberation. The empowerment came from the group itself. Clearly a new sense of what could be done was an important element of the change that gripped blacks. It suddenly seemed possible that whites could be resisted, that fighting back was not merely committing suicide. Part and parcel of that new sense of possibility was a new and more intense sense of injustice.

Blacks did not suddenly discover that they were oppressed. They had always known that. The weight of racial oppression had always been felt intensely. But they felt more urgently the unbearable injustice of that oppression. Oppressive regimes work hard to convince the oppressed that oppression is inescapable. They do this through brute show of force. But they also do it by damaging the sense the oppressed have of their own power. The change that comes with empowerment is a partial emergence from that internalized oppression into a more forceful sense that one deserves better, that no human being deserves the treatment one receives. Such a new sense of worth is closely tied to a new sense of one's capabilities. White supremacy lost some of its air of invincibility. New possibilities for action opened up for people who felt new power.

The emergence of a protest movement entails a transformation both of consciousness and of behavior. First, "the system" ... loses legitimacy. Large numbers of men and women who ordinarily accept the authority of their rulers and the legitimacy of institutional arrangements come to believe in some measure that these rulers and these arrangements are unjust and wrong. Second, people who are ordinarily fatalistic, who believe that existing arrangements are inevitable, begin to assert "rights" that imply demands for change. Third, there is a new sense of efficacy. (Piven and Cloward, 1979:3)

These changes go hand in hand. Existing structures of domination lose their legitimacy to the extent that the dominated have a new sense of their own powers and their own possibilities. These changes take place and manifest themselves in the continued action of groups. There were meetings in which people spoke in ways that they had never dared to speak in public before, marches in places where blacks had never dared to go before, a new and very public solidarity between young and old—all elements of this self-empowerment. These new ways of acting, moreover, were accepted in and validated by the group. New ways of speaking in meetings that would earlier have been met by an embarrassed and perhaps disapproving silence were cheered. Disrespect to established leaders who now seemed too timid was praised, whereas before it would have led to criticism and isolation from the group. So was a shift of loyalties from the old, established black leadership that had mediated between blacks and whites to a new leadership that was activist, angry, and rebellious. New organizations arose with new leaders to execute new plans. In these new social settings individuals not only felt differently, but they also could do what they had never been able to do before. They could see possibilities that had never seemed real before, and they could exploit those possibilities and make changes in their social position.

Here empowerment is no longer the experience or action of separate individuals; nor is it merely a matter of gaining power-over others. Clearly the civil rights movement had that effect. But it first changed blacks themselves. It destroyed the old world in which white terrorism was never legitimate, and was always resisted in some ways, but where the battle seemed hopelessly uneven. It created a new world in which struggle over racism would never disappear again. From different quarters comes the same insight: Empowerment is a joint effort of groups. Social ties helped the survivors of the Holocaust immeasurably (Gottlieb, 1990:150ff.). However oppressed in the world of men, women have always supported and validated one another as women (Raymond, 1986).

We encountered that kind of empowerment in groups earlier in the discussion of knowing in-relation (Chapter 7). One frequent example of that is women's consciousness-raising groups of the 1970s where women discovered, for instance, their anger at partners, parents, and children and learned to acknowledge that anger. Learning here is not merely intellectual. Women did not merely say, I am angry. They raged, felt the fear and anxiety aroused by the avoval of anger, and then learned to overcome those fears. They changed because they learned to do something they had not been able to do before, namely, to be aware of a deep sense of oppression and devaluation. What matters in this story as an example of empowerment is that they acquired new skills. They learned to resist in spite of the fears that had kept them docile before. Empowerment involves feelings one had not been aware of before and learning to do what one could not do before because of unavowed feelings that held one back.

What may seem, at first, a very different kind of example will throw some light on the transformations that one undergoes when learning in-relation and being empowered by it. Naomi Scheman relates a conversation between Jewish and African-American feminists in which she talked about Jews having traditionally displayed solidarity with African Americans. Some African-American women agreed but added that this solidarity was always moderated by the Jews' assumption that they were superior. They always saw themselves as benefactors rather than as equals (Scheman, 1993:237). Here Scheman learns to see herself in a new light, namely through the eyes of African-American women, whose perception of the role of Jews in the struggle for civil rights is rather different from her own as a Jew. Had the observation been made in a different setting, she might have turned away from it or dismissed it as unfair or antisemitic. But in a setting of feminists, of women reaching for learning in-relation, she could hear this very different story about herself and accept it. It was empowering to replace a misrepresentation of oneself—the posturing as ally to the downtrodden—with a more complex, less vainglorious picture. It enabled her to think better (and act better) in relation to feminists who are different from her and with whom conversations can be fruitful but are difficult. Learning to surrender certain postures makes it possible to learn from persons whom before one could not take seriously because their critical views were too painful. In a suitably supportive environment, she could hear what made her understand her own place in the world in more complex and useful ways.

Thus empowerment comes when one learns to see oneself more clearly. But that new view of oneself is not merely an intellectual change: It consists of one's being transformed, of becoming a different person. Knowing in-relation transforms. One overcomes one bit of alienation by learning to reject the definition imposed on one by others and, instead, names oneself. The women who learn of their own anger also learn to see themselves more accurately as excessively conciliatory, too timid to express their needs, too worried to find approval in the eyes of this authority or that. They learn to reject the definition of women as always making peace, being compliant, and worshiping the ground their men walk on. This learning is easier in a group because one sees one's own timidity reflected in that of others. Like Aristotle's friends, one knows oneself better by knowing the other. Empowerment means learning to play a new role in the world—a role that is, in this case, less submissive, more autonomous in-relation, and more expansive or, in the first case, less patronizing and less closed off against the people with whom one is trying to ally oneself. One gains empowerment in those ways by learning to see oneself from the outside—often in a group—and discarding the postures and pretenses that held one back before as one learns of the fears and injuries that taught one to adopt those postures. Thus one counters alienation.

These changes are, at times, set in motion by particular persons. New organizations are founded by organizers who come into a community from the outside. But these organizers do not empower people. Empowerment both gives birth to the groups that form and makes them grow. Whether groups form does not depend on the organizer. Organizers help, but they cannot organize people who do not want to be organized. No one empowers anyone else; at best one can facilitate another's self-empowerment (Boyte, 1989:91).

But self-empowerment is not a separate act. Empowerment is mutual. It is the act of a group. Empowerment provides power not in the sense of power-over, power against, and power to dominate but power in the sense of being creative, inventive, able to do what is difficult, and able to persevere, learn, and improve. This is not separate power but power with. Power ceases to be *power-over* and comes to be *power with*. Power in-relation is manifest in the ability of the group to achieve its shared goals.[6]

This power in-relation is different from the power that two or more persons have when they pool their separate strengths. Take as an example framing a roof. Joan cannot do the job by herself because the rafters are too heavy for one person to lift and hold in place. Neither can Robert do the job without Joan's help. When Joan joins her power with Robert's, the two can accomplish what they could not accomplish separately because some jobs require two persons. Is theirs power in-relation? Well, so far all we have is one more instance of collective action. If all Joan needs is someone to help her lift a few heavy rafters into place, anybody with sufficient strength could do that and it makes no difference who it is. The person helping needs to be minimally related to her, and thus they just add her power to that of another but with the power of each remaining separate. But if Joan and Robert work together for a while and get to be good at what they are doing, their power becomes power in-relation as they become a team in which neither member is readily replaceable (May, 1987). If they change in the course of building this working relationship and entertain new possibilities that previously would have seemed utopian, they have come to empower themselves and one another. Some of that new power is theirs together.

To this notion of empowerment as power in-relation, readers offer a number of objections. Often, they say, empowerment is individual. She gets to go to school, they get money to buy a house, he is able to travel and broaden his outlook. But such changes, by themselves, do not empower. I may be able to acquire new skills, but if no one gives me a job in which I can use those new skills and get paid for them, they do not empower. The black family that buys a house in a white neighborhood and has crosses burned on its lawn is not empowered by home ownership. New knowledge, new property, and new opportunities empower only if they produce new relations to other persons and new standing in a network of actors. Empowerment comes only with new ways of being-in-relation with others.

A stronger objection points out that we often gain new power by separating ourselves from others. The child who can become more independent in relation to parents gains in strength. Although that is true, what is the nature of that separation? Is the runaway child empowered? Hardly. Does breaking the relation to overweaning, demanding, or possessive parents empower? Whether the ability to break such a relation, which has long been resented, is a sign of greater power remains to be seen. Many persons emerge from a very tight relation to parents to enter into the exact sort of relation with another person. No empowerment here. We want to see whether this person who is separating from parents is able to be more autonomous in other relationships. In the optimal case that is also the first step toward refashioning the relation to parents. Under the impression of separateness and separate conceptions of autonomy, we see that children distance themselves from parents. But we do not see that this distancing is usually a renegotiating of the relationship (Candib, 1995). But sometimes, the critic persists, it is just a rupture. Nothing takes the place of the relation to parents that has now been abandoned. Is that really empowering, or is it a festering sore, a permanent loss, and a source of continuing rage, however well concealed? The answers to those questions depend on the new kinds of relationship a person can enter and find autonomy in-relation. The mere separation, by itself, no more empowers than the new diploma or the new house.[7]

CHOOSING EMPOWERMENT

People empower themselves by creating new relationships in their groups. What they gain by that is not power-over one another, or, necessarily, power-over persons outside their group, but a new strength, a new sense of what they can do, a new hope, and perseverance. But the examples we have seen are not of empowerment chosen deliberately. It sometimes happens in ways that are unpredictable and often remain partially unexplained. New movements arise, and a new restlessness and vision of what life could be like takes hold of people. They come together to demand more forcefully and insistently what they believe is theirs.

But can empowerment also be chosen? In all the preceding chapters I have insisted that there is a choice between being separate and being-in-relation, between separate empathy or decisionmaking and empathy or decision in-relation, between separate knowing and knowing in-relation. It remains to make some suggestions about what sort of choice there might be between separate power— power-over—and power in-relation—empowerment.

Most of the situations in which we find ourselves are structured by power-over. In the family, at work, and in leisure-time activities different people have different degrees of power-over and use that power to tell others what to do or what not to do. Is there any room here for being-in-relation, for power in-relation, for attempts to empower ourselves and others? Any attempt to move from relationships structured by power-over to empowering relationships must transform existing social groups. I will cite some examples of such transformations in the classroom.

To transform a group structured by power-over into one that empowers its members, the relationships in the group must be altered. In a classroom, listening is central to that alteration. Listening involves centrally that everyone in the group be encouraged to participate (Kramarae and Treichler, 1990:54). Everyone must become more autonomous (in-relation) in this group. This means that each participant must make a contribution; each contribution needs to be acknowledged and taken seriously. The different roles of the various members are a matter for comment in the group. It is important that members who hang back and remain more passive are encouraged to do their part of the job. Everyone must be someone; everyone must do his or her best in the work of the whole. Everyone's individuality in the group must be acknowledged by the group. It is important that everyone's ability be marshaled and included in the power of the group, and that means that everyone must be allowed and encouraged to contribute and everyone must be heard with care.

Listening also involves hearing not only the words spoken but also what is not said: "To listen with care is to treat the text [in the present case what is said] not merely in its textuality but as an expression of a subject" (Schweickart, 1990:89). One must pay attention not only to what is said in so many words but to who it is who says that and how that fits with the person speaking and what it might mean said by this person rather than another. Listening goes hand in hand with speaking. A classroom is empowering to the extent that its members are listening to each other, but also to the extent that they are willing to talk, and to talk openly and fearlessly (Kreisberg, 1992:164). For such a group to choose to be openly in-relation, group identity and group accomplishments must be self-conscious. The members of the group must understand that what they accomplish in the classroom is a joint accomplishment. That understanding must, moreover, be concrete and reasonably accurate. A factitious group identity ("We are all Hoosiers" or "Are you a Red Sox fan?") is not the same as a group acknowledging that its learning is a joint achievement.

But is it not the teacher's job to know more, be an authority, choose topics, explain to students what they do not understand, correct their work, and urge them on to greater effort? No sensible person would deny that. The teacher's job is to teach. But the question is how best to do that. Traditional pedagogy relies heavily on power-over: The teacher tells the student what to do, how to do it, and when to do it. The teacher imparts information. The teacher checks whether students have learned what they were supposed to learn by giving examinations.

But that mode of teaching disempowers students. An alternative is to encourage students to make as many decisions in the classroom together as possible. The teacher's role here is no longer to be in command but to supply information, to point students toward resources, to lay out alternative views to theirs, and to propose alternative projects or different ways of going about a particular project. The teacher's role is to encourage students to listen carefully and respectfully to one another and to encourage the development of cooperative skills in students, whom the society at large expects to cooperate with their superiors but to compete against one another (Kreisberg, 1992). Here central attention is paid not just to the transmission of information or skills but to enabling students, as a group, to uncover information, to develop projects, and to consider issues open-mindedly and critically.

Elaine Garan reports on her observations in a first-grade classroom in an urban school in Buffalo, New York. Here the teacher made a very deliberate attempt to surrender some of her authority by teaching children to take responsibility for the various activities in the classroom. As Garan reports, the effort worked. In the beginning of the year, when the phone rang the teacher asked one of the children to answer it; by the end of the year, the teacher barely notices the ringing phone because a student answers and takes care of whatever needs to be done. Early in the year, the teacher reminds children whose attention is wandering off the task at hand. By the end of the year, children will recall each other to the work in their group and the child whose attention strayed for a moment will return to the work without any difficulty. Spelling words are posted on the wall, and the children get in the habit of asking each other and showing the word in question to the child who asks. The conversations in the work groups change from being conversations between individual students and the teacher to conversations among all the members of a group (Garan, 1994).

The teacher still has a special position in the classroom by virtue of knowing more, being older, being more skilled in arguments, and being more experienced in helping groups to do their work together. This is the teacher's power (in the most general sense of that term) to marshall a range of material, to explain certain matters clearly, and to teach a given subject matter to persons who lack this particular power. Such power easily produces power-over. As a teacher I organize my courses; that is, I tell my students what work they must do. The doctor's power by virtue of medical knowledge easily transmutes itself into power-over the patient, who is told what to eat and how to live. Once we are openly in-relation, decisions need to be made about the privileges, if any, that accrue to teachers: whether they will have more time to speak and to what extent they will organize a course of study—both of them forms of power-over. If the one who has more power-over wants to use that power, permission must first be obtained. You cannot be in-relation to someone you are also trying to coerce.

Earlier in this chapter I distinguished power—the ability to do certain things, which was exemplified by the teacher's or the doctor's knowledge—from power-over—the very specific ability to make others do what they do not want to do. Power, as we just saw, leads easily to power-over but need not do so. But as noticed earlier in this chapter, a good deal of power-over that teachers, for instance, have in the society at large, manifested, for instance, in the power to grade students, is not a result of the teacher's power. Nor does it belong to the teacher individually. It is a form of being covertly in-relation. This power-over does not flow naturally from the teacher's greater power but is constructed by the society at large. The individual teacher or doctor therefore cannot shed this power-over at will without giving up the social role of teacher or doctor. Hence the power-over that accrues to me by virtue of my position cannot be gotten rid of short of re-making the society from the bottom up. But like the power that comes to me by virtue of my knowledge as a philosopher and experience as a teacher, this power-over cannot be used by me except in consultation with students if I want to be in-relation with them and to seek mutual empowerment with them. You cannot be in-relation to someone you are coercing, but differences in power, or in power-over, are open to negotiation among those who seek power in-relation together.

The choice of empowerment is a difficult choice because society at large, being committed to separateness, discourages it. But even in a more supportive society the choice would be difficult, for reasons discussed in the preceding chapter. We saw that knowing in-relation ceases to be oppressive only if it stops being exclusive. Only if we try to know in-relation even with those who are very different will knowledge no longer be a means of excluding some from the preferred role of knower. In corresponding ways, power in-relation that binds only some people together can all too easily become power-over those on the outside. The bonding of males has always been used to oppress women. The intimate ties among the members of ruling groups have closed those groups off to entry from the ranks of the ruled. If power in-relation is not to be simply a marshaling of resources for being better able to oppress and exclude, power in-relation must be sought also between persons and groups that are very different—groups that, for instance, bear grievances of long standing toward each other. Here each must approach the other, being prepared to change in ways that would make this relationship possible. Each must surrender old prejudices and the ways of acting that keep those alive today. Here different groups come to each other and themselves in new ways and together gain new strength, new hope, and new ideas for the future. In gaining knowledge in-relation, they are empowered.

The choice to seek power in-relation is, like all the choices to be in-relation, not an individual choice. We can be fully in-relation only in a society where that is the norm and separateness the deviant state. Until the choice of being openly in-relation and mutually empowered is the rule, the empowerment of some groups will in the end serve to make them better oppressors of other groups. Seeking mutual empowerment selectively only enables some groups to exclude others more effectively, to compete more mercilessly, and to do more damage indulging their prejudices. Power in-relation will contribute to a genuinely freer society only if it can become the rule and separate power or covertly in-relation power the deviant exception.

As I suggested at the end of Chapter 6, a society in which being-in-relation is the norm will be a society free from coercion. It will be a genuinely free society. But what I have said so far does not fully support that pronouncement. We have seen in this chapter that separateness tends to transform power into power-over. A society that turns its back on separateness will be less coercive than ours. But I have not shown that separateness is the only source of coercive uses of power and hence have not shown that the diminution of separateness will liberate us from all coercion. Power in-relation—empowerment—slowly frees us from the pretense and posturing that conceals our weaknesses and hides recourse to power-over. Empowerment, I argued earlier, consists in part of joining others who are quite different to divest oneself of power-over or divest oneself of fear of that power-over to enable one to resist it better. Both will work toward a decrease in coercion but neither guarantees that it will eliminate it completely.

Besides, there are other sources of coercion: If I believe that I absolutely need to get this job, I will do anything, even if it is coercive, to secure it. Will seeking empowerment make me better able to surrender goals that I can reach only with the use of power-over? Will empowerment make me willing to give up those goals that drive me to act coercively toward others? There are many questions like this one that need to be answered before we can be assured that being-in-relation will assure us the peaceful world we seek. All we know now is that it will move us in the right direction.

SOME FINAL THOUGHTS

In the background of this entire discussion looms a difficult question: Why is separateness dominant, and why do we choose to knuckle under and support the claims to separate power of those who oppress us? The answer to that question is by no means clear. But there is, as I pointed out in the Preface, a venerable tradition that contrasts the power of social ties that were very local, that connected and were maintained by persons in their own communities, to the atomization of society, to the attendant rationalization of social ties, and to the increasing power of central states and large economic units. Without question the transition to capitalism is deeply implicated in this transformation. Capitalism transformed group members into single, separate economic agents. It replaced the guidance of specific local communities and their norms by the impersonal regulation of the market and the distant legislation of national governments. Whether the rise of capitalism is the root cause or merely the description of the salient features of the new society in which separateness rules supreme, it seems clear that as long as capitalism is maintained unchastened, being-in-relation will remain partial and covert and oppression and alienation will remain central in social life (Glasman, 1994).

The preceding discussion suggests why those who dominate others are interested in maintaining separateness. It gives them the surreptitious support of the dominated without their having to do their part to foster the empowerment that arises in-relation. For those who have separate power to dominate, it certainly pays to continue to pretend that persons are separate and to enforce that pretense with all the power at their disposal. The teacher who dominates does not have to face the questions and criticisms of students. The capitalist who arrogates all power does not have to pay higher wages or improve working conditions. The husband who claims traditional patriarchal power receives around-the-clock services and needs not provide much in return. Our current practices, incoherent and unstable though they be, give great rewards to some and impose great burdens on others. Hence the interest in perpetuating these practices on the part of those who profit.

If we are to free ourselves from the burdens of that domination, we need to do more than take power away from those who dominate: We need to transform power itself. Short of that, domination will just be in different hands. To be sure, if one must be dominated, some powers are much less onerous in their domination than others. But simply gaining a different group to dominate us is not liberation. We misunderstand liberation as long as we interpret it as merely replacing the existing ruling groups. Only when vast numbers of people learn to choose to be openly in-relation, with respect to power as well as to knowledge, will oppression be less frequent and less onerous than it is now.

But that change is, of course, extremely difficult. It is difficult in one's private life to withstand the temptation to separate oneself and to dominate. But in most situations, individual choices of being openly in-relation are bound to be frustrated by institutional constraints. Separateness is not just something we choose individually. It is embedded in the hierarchical institutions that govern all aspects of our lives. I may try to reduce domination in my classroom, but I am expected to give grades and to affect my students' future in significant ways. The system in which I operate is hierarchical and authoritarian, and thus my effectiveness in transforming power is very limited. To make being-in-relation the preferred mode of being, we need to change not only ourselves but also our institutions.

The people who maintain the current distribution of power also maintain the current definition and practices of power as separate. They do not want to surrender that separate power and empower themselves by being-in-relation to a bunch of radicals, feminists, people of color, or homosexuals. How then shall we transform the nature of power from power to dominate into empowerment? That is a difficult question to which I do not have an answer.[8] The conclusion that is usually drawn from the apparent impossibility of changing the fundamental assumptions and practices of those in power is that we need to overcome those who hold and define power today by adopting their definitions and practices. But this book has shown that that would surely be a mistake. Kathy Ferguson has argued eloquently that the adoption of prevailing bureaucratic methods of political action makes it impossible to prevail against the bureaucracy (Ferguson, 1984). I believe that the same is true of alternative conceptions of power. You cannot compel people to empower themselves in-relation by using force or manipulating them. What is left to us is Barbara Deming's advice: "It has to be invented, you know" (Deming, 1985:223).

Notes

Chapter 1

1. The scope of these reflections about separateness and being-in-relation is problematic. On the one hand, the observations I will make apply much more readily to men and women in North America, who are primarily white, primarily middle class. On the other hand, philosophers have for a long time taken separateness for granted. Paradigmatic "man" was always separate. A critique of that particular philosophical commonplace is thus of some interest even to those in whose lives separateness is less of a problem than it is in the lives of persons like myself because dominant philosophical preconceptions have some effect also on them.

2. In the discussion that follows I will use "being one's own person" and "being oneself" or "having a self of one's own" interchangeably. Although "self" and "person" are not ordinarily synonymous, the two terms are used in the same sense as they occur in the various idiomatic expressions cited.

3. To this Hegel replies that I demonstrate that I own myself by harming or destroying myself (Hegel, 1949:43). But this is a special kind of harm or destruction of property that automatically also harms or destroys the owner. This is just the sort of contradiction that Hegel is looking for to drive the dialectic beyond an untenable conception of self as self-owner.

4. Nozick agrees that property is alienable. He defines property relations as the power to decide how something is to be used (Nozick, 1974:281). But that is, of course, too weak a sense of ownership to allow us to talk sensibly of self-ownership. For as self-owner I cannot only decide what should be done with myself, but I can *do* it. I can raise my arm. Another can only order or coerce me into raising my arm. Being oneself is a more intimate relation than owning oneself.

5. That view is initially plausible. It responds to the insight that one kind of autonomy consists of a life led deliberately: What one does is carefully chosen. The stands one takes are taken in full knowledge of what they entail, and one's deliberateness extends to taking full responsibility for consequences, expected or not, of one's choices. It is that sort of picture that, I think, stands behind the talk about "identifying" with one's desires. But if one also assumes human separateness, then the acts of deliberation and choice are all internal to the person. Their efficacy does not depend on the actions of anyone else. The notion of "identifying" then loses most of its content or is reduced to having strong feelings about certain choices one makes. But the picture of the autonomous person who makes explicit choices and who follows a course laid down by himself or herself is powerful because, ordinarily, these choices are *social* acts: One presents oneself to the world as a certain person. One is recognized and acknowledged as such a person and thus one's autonomy is a social stance. One is dependent in one's autonomy on the recognition by others. This is no longer

separate autonomy but is what I shall call in the next chapter "covert being-in-relation." This account of separate autonomy turns out not to be so separate after all.

6. But could it not be worth striving for even if we did not know whether we ever manage to achieve autonomy? O'Neill ascribes the view to Kant that autonomy should be pursued even if we cannot be sure that we ever are fully autonomous (O'Neill, 1992:219). There are goals that some people achieve and are therefore worth pursuing for me, even though I may not know whether I can achieve them. But goals of which we do not know whether anyone ever achieves them, do not seem worth pursuing. Now if autonomy is capable of degrees, we might say that we do not know whether anyone has ever been *completely* autonomous, but it is still worth trying to be partially autonomous. But the problem of socialization not only prevents us from knowing whether we are ever completely autonomous—given prevailing senses of that term—but just as much prevents us from knowing whether we are autonomous to any degree.

Chapter 2

1. There is a powerful temptation here to use the language of property to explicate this "having" of ideas, values, beliefs, and so on. But we have already seen that that would only confuse the issue. I shall sometimes speak of that knowledge, or belief, or other states as "belonging" to persons separately, but that should not be read as implying that they are the property of persons in any ordinary sense.

2. This passage occurs in the middle of a complex argument that leftists should take Nozick's metaphor of "self-ownership" seriously. (See also Cohen, 1991.) I have given my reasons in the preceding chapter for not thinking that self-ownership is a useful metaphor. The passage cited is offered as one more, informal, reason for adopting the self-ownership metaphor. Instead, I believe, it is one more reason for rejecting it.

3. Early in the preceding chapter I differentiated the distinctness of our bodies from the (possible) separateness of our persons and actions.

4. In his second article on self-ownership, Cohen also conflates the two different senses of "separateness." He argues there that joint ownership of resources is incompatible with self-ownership because the former implies that one can do nothing without the consent of others. But self-ownership, Cohen simply assumes, implies that I can make decisions by myself exclusively. Decisions in which others participate are inconsistent with self-ownership because that is assumed to mean that I own myself *exclusively*. Joint ownership in oneself is not considered a possibility (Cohen, 1986b).

5. That we feel our feelings in our bodies and no one else feels those feelings directly is hardly a complete argument for equality, for the inviolability of human lives, or of human freedom. After all, animals also are distinct in their bodies and so are plants. If one were to take these arguments seriously, one could only be a very rigorous vegetarian, and perhaps not even that. No libertarianism without vegetarianism!

6. I have treated this controversy in more detail in "Methodological Individualism, Psychological Individualism, and the Defense of Reason" (Schmitt, 1989).

7. If I am right and methodological individualism is not defensible, then a fortiori ontological individualism must also be given up.

8. Supporting a consensus with which one is privately not entirely at ease is different from adopting a group resolution that one disapproves of but does not want to oppose in the group discussion either for fear of being excluded from the group, being ridiculed or

marginalized, or for the sake of the unity of the group. Participating in a joint decision is different from being unprincipled, being coerced into assent one does not actually support, or sacrificing one's own views for the sake of group unity. Being-in-relation does not countenance any of those. On the contrary, the clear respect for difference is essential to it. I will return to this in Chapter 5.

Chapter 3

1. For more about objectivity, see Chapter 7.

2. Virginia Woolf described life in pre–World War I England. A lot has changed since then. The conflicting evidence about change in stereotypical men is examined in considerable detail in Lynne Segal's *Slow Motion* (1990).

3. The final two criticisms will be discussed at length in Chapter 7.

4. One could try to avoid these problems by thinking of fathering as a purely biological act. That might preserve autonomy but only because it would make out the autonomous man as one who chooses his acts carefully and autonomously but does not take responsibility for the consequences. He satisfies his sexual needs, after due consideration, but then lets others take care of the consequences. If children result, that is the woman's lookout. Well, you say, is not that the way it has always been and still is? But that certainly makes it seem as if the autonomous man who decides on actions and leaves the consequences to others to take care of is just being irresponsible. But irresponsiblity is not what philosophers have urged on us when they recommended their separate kind of autonomy to us so enthusiastically.

5. That is not, strictly speaking, accurate. I can have commitments, moral and otherwise, and still be autonomous in the separate sense. For instance, I can commit myself to lose ten pounds. That commitment is reaffirmed with every dessert I refuse and every tempting snack I resist. In each reaffirmation of the commitment I reaffirm my autonomy. But once commitments become social ties that give others claims on me—on my choices and actions—my autonomy is compromised. When my children remind me that I promised to lose weight as I am about to take a third helping of lasagna, then my autonomy is restricted by that commitment. The same applies to friendship or to devotion to a cause. The question always is who is holding me to keeping my commitment. As long as I do that myself, I remain autonomous in the separate sense.

6. Many philosophers stress the centrality of self-reflective thinking, or taking a critical stance toward prevailing views of the good life and of action, including their own views and earlier commitments. But if we look carefully we find that these philosophers regard only self-reflection as necessary for autonomy (Moore, 1993:185). Also necessary for autonomy is that one *act*. Not only careful evaluation and reevaluation of one's life are needed but also "the resolve, the fortitude, to act from the results of such deliberations" (Macedo, 1990: 225).

7. It is very important to remember that, as Lugones points out, most persons inhabit several worlds and inhabit them in more than one way. In some worlds we are perceived arrogantly or perhaps ignored and thereby deprived of substance. In others we are more or less at home; we are ourselves, strong and full of joy (Collins, 1991:91ff).

8. It is important to see the implication of this observation: One cannot argue against separateness on the grounds that our choices, our actions, and even our persons are "socially constituted," that is, depend heavily on the social context in which they take place.

For the choice of separateness is also dependent on such social support. Both separateness and being-in-relation are, in the respects suggested, social phenomena.

9. Feminist theorists are well aware of that. They do not claim that we are, as a matter of fact, in-relation because we are, for example, dependent as children or because as parents we have children depend on us. Instead they urge that we model our theories of conduct not on the separate relations in men's clubs or in the economic marketplace but on the relationships between children and their caregivers (Held, 1987; Baier, 1986). Other theorists have been wary of the caregiver–dependent person paradigm and have instead suggested that our theories of conduct be modeled on friendship (Code, 1987b). Being-in-relation is not presented to us as fact but as a desirable choice.

Chapter 4

1. If we are willing to countenance collective agents, we face a difficulty. On the prevailing assumption of separateness, every action is exclusively owned by a specific agent. Every act has one specific agent. In the case of collective acts that means that there are collective agents, which are not identical with the individual persons who make up that collective. Under the assumption of separateness we must say that the action of a collective is performed by the collective and not by its members. You and I play tennis, but I do not play tennis and neither do you. The nation goes to war, but its citizens do not. But that is a very strange view. We can deny it either by denying that there are collective acts or by giving up separateness. The former is the common strategy; I am arguing for the latter.

2. Hence criticisms of Gilligan's claim that there is some sort of incommensurability between the two ethics tends to be misdirected. Critics claim that the ethics of care differs from an ethics of justice simply in appealing to different moral principles. Whereas the ethics of justice appeals to principles about fairness, the ethics of care rests on principles like "one should promote the well-being of others to whom one is affiliated and refrain from harming them" (Mason, 1990:169). (See also Flanagan and Jackson, 1990; Brell, 1989; Calhoun, 1988; Blustein, 1991). Such readings of Gilligan completely overlook the change of meaning that the term "ethics" undergoes when we move from an "ethics of care" to an "ethics of justice"—a change discussed by feminist philosophers (Walker, 1992). Once we move from separateness to being-in-relation, the whole complexion of ethical issues changes because we are talking about very different sorts of relationships between agents from what ethics usually talks about. The difference between the two ethics is, for instance, not one between different ethical principles but between the very different role played by ethical principles in each. That difference may well be described as a form of "incommensurability."

3. At least one philosopher has argued at great length that reciprocity-in-exchange is the only kind of reciprocity there is (Becker, 1986).

4. That view is controversial even among feminists. Joan Tronto rejects it as "clearly wrong" (Tronto, 1989:178). See also Curtin, 1991.

5. We notice here that for a full understanding of being-in-relation we need to think about power. I will do that in Chapter 8.

6. It is also important to note that although being-in-relation is chosen, we may not always be able to be in-relation to a person with whom we would like to be openly in-relation. Sometimes we may choose to have a particular joint project with others but fail. Even persons of goodwill do not always get along. The desire to be engaged in this or that joint

project does not always suffice. The project may not be possible for us; it may not be possible at this time or under these circumstances. Goodwill is necessary but not sufficient for collective projects of all kinds. The time must be right, fortune must smile on the project, and the participants need all sorts of skills and knowledge. Just choosing to be in-relation does not establish an openly in-relation connection.

Chapter 5

1. Not all psychologists. See Judith Jordan's characterization of empathy: "Empathy leads to an understanding of the other as subject, not object. ... Mutuality is sought. I look for a sense of connection and relational expansion rather than control. ... You are experienced as having your own subjective needs ... which may or may not be in harmony with mine. If they are not, the differences are acknowledged and some work on areas of conflict is necessary ..." (Jordan, 1987:5).

2. This is one more instance of the failures of separate empathy. Offering support or sympathy to someone who does not want it at all, or offering it in a form the other finds difficult to accept or ridiculous, is surely lacking in genuine fellow feeling. But separate empathy is incapable of these fine discriminations.

3. Conversations require several voices and to that extent are collective enterprises. They require several persons working together. So is, we saw earlier, empathy. So are games of tennis and many other games. Collective activities may be undertaken by persons who are quite separate. Playing tennis is not a form of being-in-relation; neither is a "conversation" between thinkers who are not contemporaries. Collective activities include speaking a language, but the different speakers may be quite separate from one another. The element of being-in-relation is first introduced when the rules of a game are worked on by the different players as they play, in just the way in which persons talking to one another reaffirm or change the rules of the language. Innovative uses of language may be imitated by others and thereby be incorporated into the stock of permitted usages or be rejected as deviant. Here, the maintenance and innovation of a shared language is a joint project. The participants may deny that, and being covertly-in-relation, they may show only their separateness to one another. They may, alternatively, openly choose to be in-relation.

4. This does not show that all philosophers are in-relation with one another. Philosophy is a collective project, but the participants usually are quite separate from one another. But they could, of course, choose to be in-relation.

5. This is the conception of autonomy that Lori Stern, one of Carol Gilligan's associates, heard from the adolescent students at Emma Willards School (Stern, 1990).

6. We need to remind ourselves of the importance of distinctness because many of the discussions of separateness and being-in-relation do not draw a clear line between bodily distinctness and separateness. Hence in rejecting separateness, authors often also reject bodily distinctness and thus expose themselves to obvious and powerful criticisms. Thus most recently Tom Digby's "No *One* is Guilty: Crime, Patriarchy, and Individualism" (Digby, 1994).

7. Dealing with difference and persons who are very different is often difficult. But those are just the differences we must not overlook or evade. For more on that see Chapter 7.

8. This is the beginning of long and complex discussions of the ways in which prevailing privatism and the assumption of separateness have affected the practice of artists and writers. Would collective work be easier in a world that was less fixated on separateness? But

hooks's central point remains true and important: Groups cannot think collectively if their members cannot think for themselves. The converse is also true however: Individuals cannot think for themselves if they cannot think in groups. They think badly if they are not thinking in groups.

Chapter 6

1. Anyone looking for an exhaustive discussion of current views of love should consult Alan Soble's *The Structure of Love* (1990).

2. We saw a very similar development much earlier with relation to the concept of autonomy: Starting at the conception of persons as separate we soon found that separate autonomy was purely a mental state internal to a person but did not involve acting in any particular way. From being separate it moved to being utterly private.

3. This problem, of course, does not arise if we assume that the other's role is not also bestowal but rather having value bestowed upon him or her. The surface plausibility of these views rests on the tacit assumption of a gendered paradigm in which the male is active and bestows value and the woman is passive in accepting the value bestowed on her. They make no sense without that paradigm. They are repugnant with it.

4. Could one defend the separate view of love by strengthening the concept of "reciprocity"? Suppose we require not only that love involve contemporaneous feelings, acts, and so on but also that the feelings of one person be caused by the feelings of the other. For such a suggestion to help the defenders of separateness, all causal connections must be between separate entities or events. At first that appears quite plausible. But then we notice that the acts of the lover have their specific efficacy on the beloved only in a setting that is the joint product of both lover and beloved. We need to make use of the concept of love as a form of being-in-relation in order to give a causal analysis of love.

5. Buber confronts the same problem and is no better able to resolve it as readers of *I and Thou* can easily ascertain. Similarly, Nozick insists, "Love, romantic love, is *wanting* to form a *we* ... a new web of relationships between them that makes them no longer separate." Forming this *we* involves loosening the boundaries of one's identity (Nozick, 1991). This is very promising, but when he tries to explicate these general hints, Nozick has little to say.

6. I see myself not only because we do some of the same things. Aristotle insists that in seeing actions of his friend a man sees "worthy actions and actions that are his own" (1170a3). The most natural reading of that phrase is that there are some actions that are neither exclusively mine nor exclusively yours but ours.

7. I owe this reading of Aristotle to A. W. Price, *Love and Friendship in Plato and Aristotle* (1989).

8. I am oversimplifying a complex controversy about self-knowledge. But the disagreements that philosophers have fought out for a long time do not serve to clarify being-in-relation any further. So we may ignore them here.

Chapter 7

1. For one German eugenicist, Fritz Lenz, degeneracy "was virtually synonymous with lack of culture" (Weiss, 1990:32). Alfred Ploetz, another leader of the early eugenics movement in Germany, tended to "equate fitness with class" (Weiss, 1990:24). It was a part of the

eugenicists' program to encourage members of the upper class to have large families. Surely in the background of eugenics there was a picture of the world divided into us, the superior people—the white (male) middle class—and them, the inferior people—foreigners, poor folks, Negroes, and so on. Clear class and ethnic prejudices supported the move from Mendelian genetics to the actual practice of compulsory sterilization of inmates of institutions. But these prejudices remained unstated and uncriticized.

2. More generally all mental acts—knowing, believing, doubting—are thought of as "propositional attitudes." In each case a person is said to "have a relation" to a proposition.

3. A practice is oppressive if it injures undeservedly and/or for inadequate reasons. Tutelage of children is perhaps not deserved but is sometimes supported by good reasons. It is therefore not oppressive. Incarceration of rapists is deserved and has good reasons and thus also does not oppress. This section shows that exclusion from the domain of knowledge by class, race, and gender is not for good reasons; it injures undeservedly. Working people and women, both white and not, are not regarded as "real" knowers because they have limited theoretical knowledge. But that is not a defensible restriction of the concept of knowledge. The exclusions that are a consequence of this unjustified restriction of what is to count as knowledge are undeserved. The separate conception of knowledge is therefore oppressive.

4. This does not mean that propositional knowledge does not count for anything but only that the professional intellectuals must situate themselves with respect to and for the persons they speak about or even speak for (Collins, 1991). They must also, as we shall see, expose themselves to the views those others have of them.

5. The controversy over Rosalind Franklin's contribution to the discovery of the structure of DNA is another interesting case history of the ways in which scientific research is both separate but also covertly in-relation (Sayre, 1975).

6. But unlike mainstream philosophy, which has quite consistently ignored critiques by feminists and by philosophers of color, feminism has acknowledged, published, and discussed these criticisms.

7. Mainstream ethics expresses that by talking about "impartiality." We have seen reasons for being suspicious of that picture of the moral agent without a standpoint. But the mainstream position does, of course, contain an important insight: Women, people of color, and those of us who are "different" politically or in the way we lead our lives have long been outraged by a society that makes large moral claims for itself but plays favorites in the most blatant ways. What we demand is that we be treated fairly in a way that does not play favorites. How that moral stance without favoritism is to be formulated is not easy to say.

8. The phrase and many important suggestions for specifying its precise meaning are provided in Lorraine Code's *Epistemic Responsibility* (1987a).

9. I am indebted for this insight that critical respect is of the essence to Jane Braaten's so far unpublished work on Adorno.

Chapter 8

1. For other ways in which the options facing us are manipulated so that those in power do not need to determine our decisions directly or coercively, see Bachrach and Baratz, 1962, and Lukes, 1973.

2. That is, of course, quite consistent with each agent in this network being quite separate. The relation between the judge and the bailiff and the clerk of the court are quite separate. All are employees of the state. Their mutual relations are strictly hierarchical and although there is a certain rhetoric about teamwork, no one takes that terribly seriously. Not every activity that requires more than one actor is a counterexample to the thesis that human beings are separate. I distinguished earlier between collective activities, such as playing tennis, where more than one actor is required, but the two do not need to be in-relation and a covertly in-relation activity. In this latter case the agents must have some sort of shared understanding of what they are doing, and how it should be done, but may act very separate once that initial joint understanding has been reached. The example here is a number of people writing a book together: After the initial understanding about the topic and timetable has been reached, every person goes off to write his or her chapter and there is no more communication between the participants. The criminal justice system may very well be an instance of a collective activity that leaves the individual members of the whole network of agents quite separate from one another. It will seem more plausible in the end to regard the criminal justice system, also, as a case of being covertly in-relation. But to prove that we need to say more than that many people are needed to enable the judge to judge.

3. One might try to resolve that contradiction by drawing a distinction. Power, one might suggest, is the sort of thing that people have always said it is, namely, the ability of one person to make a second person do what he or she would rather not do. The communicative medium is not power but a presupposition of power. But that would not seem to be satisfactory because we want to say that having limits set to our lives and choices, being made to believe that we ought to fill certain roles in certain ways, and having our desires defined really is power-over us. If that sort of capacity over the lives and persons of others is not power, it is difficult to say what power might be.

The alternative would be to say that there are two kinds of power: (1) personal, separate power-over of the bully or the holdup artist and then (2) the diffuse, systemic, "structural power" of the capitalists, or of the patriarchy. But that solution is no better. On the one hand, as I observed earlier, the actions of the white bullying a person of color, or of a man battering a woman, do not just manifest the separate power of each but show the power of whites over persons of color, of men over women. Both individual and group power come into play here. On the other hand, the power of the capitalist class, or of the patriarchy, is the power of identifiable groups—I belong to the latter but not to the former. The master of the patriarchal regime may not be identifiable without some effort, but he is identifiable.

4. The implicit argument here parallels that suggested in the first note to Chapter 4: According to the view that human beings are separate, all attributes are owned by separate individuals. Each attribute therefore has a single owner. Insofar as power is separate power it is the power of this person or of that other one. Power that is not so owned by identifiable individuals must have a superindividual owner. In that sense, Foucault often refers to power as a superindividual agent. Power owns itself; it is a superindividual being.

5. Let no one confuse this dependence on one's status with the genuine power of empowerment. Status is owned by separate persons. Professional status separates and oppresses in ways that should by now be familiar. This dependence on status is the very opposite of empowerment.

6. Hannah Arendt recognized this sense of power in-relation in her claim that "power springs up wherever people get together and act in concert" (Arendt, 1970:52). Power be-

longs to groups, and groups are powerful when they can marshall their resources as effectively as possible to achieve shared ends. The power of separate individuals, what Arendt calls "violence," disrupts power in-relation.

7. Obviously these matters are still much more complicated. Few parents are *only* possessive or overly demanding; they are also loving and respectful. Sometimes they are respectful because they have too little distance from the child. Their respect for the child is self-respect. To untangle the strands of separateness and being-in-relation in such a situation is very difficult. (I owe this observation to Sandra Bartky).

8. The answer to that question is obviously a long one. To understand empowerment we need to understand alienation in more detail. Understanding alienation requires that we be clear of what we mean by the "self" and what we mean therefore when we say that we are alienated and not quite ourselves. I will try to adress some of these questions in another book.

References

Agich, G. J. (1990) "Assessing the Autonomy of Long-Term Care." *Hastings Center Report* 20:12–20.

Alcoff, L. (1993) "How Is Epistemology Political?" in R. Gottlieb, ed., *Radical Philosophy: Tradition, Counter-Tradition, Politics* (Philadelphia: Temple University Press), 65–85.

Alinsky, S. (1972) *Rules for Radicals* (New York: Vintage).

Annas, G. J., and Grodin, M. A., eds. (1992) *The Nazi Doctors and the Nuremberg Code: Human Rights and Human Experimentation* (New York: Oxford University Press).

Antony, L. M. (1993) "Quine as Feminist: The Radical Import of Naturalized Epistemology," in L. M. Antony and C. Witt, eds., *A Mind of One's Own: Feminist Essays on Reason and Objectivity* (Boulder: Westview Press), 185–226.

Archard, David. (1992) "Autonomy, Character and Situation," in David Milligan and David Watts Miller, eds., *Liberalism, Citizenship and Autonomy* (Aldershot: Avebury), 157–170.

Arendt, H. (1970) *On Violence* (New York: Harvest Books).

Aristotle. (1941) *Nichomachean Ethics* (New York: Random House).

Babbit, S. (1993) "Feminism and Objective Interests: The Role of Personal Transformation Experiences in Rational Deliberation," in L. Alcoff and E. Potter, eds., *Feminist Epistemologies* (New York: Routledge and Kegan Paul), 245–264.

Bachrach, P., and Baratz, M. S. (1962) "The Two Faces of Power." *American Political Science Review* 65:947–952.

Baier, A. (1986) "Trust and Anti-Trust." *Ethics* 96:231–260.

Barnes, B. (1988) *The Nature of Power* (Urbana: University of Illinois Press).

Becker, Lawrence. (1986) *Reciprocity* (London: Routledge and Kegan Paul).

Benhabib, S. (1987) "The Generalized and the Concrete Other," in S. Benhabib and D. Cornell, eds., *Feminism as Critique* (Minneapolis: University of Minnesota Press), 77–95.

Benn, S. I. (1975–1976) "Freedom, Autonomy and the Concept of a Person." *Proceedings of the Aristotelian Society*, n.s. 76:109–130.

————. (1982) "Individuality, Autonomy and Community," in E. Kamenka, ed., *Community as Social Value* (New York: St. Martin's Press), 43–62.

Benson, J. (1983) "Who Is the Autonomous Man?" *Philosophy* 58:5–17.

Bergmann, F. (1977) *On Being Free* (South Bend, Ind.: Notre Dame University Press).

Bernick, S. E. (1991) "Towards a Value-Laden Theory: Feminism and Social Science." *Hypatia* 6:118–136.

Bernstein, M. (1983) "Socialization and Autonomy." *Mind* 92:120–123.

Bettelheim, B. (1960) *The Informed Heart* (New York: Free Press).

Billson, J. M. (1991) "The Progressive Verification Method: Toward a Feminist Methodology for Studying Women Cross-Culturally." *Women's Studies International Forum* 14:201–215.

Blustein, J. (1991) *Care and Commitment: Taking the Personal Point of View* (New York: Oxford University Press).

Bock, G. (1986) *Zwangssterilisation im Nationalsozialismus* (Opladen: Deutscher Verlag).

Bonjour, L. (1986) "Can Empirical Knowledge Have a Foundation?" in P. K. Moser, ed., *Empirical Knowledge: Readings in Contemporary Epistemology* (Totowa, N.J.: Rowman and Littlefield).

Boulding, K. (1989) *The Three Faces of Power* (Newbury Park, Calif.: Sage).

Boyte, H. (1989) *CommonWealth: A Return to Citizen Politics* (New York: Free Press).

———. (1993) "Public Freedom," in R. Schmitt and T. E. Moody, eds., *Alienation and Social Criticism* (Atlantic Highlands, N.J.: Humanities Press), 235–245.

Brell, C. D. (1989) "Justice and Caring and the Problem of Moral Relativism: Reframing the Gender Question in Ethics." *Journal of Moral Education* 18:101–111.

Brown, R. (1987) *Analyzing Love* (Cambridge: Cambridge University Press).

Buber, M. (1958) *I and Thou* (New York: Charles Scribner's).

Bunkle, P. (1993) "Calling the Shots: The International Politics of Depo-Provera," in S. Harding, ed., *The "Racial" Economy of Science: Toward a Democratic Future* (Bloomington: Indiana University Press), 287–302.

Calhoun, C. (1988) "Justice, Care and Gender Bias." *Journal of Philosophy* 95:451–463.

Callahan, D. (1984) "Autonomy: A Moral Good Not a Moral Obsession." *Hastings Center Report* 14:40–42.

Candib, L. (1995) *Medicine and the Family* (New York: Basic Books).

Chodorow, N. (1978) *The Reproduction of Mothering* (Berkeley: University of California Press).

Christman, J. (1987) "Autonomy: A Defense of the Split Level Self." *Southern Journal of Philosophy* 25:281–293.

Cocks, J. (1989) *The Oppositional Imagination: Feminism, Critique and Political Theory* (London: Routledge and Kegan Paul).

Code, L. (1987a) *Epistemic Responsibility* (Hanover, N.H.: University Press of New England).

———. (1987b) "Second Persons," in M. Hanen and K. Nielsen, eds., *Science, Morality and Feminist Theory.* Canadian Journal of Philosophy Supplementary Volume 13, Calgary.

———. (1993) "Taking Subjectivity into Account," in L. Alcoff and E. Potter, eds., *Feminist Epistemologies* (New York: Routledge and Kegan Paul), 15–48.

Cohen, G. A. (1986a) "Self-Ownership, World Ownership, and Equality," in F. S. Lucash, ed., *Justice and Equality Here and Now* (Ithaca: Cornell University Press), 108–135.

———. (1986b) "Self-Ownership, World Ownership and Equality II." *Social Philosophy and Policy* 3:77–96.

———. (1991) "The Future of a Disillusion." *New Left Review,* no. 190:9–20.

Collins, P. H. (1986) "Learning from the Outsider Within: The Sociological Significance of Black Feminist Thought." *Social Problems* 33:514–532.

———. (1991) *Black Feminist Thought: Knowledge, Consciousness and the Politics of Empowerment* (New York: Routledge and Kegan Paul).

Comay, R. (1987) "Interrupting the Conversations: Notes on Rorty," in E. Simpson, ed., *Anti-Foundationalism and Practical Reason* (Edmonton: Academic Printing and Publishing), 83–98.

Curtin, D. (1991) "Toward an Ecological Ethic of Care." *Hypatia* 6:60–74.

Dahl, R. A. (1957) "The Concept of Power." *Behavioral Science* 2:201–205.

———. (1985) *A Preface to Economic Democracy* (Berkeley: University of California Press).

Dalmiya, V., and Alcoff, L. (1993) "Are 'Old Wives' Tales' Justified?" in L. Alcoff and E. Potter, eds., *Feminist Epistemologies* (New York: Routledge and Kegan Paul), 217–244.

Deming, B. (1985) *Prisons That Could Not Hold* (San Francisco: Spinster's Ink).

Descartes, R. (1951) *Meditations* (New York: Library of Liberal Arts).

———. (1956) *Discourse on Method* (New York: Library of Liberal Arts).

Dewey, J. (1938) *Logic: The Theory of Inquiry* (New York: Henry Holt).

Digby, T. F. (1994) "No *One* Is Guilty: Crime, Patriarchy, and Individualism." *Journal of Social Philosophy* 25:180–205.

Dilham, I. (1987) *Love and Human Separateness* (Oxford: Basil Blackwell).

Dillon, R. (1992) "Care and Respect," in Eve Browning Cole and Susan Coultrap McQuin, eds., *Explorations in Feminist Ethics: Theory and Practice* (Bloomington: Indiana University Press), 68–81.

Duelli-Klein, R. (1983) "How To Do What We Want to Do: Thoughts About Feminist Methodology," in G. Bowles and R. Duelli-Klein, eds., *Theories of Women's Studies* (London: Routledge and Kegan Paul), 88–104.

Dworkin, G. (1988) *The Theory and Practice of Autonomy* (Cambridge: Cambridge University Press).

———. (1989) "The Concept of Autonomy," in J. Christman, ed., *The Hidden Citadel* (New York: Oxford University Press), 54–62.

Dworkin, R. (1984) "Liberalism," in M. Sandel, ed., *Liberalism and Its Critics* (New York: New York University Press), 60–79.

Elster, J. (1985a) *Making Sense of Marx* (Cambridge: Cambridge University Press).

———. (1985b) *Sour Grapes* (Cambridge: Cambridge University Press).

Emmet, D. (1953) "The Concept of Power." *Proceedings of the Aristotelian Society* n.s. 54:1–26.

Fausto-Sterling, A. (1985) *Myths of Gender: Biological Theories About Women and Men* (New York: Basic Books).

Feinberg, J. (1980) "The Idea of a Free Man," in *Rights, Justice and the Bounds of Liberty* (Princeton: Princeton University Press), 3–29.

———. (1989) "Autonomy," in J. Christman, ed., *The Inner Citadel* (New York: Oxford University Press), 27–53.

Ferguson, A. (1991) *Sexual Democracy: Women, Oppression and Revolution* (Boulder: Westview Press).

Ferguson, K. E. (1984) *The Feminist Case Against Bureaucracy* (Philadelphia: Temple University Press).

Fisk, M. (1989) *The State and Justice* (Cambridge: Cambridge University Press).

Flanagan, O., and Jackson, K. (1990) "Justice, Care, and Gender: The Kohlberg-Gilligan Debate Revisited," in C. Sunstein, ed., *Feminism and Political Theory* (Chicago: University of Chicago Press), 37–52.

Fontaine, W. T. (1983) "'Social Determination' in the Writings of Negro Scholars (Commentary by E. Franklin Frazier)," in L. Harris, ed., *Philosophy Born of Struggle* (Dubuque, Ia.: Kendall/Hunt).

Foucault, M. (1980) *Power/Knowledge* (New York: Pantheon).

Frankfurt, H. (1971) "Freedom of the Will and the Concept of a Person." *Journal of Philosophy* 68:5–21.

————. (1982) "The Importance of What We Care About." *Synthese* 53:257–272.

Friedman, M. (1986) "Autonomy and the Split-Level Self." *Southern Journal of Philosophy* 24:19–35.

————. (1990) "Feminism and Modern Friendship: Dislocating the Community," in C. Sunstein, ed., *Feminism and Political Theory* (Chicago: University of Chicago Press), 143–158.

Fromm, E. (1970) *The Art of Loving* (New York: Harper and Brothers).

Fry, S. T. (1992) "The Role of Caring in a Theory of Nursing Ethics," in H. B. Holmes and L. M. Purdy, eds., *Feminist Perspectives in Medical Ethics* (Bloomington: Indiana University Press), 93–106.

Frye, M. (1983) *The Politics of Reality: Essays in Feminist Theory* (Trumansburg, N.Y.: Crossing Press).

Fuller, S. (1989) *Philosophy of Science and Its Discontents* (Boulder: Westview Press).

Garan, E. (1994) "Who's in Control? Is There Enough Empowerment to Go Around?" *Language Arts* 71:192–199.

Gardiner, J. K. (1987) "Self-Psychology as Feminist Theory." *Signs* 12:763–776.

Gibson, M. (1985) *To Breathe Freely* (Totowa, N.J.: Rowman and Allanheld).

Gilbert, M. (1992) *On Social Facts* (Princeton: Princeton University Press).

Gill, A. (1988) *The Journey Back from Hell: An Oral History of Conversations with Concentration Camp Survivors* (New York: William Morrow).

Gilligan, C. (1982) *In a Different Voice* (Cambridge: Harvard University Press).

————. (1987) "Moral Orientation and Moral Development," in E. F. Kittay and D. T. Meyers, eds., *Women and Moral Theory* (Totowa, N.J.: Rowman and Littlefield), 19–36.

Gilman, C. P. (1973) *The Yellow Wallpaper* (New York: Feminist Press).

Glasman, M. (1994) "The Great Deformation: Polanyi, Poland, and the Terrors of Planned Spontaneity." *NLR* 205:59–96.

Goldman, A. (1972) "Towards a Theory of Social Power." *Philosophical Studies* 23:221–268.

Gottlieb, R., ed. (1990) *Thinking the Unthinkable: Meanings of the Holocaust* (New York: Paulist Press).

Gould, S. J. (1981) *The Mismeasure of Man* (New York: Norton).

Govier, T. (1993) "Self-Trust, Autonomy and Self-Esteem." *Hypatia* 8:99–120.

Grayling, A. C. (1985) *The Refutation of Scepticism* (LaSalle, Ill.: Open Court).

Greenspan, P. S. (1986) "Identificatory Love." *Philosophical Studies* 50:321–341.

Gregory, P. (1986) "The Two Sides of Love." *Journal of Applied Philosophy* 3:229–233.

Griffiths, M. (1992) "Autonomy and the Fear of Dependence." *Women's Studies International Forum* 15:351–362.

Grimshaw, J. (1986) *Philosophy and Feminist Thinking* (Minneapolis: University of Minnesota Press).

————. (1988) "Autonomy and Identity in Feminist Thinking," in M. Griffiths and M. Whitford, eds., *Feminist Perspectives in Philosophy* (Bloomington: Indiana University Press), 90–108.

Gutman, A. (1989) "Undemocratic Education," in N. Rosenblum, ed., *Liberalism and the Moral Life* (Cambridge: Harvard University Press), 71–88.

Gwaltney, J. L. (1980) *Drylongso: A Self-Portrait of Black America* (New York: Random House).

Haller, J. S. (1971) *Outcasts from Evolution: Scientific Attitudes of Racial Inferiority, 1895–1900* (New York: McGraw-Hill).

Harding, S. (1993a) "Rethinking Standpoint Epistemology: 'What Is Strong Objectivity'?" in L. Alcoff and E. Potter, eds., *Feminist Epistemologies* (New York: Routledge), 49–82.

———. ed. (1993b) *The "Racial" Economy of Science* (Bloomington: Indiana University Press).

Hardwig, J. (1985) "Epistemic Dependence." *Journal of Philosophy* 82:335–349.

Haworth, L. (1986) *Autonomy: An Essay in Philosophical Psychology and Ethics* (New Haven: Yale University Press).

Hegel, G.W.F. (1931) *The Phenomenology of Mind*, trans. J. B. Gallie (London: George Allen and Unwin).

———. (1949) *The Philosophy of Right* (Oxford: Oxford University Press).

———. (1953) *Reason in History* (New York: Little Library of Liberal Arts).

Held, V. (1987) "Feminism and Moral Theory," in E. F. Kittay and D. T. Meyers, eds., *Women and Moral Theory* (Totowa, N.J.: Rowman and Littlefield), 111–128.

Hill, T. E., Jr. (1987) "The Importance of Autonomy," in E. F. Kittay and D. T. Meyers, eds., *Women and Moral Theory* (Totowa, N.J.: Rowman and Littlefield), 129–138.

Hoagland, S. L. (1990) "A Note on a Bind." *APA Newsletter on Feminism* 88:39.

Hobbes, T. (n.d.) *Leviathan* (Oxford: Basil Blackwell).

Hoffman, F. L. (1991) "Feminism and Nursing." *NWSA Journal* 3:53–69.

Holmes, S. (1989) "The Permanent Structure of Anti-Liberal Thought," in N. Rosenblum, ed., *Liberalism and the Moral Life* (Cambridge: Harvard University Press), 227–254.

hooks, b. (1989) *Talking Back: Thinking Feminist, Thinking Black* (Boston: South End Press).

———. (1993) *Sisters of the Yam* (Boston: South End Press).

hooks, b., and West, C. (1991) *Breaking Bread: Insurgent Black Intellectual Life* (Boston: South End Press).

Houston, B. (1989) "Caring and Exploitation" *Hypatia* 5:115–119.

Isaac, J. (1987) *Power and Marxist Theory* (Ithaca: Cornell University Press).

Jones, J. (1993) "The Tuskeegee Syphilis Experiment: 'A Moral Astigmatism,'" in S. Harding, ed., *The "Racial" Economy of Science: Toward a Democratic Future* (Bloomington: Indiana University Press), 275–286.

Jordan, J. V. (1983) "Empathy and the Mother-Daughter Relationship." *Work in Progress* 82-02:2–5.

———. (1984) "Empathy and Self Boundaries." *Work in Progress* 16:1–14.

———. (1987) "Clarity in Connection: Empathic Knowing, Desire and Sexuality." *Work in Progress* 29:1–26.

Jordan, J. V., Kaplan, A. G., Miller, J. B., Stiver, I. P., and Surrey, J. L. (1991) *Women's Growth in Connection: Writings from the Stone Center* (New York: Guilford).

Kateb, G. (1989) "Democratic Individuality and the Meaning of Rights," in Nancy L. Rosenbloom, ed., *Liberalism and the Moral Life* (Cambridge: Harvard University Press), 183–206.

Keller, C. (1986) *From a Broken Web* (Boston: Beacon Press).

Keller, E. F. (1983) *A Feeling for the Organism* (New York: Freeman and Co.).

Kernohan, A. (1989) "Capitalism and Self-Ownership." *Social Philosophy and Policy* 6:60–76.

Koller, A. (1990) *The Stations of Solitude* (New York: Morrow).

Krafmarae, C., and Treichler, P. A. (1990) "Power Relationships in the Classroom," in S. L. Gabriel and I. Smithson, eds., *Gender in the Classroom* (Urbana: University of Illinois Press), 78–95.

Kreisberg, S. (1992) *Transforming Power: Domination, Empowerment and Education* (Albany: SUNY Press).

Kuflik, A. (1984) "The Inalienability of Autonomy." *Philosophy and Public Affairs* 13:271–298.

Kuhn, T. S. (1977) *The Essential Tension: Selected Studies in Scientific Tradition and Change* (Chicago: University of Chicago Press).

Kupfer, J. (1987) "Privacy, Autonomy and Self-Concept." *APQ* 24, 81–89.

Kymlicka, W. (1989) *Liberalism, Community and Culture* (Oxford: Clarendon Press).

———. (1990) *Contemporary Political Philosophy* (Oxford: Oxford University Press).

Lâm, M. C. (1994) "Feeling Foreign in Feminism." *Signs* 19:865–893.

Latour, B., and Woolgar, S. (1979) *Laboratory Life: The Social Construction of Scientific Fact* (Beverly Hills, Calif.: Sage).

Lehrer, K. (1974) *Knowledge* (Oxford: Clarendon Press).

———. (1977) "Social Information." *Monist* 60:473–487.

Levi, P. (1961) *Survival in Auschwitz* (New York: Collier Books).

Levins, R., and Lewontin, R. (1993) "Applied Biology in the Third World: The Struggle for Revolutionary Science," in S. Harding, ed., *The "Racial" Economy of Science: Toward a Democratic Future* (Bloomington: Indiana University Press), 315–325.

Lifton, R. J. (1986) *The Nazi Doctors: Medical Killing and the Psychology of Genocide* (New York: Basic Books).

Lloyd, G. (1984) *The Man of Reason: 'Male' and 'Female' in Western Philosophy* (Minneapolis: University of Minnesota Press).

Longino, H. E. (1990) *Science as Social Knowledge* (Princeton: Princeton University Press).

Lugones, M. (1987) "Playfulness, 'World'-Travelling and Loving Perception." *Hypatia* 2:3–19.

———. (1991) "On the Logic of Pluralist Feminism," in C. Card, ed., *Feminist Ethics* (Lawrence: University Press of Kansas), 35–44.

Luhmann, N. (1975) *Macht* (Stuttgart: Enke Verlag).

Lukes, S. (1973) *Individualism* (New York: Harper Torchbooks).

———. (1974) *Power: A Radical View* (London: Macmillan).

Macedo, S. (1990) *Liberal Virtues: Citizenship, Virtue, and Community in Liberal Constitutionalism* (Oxford: Clarendon Press).

Manning, R. (1992) "Just Caring," in E. Browning Cole and S. Coultrap McQuin, eds., *Explorations in Feminist Ethics: Theory and Practice* (Bloomington: Indiana University Press), 38–44.

Martin, R. (1977) *The Sociology of Power* (London: Routledge and Kegan Paul).

Marx, K. (1967) *Capital*, vol. 1 (New York: International Publishers).

Marx, K., and Engels, F. (1978) *The Marx-Engels Reader*, ed. R. Tucker (New York: Norton).

Mason, A. (1990) "Gilligan's Conception of Moral Maturity." *Journal for the Theory of Social Behavior* 20:167–177.

———. (1992) "Personal Autonomy and Identification with a Community," in D. Milligan and W. Watts Miller, eds., *Liberalism, Citizenship and Autonomy* (Aldershot: Avebury), 171–186.

May, L. (1987) *The Morality of Groups: Collective Responsibility, Group Based Harm, and Corporate Rights* (Notre Dame, Ind.: University of Notre Dame Press).

McClendon, J. H. (1983) "Eugene C. Holmes: A Commentary on a Black Marxist Philosopher," in L. Harris, ed., *Philosophy Born of Struggle* (Dubuque, Ia.: Kendall/Hunt).

McGary, H. (1993) "Alienation and the African-American Experience," in R. Schmitt and T. E. Moody, eds., *Alienation and Social Criticism* (Atlantic Highlands, N.J.: Humanities Press), 132–146.

McKerlie, D. (1988) "Egalitarianism and the Separateness of Persons." *Canadian Journal of Philosophy* 18:205–226.

Meyers, D. T. (1989) "Personal Autonomy and the Paradox of Feminine Socialization." *Journal of Philosophy* 84:619–628.

Midgley, M. (1988) "On Not Being Afraid of Natural Sexual Differences," in M. Griffiths and M. Whitford, eds., *Feminist Perspectives in Philosophy* (Bloomington: Indiana University Press), 29–41.

Mill, J. S. (1948) *On Liberty* (Oxford: Blackwell's).

Miller, J. B. (1976) *Towards a New Psychology for Women* (Boston: Beacon Press).

———. (1983) "The Construction of Anger in Men and Women." *Work in Progress* 83-01:1–15.

———. (1986) "What Do We Mean by Relationships?" *Work in Progress* 22:1–23.

Moore, M. (1993) *Foundations of Liberalism* (Oxford: Clarendon Press).

Mueller-Hill, B. (1988) *Murderous Science* (Oxford: Oxford University Press).

Mullett, S. (1987) "Only Connect: The Place of Self-Knowledge in Ethics," in M. Hanen and K. Nielsen, eds., *Science, Morality and Feminist Theory* (Calgary: Canadian Journal of Philosophy), 309–338.

Murdoch, I. (1970) *The Sovereignty of Good* (New York: Ark Paperbacks).

Nagel, T. (1986) *The View from Nowhere* (Oxford: Oxford University Press).

Nedelsky, J. (1990) "Law, Boundaries, and Bounded Self." *Representations* 30:162–189.

Nelson, L. H. (1990) *Who Knows: From Quine to Feminist Empiricism* (Philadelphia: Temple University Press).

———. (1993) "Epistemological Communities," in L. Alcoff and E. Potter, eds., *Feminist Epistemologies* (New York: Routledge and Kegan Paul), 121–160.

Newton-Smith, W. (1973) "A Conceptual Investigation of Love," in A. Montefiore, ed., *Philosophy and Personal Relations* (Montreal: McGill-Queens University Press), 113–135.

Nietzsche, F. (1976) *The Portable Nietzsche* (Harmondsworth: Penguin).

Noddings, N. (1984) *Caring: A Feminist Approach to Ethics and Moral Education* (Berkeley: University of California Press).

Nozick, R. (1974) *Anarchy, State and Utopia* (New York: Basic Books).

———. (1991) "Love's Bond," in R. C. Solomon and K. M. Higgins, eds., *The Philosophy of Erotic Love* (Lawrence: University of Kansas Press), 417–432.

Nussbaum, M. C. (1980) "Shame, Separateness and Political Unity: Aristotle's Criticsm of Plato," in A. O. Rorty, ed., *Essays in Aristotle's Ethics* (Berkeley: University of California Press), 395–435.

———. (1986) "Love and the Individual: Romantic Rightness and Platonic Aspiration," in T. C. Heller, M. Sosna, D. E. Wellbery, eds., *Reconstructing Individualism* (Stanford: Stanford University Press), 253–277.

———. (1988) "Narrative Emotions: Beckett's Genealogy of Love." *Ethics* 98:225–254.

Nye, A. (1990) *Words of Power* (New York: Routledge and Kegan Paul).

Oakley, A. (1981) "Interviewing Women: A Contradiction in Terms," in H. Roberts, ed., *Doing Feminist Research* (London: Routledge and Kegan Paul).

Okin, S. M. (1991) "Humanist Liberalism," in N. L. Rosenblum, ed., *Liberalism and the Moral Life* (Cambridge: Harvard University Press), 39–53.

Ollman, B. (1971) *Alienation: Marx's Conception of Man in Capitalist Society* (Cambridge: Cambridge University Press).

Olsen, R. (1978) *Karl Marx* (Boston: Twayne).

O'Neill, O. (1992) "Autonomy, Coherence and Independence," in D. Milligan and W. Watts Miller, eds., *Liberalism, Citizenship and Autonomy* (Aldershot: Avebury), 203–225.

Outlaw, L. (1991) "Lifeworlds, Modernity and Philosophical Praxis: Race, Ethnicity and Critical Social Theory," in E. Deutsch, ed., *Culture and Modernity: East-West Philosophical Perspectives* (Honolulu: University of Hawaii Press), 21–49.

Parfit, D. (1986) *Reasons and Persons* (Oxford: Oxford University Press).

Parsons, T. (1963) "On the Concept of Political Power." *Proceedings of the American Philosophical Society* 107:232–262.

Partridge, P. H. (1963) "Some Notes on the Concept of Power." *Political Studies* 11:107–125.

Piper, J. (1972) *About Love* (Chicago: Franciscan Herald Press).

Piven, F. F., and Cloward, R. A. (1979) *Poor People's Movements: Why They Succeed and How They Fail* (New York: Vintage).

Popper, K. (1971) *The Open Society and Its Enemies,* Vol. 2 (Princeton: Princeton University Press).

Price, A. W. (1989) *Love and Friendship in Plato and Aristotle* (Oxford: Clarendon Press).

Prince, M. (1988) "The History of Mary Prince, a West Indian Slave," in H. L. Gates, ed., *Six Women's Slave Narratives* (Oxford: Oxford University Press).

Quine, W.V.O. (1969) *Ontological Relativity and Other Essays* (New York: Columbia University Press).

Ratushinskaya, I. (1989) *Grey Is the Color of Hope* (New York: Vintage International).

Rawls, J. (1971) *A Theory of Justice* (Cambridge: Harvard University Press).

Raymond, P. (1986) *A Passion for Friends: Toward a Philosophy of Female Affection* (Boston: Beacon Press).

Raz, J. (1986) *The Morality of Freedom* (Oxford: Oxford University Press).

Reagon, B. (1979) "The Borning Struggle," in D. Cluster, ed., *They Should Have Served That Cup of Coffee: Seven Radicals Remember the Sixties* (Boston: South End Press), 1–40.

Reeve, A. (1987) *Property* (Atlantic Highlands, N.J.: Humanities Press).

Reilly, P. R. (1991) *The Surgical Solution: A History of Involuntary Sterilization in the United States* (Baltimore: Johns Hopkins Press).

Reiman, J. H. (1976) "Privacy, Intimacy and Personhood." *Philosophy and Public Affairs* 6: 26–44.

Reinharz, S. (1983) "Experiential Analysis: A Contribution to Feminist Research," in G. Bowles and R. Duelli-Klein, eds., *Theories of Women's Studies* (London: Routledge and Kegan Paul), 162–191.

Riessman, C. K. (1987) "When Gender Is Not Enough: Women Interviewing Women." *Gender and Society* 1:172–207.

Rigterink, R. J. (1992) "Warning: The Surgeon Moralist Has Determined That Claims to Rights Can Be Detrimental to Everyone's Interests," in E. Browning Cole and S.

Coultrap McQuin, eds., *Explorations in Feminist Ethics: Theory and Practice* (Bloomington: Indiana University Press), 38–44.

Ripstein, A. (1987) "Explanation and Empathy." *Review of Metaphysics* 40:465–482.

Rorty, R. (1979) *Philosophy and the Mirror of Nature* (Princeton: Princeton University Press).

———. (1989) *Contingency, Irony and Solidarity* (Cambridge: Cambridge University Press).

Rossiter, M. (1982) *Women Scientists in America: Struggles and Strategies to 1940.* (Baltimore: Johns Hopkins Press).

Ruddick, S. (1989) *Maternal Thinking: Toward a Politics of Peace* (Boston: Beacon Press).

Sales, R. (1990) "In Our Own Words: An Interview." *Women's Review of Books* 7:24–27.

Sarton, M. (1982) *Anger* (New York: W. W. Norton).

Sayre, A. (1975) *Rosalind Franklin and DNA* (New York: Norton).

Schaff, A. (1970) *Marxism and the Human Individual* (New York: McGraw-Hill).

Scheler, M. (1931) *Wesen und Formen der Sympathie* (Bonn: Friedrich Cohen).

Scheman, N. (1980) "Anger and the Politics of Naming," in S. McConnell-Gine, R. Borker, and N. Furman, eds., *Women and Language* (New York: Praeger).

———. (1983) "Individualism and the Objects of Psychology," in S. Harding and M. L. Hintikka, eds., *Discovering Reality* (Dordrecht: Reidel), 225–244.

———. (1993) *Engendering: Constructions of Knowledge, Authority and Privilege* (New York: Routledge and Kegan Paul).

Schmitt, R. (1989) "Methodological Individualism, Psychological Individualism and the Defense of Reason," in R. Ware and K. Nielsen, eds., *Analyzing Marxism: New Essays on Analytical Marxism* (Calgary: Canadian Journal of Philosophy), 231–256.

———. (1993) "Why Is the Concept of Alienation Important?" in R. Schmitt and T. E. Moody, eds., *Alienation and Social Criticism* (Atlantic Highlands, N.J.: Humanities Press), 1–23.

Schweickart, P. P. (1990) "Reading, Teaching, and the Ethic of Care," in S. L. Gabriel and I. Smithson, eds., *Gender in the Classroom: Power and Pedagogy* (Chicago: University of Illinois Press), 78–95.

Segal, L. (1990) *Slow Motion: Changing Masculinities, Changing Men* (New Brunswick, N.J.: Rutgers University Press).

Shiva, V. (1993) "Colonialism and the Evolution of Masculinist Forestry," in S. Harding, ed., *The "Racial" Economy of Science: Toward a Democratic Future* (Bloomington: Indiana University Press), 303–314.

Singer, I. (1984) *The Nature of Love,* vol. 1 (Chicago: University of Chicago Press).

Smith, D. W. (1989) *The Circle of Acquaintance* (Dordrecht: Kluwer).

Soble, A. (1990) *The Structure of Love* (New Haven: Yale University Press).

Spelman, E. V. (1988) *Inessential Woman: Problems of Exclusion in Feminist Thought* (Boston: Beacon Press).

———. (1991) "The Virtue of Feeling and the Feeling of Virtue," in C. Card, ed., *Feminist Ethics* (Lawrence: University Press of Kansas), 213–232.

Stern, L. (1990) "Conceptions of Separation and Connection in Female Adolescents," in C. Gilligan, N. L. Lyons, and T. J. Hanmer, eds., *Making Connections: The Relational Worlds of Adolescent Girls at Emma Willard School* (Cambridge: Harvard University Press), 73–87.

Stiver, I. P. (1991) "Beyond the Oedipus Complex: Mothers and Daughters," in J. V. Jordan, A. G. Kaplan, J. B. Miller, I. P. Stiver, and J. L. Surrey, eds., *Women's Growth in Connection* (New York: Guilford Press), 97–121.

Taylor, C. (1985) "Interpretation and the Sciences of Man," in *Philosophy and the Human Sciences: Philosophical Papers*, vol. 2 (Cambridge: Cambridge University Press).

———. (1989) "Cross-Purposes: The Liberal-Communitarian Debate," in N. Rosenblum, ed., *Liberalism and the Moral Life* (Cambridge: Harvard University Press), 159–182.

———. (1992) *The Ethics of Authenticity* (Cambridge: Harvard University Press).

Taylor, G. (1986) "Love." *Proceedings of the Aristotelian Society*, n.s. 87:148–166.

Thomas, S. B., and Quinn, S. C. (1991) "Public Health Then and Now: The Tuskeegee Syphilis Study 1932 to 1972." *American Journal of Public Health* 81:1498–1505.

Tov-Ruach, L. (1980) "Jealousy, Attention and Loss," in A. O. Rorty, ed., *The Identities of Persons* (Berkeley: University of California Press), 465–488.

Tronto, J. C. (1987) "Beyond Gender Difference to a Theory of Care." *Signs* 12:644–663.

———. (1989) "Women and Caring: What Can Feminists Learn About Morality from Caring?" in A. M. Jaggar and S. R. Bordo, eds., *Gender/Body/Knowledge/Feminist Reconstructions of Being and Knowing* (New Brunswick, N.J.: Rutgers University Press), 172–187.

Trout, J. D. (1992) "Theory-Conjunction and Mercenary Reliance." *Philosophy of Science* 59: 231–245.

Tucker, R., ed. (1978) *The Marx-Engels Reader* (New York: Norton).

Waldron, J. (1993) *Legal Rights: Collected Papers, 1981–1991* (Cambridge: Cambridge University Press).

Walker, M. U. (1992) "Moral Understandings: Alternative 'Epistemology' for a Feminist Ethics," in E. Browning Cole and S. Coultrap McQuin, eds., *Explorations in Feminist Ethics: Theory and Practice* (Bloomington: Indiana University Press), 164–175.

Wartenberg, T. (1990) *The Forms of Power: An Essay in Social Ontology* (Philadelphia: Temple University Press).

Weiss, S. F. (1990) "The Race Hygiene Movement in Germany, 1904–1945," in M. B. Adams, ed., *The Well-Born Science: Eugenics in Germany, France, Brazil and Russia* (Oxford: Oxford University Press), 8–68.

Williams, B. (1983) "Descartes' Use of Scepticism," in M. Burnyeat, ed., *The Sceptical Tradition* (Berkeley: University of California Press), 337–352.

Williams, R. C. (1983) "W.E.B. DuBois: Afro-American Philosopher of Social Reality," in L. Harris, ed., *Philosphy Born of Struggle* (Dubuque, Ia.: Kendall/Hunt), 11–20.

Wolf, S. (1989) "Sanity and the Responsibility of Metaphysics," in J. Christman, ed., *The Inner Citadel* (New York: Oxford University Press), 137–151.

Woolf, V. (1927) *To the Lighthouse* (New York: Harcourt, Brace and Co.).

Wrong, D. (1979) *Power* (New York: Harper and Row).

Yanay, N., and Birns, B. (1990) "Autonomy as Emotion: The Phenomenology of Independence in Academic Women." *Women's Studies International Forum* 13:249–260.

Young, I. M. (1990) *Justice and the Politics of Difference* (Princeton: Princeton University Press).

Young, R. (1980) "Autonomy and Socialization." *Mind* 89:565–576.

About the Book and Author

Two very different views of persons permeate our thinking. On the one hand, we are impressed by the many social influences that affect us all. On the other hand, we also demand autonomy and individual rights. We have, at present, no suitable vocabulary for giving their due both to our social nature and to the ways in which we are distinct from one another.

In this ambitious and original book, Richard Schmitt criticizes the assumption that human beings are separate from one another—an assumption that underlies much of mainstream Anglo-American philosophy. Instead he proposes, following two decades of work by feminist theorists, that we consider ourselves as being-in-relation. A large part of the book is dedicated to clarifying these two competing views of persons. In the course of this effort the author examines different conceptions of autonomy, empathy, love, knowing, and power.

From these discussions emerges a view of persons that illuminates the ways in which each of us is distinct from others and at the same time does justice to our participation in social networks. Schmitt shows that persons have considerable choice over whether to be separate or in-relation. The controversy between these two views is not primarily theoretical but about practice—specifically, political practice.

Richard Schmitt is professor of philosophy at Brown University and the author of many books and articles on themes in continental philosophy and political and social thought. Among his several books is *Introduction to Marx and Engels: A Critical Reconstruction* (Westview).

Index

Abstractions, 14, 35, 36
Action
    joint, 3, 26–33, 46, 58. *See also* Decisions,
        joint
    common, 20, 28
African Americans. *See* Blacks
Agape, 123
Aggression, 116, 122, 155
Alienable possessions, 7–8
Alienation, 162–165, 167, 170, 171, 176,
    187(n8)
Alinsky, Saul, 166
Aloneness, 97–98. *See also* Separateness
Altruism, 39, 40
Ambivalence, 69, 70, 100, 105, 122
Anger, 84, 117, 118, 119–120, 122, 145, 169,
    170
Anger (Sarton), 117–120, 121
Antisemitism, 130
Arendt, Hannah, 151, 186(n6)
Aristotle, 109, 111–112, 122, 132, 184(n6)
Armies, 154
Attention. *See* Paying attention
Auschwitz, 128
Autonomy, 1–16, 112, 179(n5), 181(n6)
    as being one's own person, 4–7, 15, 41,
        45, 50, 70, 93
    and conformity, 88–90
    as empirical issue, 13, 14
    incoherent, 44
    in-relation, 90–97, 98, 146, 150, 165
    internal conditions for, 5, 11, 23, 91
    letting others be autonomous, 95–96
    and men, 34, 35, 41–42, 45, 48–50
    options concerning, 59
    personal, 4, 5, 11
    in philosophy, 4–6
    political/social, 3–4, 11

procedural conception of, 45–46, 47, 48,
    91, 92
redefining, 46–47
separate, 34, 38–48, 92, 97, 99, 125, 126,
    150, 159

Banks, 21, 26
Being-in-relation, 2, 29, 40, 53–55, 58–79,
    111–114, 117, 158, 171
    as chosen, 22, 26, 32, 53, 57, 58, 59, 77, 79,
        92, 93, 101, 122, 177, 182(n6)
    conflict in, 69. *See also* Conflict
    covert, 45, 55, 70, 77, 78, 79, 88, 99, 105,
        111, 138, 150, 160. *See also* Power,
        covertly in-relation
    examples of, 80–104
    minimal, 54, 55, 58–59, 138, 140
    openly, 53–54, 93, 120–122, 142, 172
    as perspective in philosophy, 104
    and reciprocity, 66–71, 102
    vs. separateness, 2, 58, 59, 73, 123
    See also Autonomy, in-relation;
        Empathy, in-relation; Power, in-
        relation
Benn, S. I., 29
Bettelheim, 166
Blacks, 94, 99–100, 136, 155, 160–161, 162,
    163, 168, 169, 170. *See also* Persons of
    color; Racism
Bly, Robert, 82–83
Bodies as distinct, 2–3, 17–18, 19, 20, 24, 25,
    57, 92, 183(n6)
Boulding, K., 154
Brown, R., 108
Buber, Martin, 109, 110, 113

Capitalism, 176

199